Public Key Cryptosystems

This book is a short book about public key cryptosystems, digital signature algorithms, and their basic cryptanalysis which are provided at a basic level so that it can be easy to understand for the undergraduate engineering students who can be defined as the core audience. To provide the necessary background, Chapters 1 and 2 are devoted to the selected fundamental concepts in cryptography mathematics and selected fundamental concepts in cryptography.

Chapter 3 is devoted to discrete logarithm problem (DLP), DLP-related public key cryptosystems, digital signature algorithms, and their cryptanalysis. In this chapter, the elliptic curve counterparts of the algorithms and the basic algorithms for the solution of DLP are also given. In Chapter 4, RSA public key cryptosystem, RSA digital signature algorithm, the basic cryptanalysis approaches, and the integer factorization methods are provided. Chapter 5 is devoted to GGH and NTRU public key cryptosystems, GGH and NTRU digital signature algorithms, and the basic cryptanalysis approaches, whereas Chapter 6 covers other topics including knapsack cryptosystems, identity-based public key cryptosystems, identity-based digital signature algorithms, Goldwasser-Micali probabilistic public key cryptosystem, and their cryptanalysis.

The book's distinctive features:

- The book provides some fundamental mathematical and conceptual preliminaries required to understand the core parts of the book.
- The book comprises the selected public key cryptosystems, digital signature algorithms, and the basic cryptanalysis approaches for these cryptosystems and algorithms.
- The cryptographic algorithms and most of the solutions of the examples are provided in a structured table format to support easy learning.
- The concepts and algorithms are illustrated with examples, some of which are revisited multiple times to present alternative approaches.
- The details of the topics covered in the book are intentionally not presented; however, several references are provided at the end of each chapter so that the reader can read those references for more details.

Esra Bas graduated from Yildiz Technical University, Istanbul, as a mechanical engineer. She obtained an MBA degree from Yeditepe University, Istanbul. She also studied at TU Berlin Global Production Engineering Master's program with the scholarship of Turkish Education Foundation (TEV)-German Academic Exchange Service (DAAD). She obtained her PhD degree from Istanbul Technical University Department of Industrial Engineering, where she works as an Assoc. Prof. During her PhD study, she has been to Columbia University's Industrial Engineering and Operations Research (IEOR) department as a Fulbright visiting scholar. Her research areas are Probability, Stochastic Processes, Cryptography, Occupational Safety and Health, and Reliability Engineering. She is the author of the books "Basics of Probability and Stochastic Processes" published in 2019, and "Einführung in Wahrscheinlichkeitsrechnung, Statistik und Stochastische Prozesse" published in 2020.

Cyber Shorts Series

Discover concise and focused books on specific cybersecurity topics with Cyber Shorts. This book series is designed for students, professionals, and enthusiasts seeking to explore specialized areas within cybersecurity. From blockchain to zero-day to ethical hacking, each book provides real-world examples and practical insights.

Ransomware
Penetration Testing and Contingency Planning
Ravindra Das

Deploying the Zero Trust Framework in MSFT Azure
Ravindra Das

Generative AI
Phishing and Cybersecurity Metrics
Ravindra Das

A Reference Manual for Data Privacy Laws and Cyber Frameworks
Ravindra Das

Offensive and Defensive Cyber Security Strategies
Fundamentals, Theory and Practices
Mariya Ouaissa and Mariyam Ouaissa

Public Key Cryptosystems
Esra Bas

For more information about this series, please visit: www.routledge.com/Cyber-Shorts/book-series/CYBSH

Public Key Cryptosystems

Esra Bas

CRC Press
Taylor & Francis Group
Boca Raton London New York

CRC Press is an imprint of the
Taylor & Francis Group, an **informa** business

Designed cover image: © Shutterstock

First edition published 2025
by CRC Press
2385 NW Executive Center Drive, Suite 320, Boca Raton FL 33431

and by CRC Press
4 Park Square, Milton Park, Abingdon, Oxon, OX14 4RN

CRC Press is an imprint of Taylor & Francis Group, LLC

ISBN: 978-1-032-82344-7 (hbk)
ISBN: 978-1-032-84623-1 (pbk)
ISBN: 978-1-003-51419-0 (ebk)

DOI: 10.1201/9781003514190

Typeset in Sabon
by KnowledgeWorks Global Ltd.

Contents

Chapter 1

Selected fundamental concepts in cryptography mathematics

1.1 INTRODUCTION

Public key cryptosystems are cryptosystems in which the encryption key is public, whereas the decryption key is private. This book is dedicated to the public key cryptosystems including digital signature algorithms, which have been developed based on mathematical fundamentals and the security of the public key cryptosystems is also based on the hardness of some mathematical problems. In Section 1.2, we first provide some basic properties of modular arithmetic since this operation is part of many public key cryptosystems. We also give the so-called fast powering algorithm related to modular arithmetic to be used for the solution of a fundamental mathematical problem in many public key cryptosystems. The "Chinese remainder theorem" is related to the solution of a set of linear congruences, and it is used in some public key cryptosystems to speed up the decryption process. Although the concepts "quadratic residue" and "quadratic nonresidue" are applicable only in some public key cryptosystems, it is still given in Section 1.2 to provide a mathematical background.

Since many public key cryptosystems work in groups, fields, or rings, Section 1.3 is devoted to the basic properties of groups, fields, and rings including some other topics such as "group homomorphism", "polynomial ring", "primitive root of a finite field", and "ring of convolution polynomials". Divisibility, greatest common divisors, and prime numbers are also critical in many public key cryptosystems; thus, Section 1.4 has been devoted to these topics including sub-topics "Fermat's little theorem", "Euclidean algorithm", and "extended Euclidean algorithm". The "Euclidean algorithm" and "extended Euclidean algorithm" can also be extended to polynomials, which are provided in Section 1.5. The main reason for providing Section 1.5 is that some special public key cryptosystems use polynomials as part of encryption and decryption steps. The security of some public key cryptosystems is based on the hardness of factoring a large integer number into two prime numbers; thus, Section 1.6 includes basic selected topics related to "integer factorization related selected mathematical fundamentals".

"Elliptic curve cryptography" is a distinctive area in cryptography and elliptic curve analogs of various public key cryptosystems and digital signature algorithms can be developed. Section 1.7 has been devoted to some

DOI: 10.1201/9781003514190-1

selected basics of elliptic curves including some subtopics such as "elliptic curves as an Abelian group", "point addition in elliptic curves", and "bilinear pairings, Weil pairings, distortion maps, and modified Weil pairings on elliptic curves". "Lattice-based cryptography" is also another distinctive area; thus, the basics of lattices will be given in Section 1.8 in comparison to vector spaces. Moreover, the lattice-related properties including fundamental domain, Hadamard's inequality, Hadamard ratio, and fundamental lattice problems will also be provided in this section. Finally, some selected basics of probability will be introduced in Section 1.9 since randomness is part of many public key cryptosystems to increase security. The topics provided in this chapter of the book are applicable in different parts of Chapters 3 to 6.

1.2 MODULAR ARITHMETIC AND RELATED TOPICS

One of the most important mathematical concepts in mathematical cryptography is the modular arithmetic, which is a fundamental operation in many cryptographic algorithms.

1.2.1 Modular arithmetic

Let x, y, m be integer numbers, where m is positive. Then $x \equiv y \pmod{m}$ means that "x is congruent to y modulo m" which also means that $(x-y)$ or $(y-x)$ can be divided by m, where m is called the "modulus" (Forman & Rash, 2015). In the case of $x \equiv 0 \pmod{m}$, x is divisible by m.

Example 1.1

$341 \equiv 16 \pmod{25}$ holds since $341 - 16 = 325$ is divisible by 25. Additionally, $-16 \equiv 10 \pmod{13}$ holds since $-16 - 10 = -26$ is divisible by 13. Moreover, since 623 is divisible by 7, $623 \equiv 0 \pmod{7}$.

1.2.2 Basic properties in modular arithmetic

Let $x_1 \equiv x_2 \pmod{m}, y_1 \equiv y_2 \pmod{m}$ hold, where x_1, x_2, y_1, y_2 are integer numbers, and m is a positive integer number. Then the basic properties in Equations (1.1) and (1.2) will follow (Contini, Kaya Koç, & Walter, 2011; Hoffstein, Pipher, & Silverman, 2008; Rosenthal, Rosenthal, & Rosenthal, 2014):

$$x_1 \pm y_1 \equiv x_2 \pm y_2 \pmod{m} \tag{1.1}$$

$$x_1 \cdot y_1 \equiv x_2 \cdot y_2 \pmod{m} \tag{1.2}$$

The following basic property is extremely important which is used in some cryptographic algorithms including the RSA public key cryptosystem that will be provided in Chapter 4.

Let m be a positive integer, and let x, y be integer numbers that satisfy $0 < x < m$ and $0 < y < m$. If $x \cdot y \equiv 1 \pmod{m}$ holds, then $y \equiv x^{-1} \pmod{m}$ is called the "multiplicative inverse" of the integer x modulo m. It is clear that $x \equiv y^{-1} \pmod{m}$ is also the "multiplicative inverse" of the integer y modulo m. Note that not every integer $0 < x < m$ has a multiplicative inverse modulo m. However, if an integer $0 < x < m$ has a multiplicative inverse modulo m, then it is unique (Meijer, 2016). Note also that the multiplicative inverse of an integer y modulo m can be again the integer y itself.

Example 1.2

Since $227 \equiv 24 \pmod{29}$, $445 \equiv 10 \pmod{29}$ hold, then $227 + 445 \equiv 24 + 10 \equiv 5 \pmod{29}$ and $227 \cdot 445 \equiv 24 \cdot 10 \equiv 8 \pmod{29}$ will result.

As another example, since $2 \cdot 3 \equiv 1 \pmod{5}$ holds, 3 is the multiplicative inverse of 2 (or 2 is the multiplicative inverse of 3) modulo 5. As the final example, 3 is the multiplicative inverse of 3 modulo 4, since $3 \cdot 3 \equiv 1 \pmod{4}$ holds.

1.2.3 Fast powering algorithm (fast exponentiation algorithm, square-and-multiply algorithm)

The problem $g^k \pmod{m}$, where $0 < g < m$ and $k > 0$ are integer numbers, is a basic problem in number theory. This calculation is also required in some cryptographic algorithms including the Diffie–Hellman key exchange and ElGamal public key cryptosystem that will be provided in Chapter 3. The fast-powering algorithm given in Table 1.1 provides an efficient solution

Table 1.1 The fast powering algorithm

The fast-powering algorithm to find $g^k \pmod{m}$	
Step 1	We write k as $k = k_0 \cdot 2^0 + k_1 \cdot 2^1 + k_2 \cdot 2^2 + k_3 \cdot 2^3 + \cdots + k_r \cdot 2^r$, where $k_0, k_1, \ldots, k_{r-1} \in \{0, 1\}, k_r = 1$.
Step 2	Let $a_0 \equiv g \pmod{m}$. Then, we write the following: $a_1 \equiv a_0^2 \equiv g^2 \pmod{m}$ $a_2 \equiv a_1^2 \equiv g^{2^2} \pmod{m}$ $a_3 \equiv a_2^2 \equiv g^{2^3} \pmod{m}$ $\ldots$ $a_r \equiv a_{r-1}^2 \equiv g^{2^r} \pmod{m}$.
Step 3	We write $g^k = g^{k_0 \cdot 2^0 + k_1 \cdot 2^1 + k_2 \cdot 2^2 + k_3 \cdot 2^3 + \cdots + k_r \cdot 2^r}$ $= (g^{2^0})^{k_0} . (g^{2^1})^{k_1} \cdot (g^{2^2})^{k_2} \cdot (g^{2^3})^{k_3} \cdot \ldots \cdot (g^{2^r})^{k_r}$ $\equiv (a_0)^{k_0} \cdot (a_1)^{k_1} \cdot (a_2)^{k_2} \cdot (a_3)^{k_3} \cdot \ldots \cdot (a_r)^{k_r} \pmod{m}$ where $k_0, k_1, \ldots, k_{r-1} \in \{0, 1\}, k_r = 1$.

Source: Adapted from Hoffstein, Pipher, and Silverman (2008) and Knuth (1998).

approach for this very basic problem. Please note that m does not have to be a prime number.

Example 1.3

We would like to calculate $3^{91} \pmod{48}$ by using the fast-powering algorithm:

Step 1: We write 91 as $91 = 2^0 + 2^1 + 2^3 + 2^4 + 2^6$.
Step 2: We let $a_0 \equiv 3 \pmod{48}$. Then, the following modulus congruences will follow:

$$a_1 \equiv 3^2 \equiv 9 \pmod{48}$$
$$a_2 \equiv 3^{2^2} \equiv 9 \cdot 9 \equiv 33 \pmod{48}$$
$$a_3 \equiv 3^{2^3} \equiv 33 \cdot 33 \equiv 33 \pmod{48}$$
$$a_4 \equiv 3^{2^4} \equiv 33 \cdot 33 \equiv 33 \pmod{48}$$
$$a_5 \equiv 3^{2^5} \equiv 33 \cdot 33 \equiv 33 \pmod{48}$$
$$a_6 \equiv 3^{2^6} \equiv 33 \cdot 33 \equiv 33 \pmod{48}$$

Step 3: By combining Steps 1 and 2, we obtain $3^{91} = 3^{2^0+2^1+2^3+2^4+2^6} = 3^{2^0} \cdot 3^{2^1} \cdot 3^{2^3} \cdot 3^{2^4} \cdot 3^{2^6} \equiv 3 \cdot 9 \cdot 33 \cdot 33 \cdot 33 \equiv 27 \bmod (48)$.

1.2.4 Chinese remainder theorem (CRT)

CRT is an old problem with different applications in number theory (Tilborg, 2011). This theorem is related to the solution of the set of the linear congruences given in Equation (1.3) to find x (Delfs & Knebl, 2015; Hoffstein et al., 2008; Schroeder, 2009)

$$x \equiv y_1 \pmod{m_1}, x \equiv y_2 \pmod{m_2}, \ldots, x \equiv y_n \pmod{m_n} \tag{1.3}$$

In Equation (1.3), $\gcd(m_i, m_j) = 1$ holds for all $i \neq j$. (For the formal definition of the greatest common divisor (gcd) of two integer numbers, please see Section 1.4.) To find the solution x in Equation (1.3), the following steps can be considered by using the notations of Schroeder (2009):

Step 1: We define $M_1 = m_2 \cdot \cdots \cdot m_{i-1} \cdot m_i \cdot m_{i+1} \cdot \cdots \cdot m_n$ and $M_i = m_1 \cdot m_2 \cdot \cdots \cdot m_{i-1} \cdot m_{i+1} \cdot \cdots \cdot m_n$ for $i = 2,.,n$.
Step 2: We find N_i for each $i = 1, 2,.,n$ that satisfies $N_i \cdot M_i \equiv 1 \pmod{m_i}$.
Step 3: Finally, the solution will be $x \equiv y_1 \cdot N_1 \cdot M_1 + y_2 \cdot N_2 \cdot M_2 + \cdots + y_n \cdot N_n \cdot M_n \pmod{m_1 \cdot m_2 \cdot \cdots \cdot m_n}$.

It can be shown that Equation (1.4) holds for two different solutions x_1 and x_2 of x (Childs, 2009; Delfs & Knebl, 2015; Hoffstein et al., 2008)

$$x_1 \equiv x_2 \pmod{m_1 \cdot m_2 \cdot \cdots \cdot m_n} \tag{1.4}$$

A special case can also be defined with only two linear congruences. CRT is particularly significant for the RSA public key cryptosystem to be provided in Chapter 4 since it can be used to speed up the decryption process in the RSA public key cryptosystem.

Example 1.4

We assume the problem of finding x by considering $x \equiv 3 \pmod{17}$ and $x \equiv 4 \pmod{19}$. We can use the following two approaches:

Approach 1: Following the approach of Schroeder (2009), we find $M_1 = m_2 = 19$, $M_2 = m_1 = 17$, and consider $19 \cdot N_1 \equiv 1 \pmod{17}$, $17 \cdot N_2 \equiv 1 \pmod{19}$ which yield $N_1 = 9, N_2 = 9$. Finally, we obtain $x \equiv 3 \cdot 9 \cdot 19 + 4 \cdot 9 \cdot 17 \equiv 156 \pmod{17 \cdot 19}$.

Approach 2: From the first congruence $x \equiv 3 \pmod{17}$, we can write $x = 3 + 17k$ $k \in \mathbb{Z}$, plug it into $x \equiv 4 \pmod{19}$, and find $3 + 17k \equiv 4 \pmod{19}$ from which $17k \equiv 1 \pmod{19}$ will follow. Finally, we must solve for k and insert it into $x = 3 + 17k$ to find x. Please note that k is the multiplicative inverse of 17 modulo 19, which can be computed by using the "extended Euclidean algorithm" provided in Section 1.4.3. Approach 2 of this example will be revisited in Section 1.4.3 for the remaining part of the solution.

1.2.5 Quadratic residue and quadratic non-residue

Let y be an integer and m be a positive odd integer, where y and m are relatively prime. If there is a solution x that satisfies $x^2 \equiv y \pmod{m}$, then y is called a "quadratic residue (QR)" modulo m, otherwise y is a "quadratic nonresidue (QN)" modulo m. It should be noted that m can be any positive odd integer or it can be an odd prime number p (Kaliski, 2011a). (Refer to Section 1.4 for the basic definitions of "relatively prime number" and "odd prime number".)

The so-called "Legendre symbol" of QR and QN was introduced for an odd prime number p as in Equation (1.5) (Gómez Pardo, 2013; Hoffstein et al., 2008; Kaliski, 2011b)

$$\left(\frac{y}{p}\right) = \begin{cases} 1 \text{ if } y \text{ is a QR modulo } p \\ -1 \text{ if } y \text{ is a QN modulo } p \\ 0 \text{ if } p \text{ divides } y \end{cases} \tag{1.5}$$

The "quadratic residuosity problem" is a special problem regarding whether $\left(\frac{y}{p}\right) = 1$ holds for a given y and p (Kaliski, 2011c). The notions of "quadratic residue" and "quadratic nonresidue" are used in some cryptographic algorithms including the Goldwasser–Micali probabilistic public key cryptosystem that will be provided in Chapter 6. There are different properties regarding the Legendre symbol of QR and QN (Gómez Pardo, 2013; Hoffstein et al., 2008; Kaliski, 2011b). However, in this section, we will provide one property that is related to the Goldwasser–Micali cryptosystem as follows:

Let y be an integer number and p,q be two odd prime numbers. Then, the equivalence in Equation (1.6) will hold (Gómez Pardo, 2013; Hoffstein et al., 2008; Kaliski, 2011b)

$$\left(\frac{y}{pq}\right)=\left(\frac{y}{p}\right)\left(\frac{y}{q}\right) \tag{1.6}$$

Note that in Equation (1.6), pq is an odd number which is not prime; thus, $\left(\frac{y}{pq}\right)$ is called the Jacobi symbol (Hoffstein et al., 2008).

1.3 RINGS, GROUPS, FIELDS

Rings, groups, and fields are of immense importance in mathematical cryptography. The distinction between these concepts is given comparatively in Table 1.2.

A "field" can alternatively be defined as a "commutative ring" in which every element other than zero has a "multiplicative inverse". A ring or field is also an "Abelian group" under $(+)$. Moreover, a field is an "Abelian group" under $(\cdot)$ if we disconsider 0. Please note from Table 1.2 that not all elements of a ring have to have "multiplicative inverses". Next, we provide some selected definitions related to rings, groups, and fields.

Definition 1.1

The set of polynomials $R[x]=\{a_0+a_1x+a_2x^2+\cdots+a_nx^n : n\geq 0,\ a_0,\ a_1,\ldots,\ a_n\in R\}$ is defined as a "polynomial ring" if they satisfy the properties of rings, where each polynomial has the degree n and the "leading coefficient" $a_n\neq 0$. If $a_n=1$ holds for a polynomial in $R[x]$, then this polynomial is called a "monic polynomial" (adapted from Becker & Weispfenning, 1993; Hibbard & Levasseur, 1999; Hoffstein et al., 2008).

Definition 1.2

A "group homomorphism" is a function $f: S\rightarrow T$, where $(S,\star)$ and $(T,\circ)$ are two different groups such that for all $x,y\in S$, $f(x\star y)=f(x)\circ f(y)$ holds, which means that the group structure is preserved in the function $f: S\rightarrow T$. In a "ring homomorphism", the group homomorphism with respect to two operations $+,\cdot$ is satisfied (adapted from Kaliski, 2005). (Please see Figure 1.1 for the illustration of a group homomorphism.)

Definition 1.3

An "ideal I of a ring R" is a subring of a ring R if the following conditions hold (Earl, 2018):

i. I is an additive subgroup of the ring $(R,+)$.
ii. For all $i\in I$ and $r\in R$, $ir\in I$ and $ri\in I$ hold.

Table 1.2 Rings, groups, fields

Ring	*Group*	*Field*
Let R be a non-empty set. Every ring $(R,+,\cdot)$ is defined for the operations $+$ and $\cdot$, where for every $a,b \in R$, $a+b \in R$ (Closed under $+$) $a \cdot b \in R$ (Closed under $\cdot$).	Let G be a non-empty set. Every group $(G, \star)$ is defined for the operation $\star$, where for every $a,b \in G$, $a \star b \in G$ (Closed under $\star$).	Let F be a non-empty set. Every field $(F,+,\cdot)$ is defined for the operations $+$ and $\cdot$, where for every $a,b \in F$, $a+b \in F$ (Closed under $+$) $a \cdot b \in F$ (Closed under $\cdot$).
Operation: $+$	**Operation:** $\star$	**Operation:** $+$
Let $a,-a,b,c \in R$.	Let $a,a^{-1},b,c \in G$.	Let $a,-a,b,c \in F$.
- Identity law $0+a=a+0=a$ holds for $\forall a \in R$, where $0 \in R$ is the unique "identity element" for the operation $+$.	- Identity law $e \star a = a \star e = a$ holds for $\forall a \in G$, where $e \in G$ is the unique "identity element" for the operation $\star$.	- Identity law $0+a=a+0=a$ holds for $\forall a \in F$, where $0 \in F$ is the unique "identity element" for the operation $+$.
- Inverse law $a+(-a)=(-a)+a=0$ holds for $\forall a \in R$, where $-a \in R$ is the unique "additive inverse" of $a \in R$.	- Inverse law $a \star a^{-1} = a^{-1} \star a = e$ holds for $\forall a \in G$, where $a^{-1} \in G$ is the unique inverse of $a \in G$.	- Inverse law $a+(-a)=(-a)+a=0$ holds for $\forall a \in F$, where $-a \in F$ is the unique "additive inverse" of $a \in F$.
- Associative law $a+(b+c)=(a+b)+c$ holds for $\forall a,b,c \in R$.	- Associative law $a \star (b \star c) = (a \star b) \star c$ holds for $\forall a,b,c \in G$.	- Associative law $a+(b+c)=(a+b)+c$ holds for $\forall a,b,c \in F$.
- Commutative law $a+b=b+a$ holds for $\forall a,b \in R$.	- Commutative law The group is called the "commutative (Abelian) group", if $a \star b = b \star a$ holds for $\forall a,b \in G$.	- Commutative law $a+b=b+a$ holds for $\forall a,b \in F$.
Operation: $\cdot$		**Operation:** $\cdot$
Let $a,b,c,u,u^{-1} \in R$		Let $a,a^{-1},b,c \in F$
- If $1 \cdot a = a \cdot 1 = a$ holds for $\forall a \in R$, then the ring is called the "ring with identity element (ring with unity)", where $1 \in R$ is the "identity element" for the operation "$\cdot$".		- $1 \cdot a = a \cdot 1 = a$ holds for $\forall a \in F$, where $1 \in F$ is the unique "identity element" for the operation "$\cdot$".
- If a nonzero element $u \in R$ has a "multiplicative inverse" u^{-1} such that $u \cdot u^{-1} = u^{-1} \cdot u = 1$ holds, then it is called a "unit".		- Inverse law $a \cdot a^{-1} = a^{-1} \cdot a = 1$ holds for each nonzero $a \in F$, where a^{-1} is the unique "multiplicative inverse" of a.
- An element $a \in R$ is "irreducible" if $a \in R$ is not a "unit", but for $a = b \cdot c$, either b or c is a "unit".		

(Continued)

Table 1.2 Rings, groups, fields *(Continued)*

Ring	*Group*	*Field*
- Associative law $a \cdot (b \cdot c) = (a \cdot b) \cdot c$ holds for $\forall a, b, c \in R$.		- Associative law $a \cdot (b \cdot c) = (a \cdot b) \cdot c$ holds for $\forall a, b, c \in F$.
- Commutative law If $a \cdot b = b \cdot a$ holds for $\forall a, b \in R$, then the ring is called a "commutative ring".		- Commutative law $a \cdot b = b \cdot a$ holds for $\forall a, b \in F$.
Other basic properties of rings	**Other basic properties of groups**	**Other basic properties of fields**
- Distributive law $a \cdot (b + c) = a \cdot b + a \cdot c$ holds for $\forall a, b, c \in R$.		- Distributive law $a \cdot (b + c) = a \cdot b + a \cdot c$ holds for $\forall a, b, c \in F$.
- Finite ring: If R has a finite number of elements, then R is a "finite ring".	- Finite group: If G has a finite number of elements, then G is a "finite group".	- Finite field: If F has a finite number of elements, then F is a "finite field". A finite field is also called the "Galois field (GF)".
- Order of R (denoted by $\lvert R \rvert$ or $\#R$): Number of elements in R, if R is a finite ring.	- Order of G (denoted by $\lvert G \rvert$ or $\#G$): Number of elements in G, if G is a finite group.	- Order of F (denoted by $\lvert F \rvert$ or $\#F$): Number of elements in F, if F is a finite field.
- Order of $a \in R$: The smallest $d \in \mathbb{Z}_+$ that satisfies $a^d = 1$ is called the order of $a \in R$.	- Order of $a \in G$: The smallest $d \in \mathbb{Z}_+$ that satisfies $a^d = a \star a \star \ldots \star a = e$ is called the order of $a \in G$.	- Order of $a \in F$: The smallest $d \in \mathbb{Z}_+$ that satisfies $a^d = 1$ is called the order of $a \in F$.

Source: Adapted from Gouvêa (2012), Hall (1999), Hoffstein et al. (2008), and Vanstone and van Oorschot (1989).

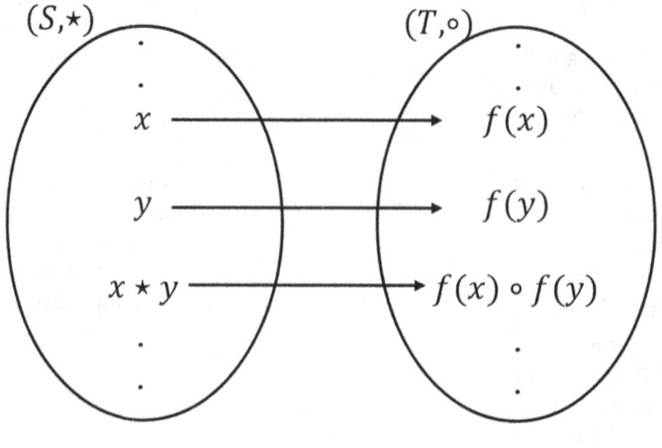

Figure 1.1 Group homomorphism.

An "ideal I of a ring R" is a "principal ideal" if there exists $a \in R$ such that $I = \langle a \rangle = \{ar \mid r \in R\}$ holds, where $\langle a \rangle$ means that a is the generator of the ideal I (adapted from Earl, 2018).

Definition 1.4

Let $r \in R$ be a fixed element of the ring R. The "coset of an ideal I" of a ring is the set of elements that are found by adding the fixed element $r \in R$ to each $i \in I$, i.e. $\{r + i \mid i \in I\}$ is a "coset of the ideal" I formed by using the so-called "coset representative" $r \in R$ (adapted from Earl, 2018).

Definition 1.5

The "quotient (factor) ring" is a ring that comprises all the "cosets of an ideal I" of a ring R denoted by $R / I = \{r + I \mid r \in R\}$ (adapted from Earl, 2018).

Example 1.5

As a very typical example, we consider $R = \mathbb{Z} = \{. -3, -2, -1, 0, +1, +2, +3, \ldots\}$. We also consider $I = 4\mathbb{Z} = \{. -12, -8, -4, 0, +4, +8, +12, \ldots\}$ as the "principal ideal" of $\mathbb{Z}$. (Please note that any integer number in $\mathbb{Z}$ will be a multiple of 4 when multiplied by any element of $I = 4\mathbb{Z}$, which means that the condition ii) in Definition 1.3 is satisfied.) It can be easily shown that the quotient ring $\mathbb{Z} / 4\mathbb{Z} = \{0 + 4\mathbb{Z}, 1 + 4\mathbb{Z}, 2 + 4\mathbb{Z}, 3 + 4\mathbb{Z}\}$ can be defined, where $0 + 4\mathbb{Z}, 1 + 4\mathbb{Z}, 2 + 4\mathbb{Z}, 3 + 4\mathbb{Z}$ are the four cosets formed by using the "principal ideal" $I = 4\mathbb{Z}$.

As a very important remark, Example 1.5 can be generalized for $R = \mathbb{Z} = \{. -3, -2, -1, 0, +1, +2, +3, \ldots\}$ and $I = m\mathbb{Z}$ as the "principal ideal" of $R = \mathbb{Z}$ such that $\mathbb{Z} / m\mathbb{Z} = \{0 + m\mathbb{Z}, 1 + m\mathbb{Z}, 2 + m\mathbb{Z}, \ldots, (m-1) + m\mathbb{Z}\}$ will hold.

In the following, we will perform the adaptations of Definitions 1.3, 1.4, and 1.5 to polynomial rings.

Definition 1.6

An "ideal $\langle f(x) \rangle$ of a polynomial ring" is a subgroup of a polynomial ring $R[x]$ obtained by multiplying $f(x) \in \langle f(x) \rangle$ by other polynomials in $R[x]$. Analogous to Definition 1.3, the following conditions hold (adapted from Norman, 2012):

i. $\langle f(x) \rangle$ is an additive subgroup of the polynomial ring $R[x]$.

ii. For all $f_i(x) \in \langle f(x) \rangle$ and $r(x) \in R(x)$, $f_i(x) r(x) \in \langle f(x) \rangle$ and $r(x) f_i(x) \in \langle f(x) \rangle$ hold.

Definition 1.7

Let $r(x) \in R[x]$ be a fixed element of the polynomial ring $R[x]$. The "coset of an ideal" of a polynomial ring is the set of elements that are found by adding the fixed polynomial $r(x) \in R[x]$ to each $f_i(x) \in \langle f(x) \rangle$, i.e. $\{r(x) + f_i(x) \mid f_i(x) \in \langle f(x) \rangle\}$ is a "coset of the ideal" $\langle f(x) \rangle$ formed by using the so-called "coset representative" $r(x) \in R[x]$ (adapted from Norman, 2012).

Definition 1.8

A "polynomial quotient (factor) ring" is a polynomial ring that comprises all the "cosets of an ideal" $\langle f(x) \rangle$ of a polynomial ring $R[x]$ denoted by $R[x]/\langle f(x) \rangle = \{r(x) + \langle f(x) \rangle \mid r(x) \in R[x]\}$. It is clear that $r(x) \equiv r_1(x) (\text{mod } f(x))$ holds for each $r(x) \in R[x]$.

Example 1.6

We assume $R[x] = \mathbb{Z}[x]$ and $\langle f(x) \rangle = \langle x^2 + 1 \rangle$, where $(x^2 + 1)p_1(x)$, $(x^2 + 1)p_2(x)$, $(x^2 + 1)p_3(x), \ldots \in \langle x^2 + 1 \rangle$ hold for $p_1(x), p_2(x), p_3(x), \ldots \in \mathbb{Z}[x]$. We consider the polynomial $r(x) = 3x^4 + 5x^3 - 6x^2 + x - 2$ in $\mathbb{Z}[x]$. It is clear that $3x^4 + 5x^3 - 6x^2 + x - 2 = (x^2 + 1)(3x^2 + 5x - 9) + (-4x + 7)$ can be obtained, which means that $3x^4 + 5x^3 - 6x^2 + x - 2 = \langle x^2 + 1 \rangle + (-4x + 7)$ holds. Accordingly, $3x^4 + 5x^3 - 6x^2 + x - 2 \equiv -4x + 7 \left(\text{mod } (x^2 + 1)\right)$ also holds. (For the formal definition of "polynomial modulo a polynomial", please see Section 1.3.3.2.)

Definition 1.9

The "characteristic of a field" $(F, +, \cdot)$, shown as char (F), is the smallest $k \in \mathbb{Z}_+$ that satisfies $k \cdot x = 0$ for all $x \in F$. If this condition is not satisfied, then the "characteristic of the field" will be 0. The characteristic of a ring can also be defined analogously (adapted from Golan, 2012; Kaliski, 2011d; Khattar & Agrawal, 2023).

Definition 1.10

A "finite multiplicative group" G is "cyclic" if it can be generated by $g \in G$ as $G = \langle g \rangle = \{g^x, x \in [0, |G| - 1]\}$ or $G = \langle g \rangle = \{g^x, x \in \mathbb{Z}\}$, where g is called the "generator" of the multiplicative group. Analogously, a "finite additive group" G is "cyclic" if it can be generated by $G = \langle g \rangle = \{gx, x \in \mathbb{Z}\}$, where g is called the "generator" of the additive group (adapted from Charpin, 2011; Childs, 1995; Kaliski, 2011e).

Example 1.7

(1) The set $\mathbb{Q}$ of rational numbers is an "infinite ring" and an infinite "Abelian group" under the operation +. If we disconsider 0, this set is also an "infinite field", and an "Abelian group" under the operation $\cdot$.

(2) The set $\mathbb{Z}$ of integer numbers is an "infinite ring" but *not* an "infinite field", since most integer numbers do not have "multiplicative inverses". This set is also an infinite "Abelian group" under the operation +.

1.3.1 Ring of integers modulo *m* and multiplicative group of units modulo *m*

Please recall that $\mathbb{Z}/m\mathbb{Z} = \{0 + m\mathbb{Z}, 1 + m\mathbb{Z}, 2 + m\mathbb{Z}, \ldots, (m-1) + m\mathbb{Z}\}$ as a special "quotient ring" from the remark after Example 1.5. Specifically, $\mathbb{Z}/m\mathbb{Z}$ is called a "ring of integers modulo m" if we define $\mathbb{Z}/m\mathbb{Z} = \{0, 1, 2, \ldots, m-1\}$ for modulo integer number m. On the other hand, $(\mathbb{Z}/m\mathbb{Z})^*$ is a "multiplicative group of units modulo m" if we define $(\mathbb{Z}/m\mathbb{Z})^* = \{a \in \mathbb{Z}/m\mathbb{Z} : a \text{ is a unit modulo } m\}$ (Hoffstein et al., 2008; Kaliski, 2011f). Since the "set of units of a ring" is closed under multiplication, this set is also a "multiplicative group" (Childs, 2009). Thus, we can call the "set of units of a ring modulo m" as "multiplicative group of units modulo m". The "Euler's phi (totient) function $\phi(m)$" is used to compute the number of elements in a "multiplicative group of units modulo m", which is defined in Equation (1.7) (Kaliski, 2011g)

$$\phi(m) = \#(\mathbb{Z}/m\mathbb{Z})^* = m\left(1 - \frac{1}{p_1}\right)\left(1 - \frac{1}{p_2}\right)\cdots\left(1 - \frac{1}{p_r}\right) \tag{1.7}$$

Note that for any integer m, $m = p_1^{e_1} \cdot p_2^{e_2} \cdot \ldots \cdot p_r^{e_r}$ is the unique factorization of m into the prime numbers $p_1, p_2, \ldots, p_r$, where $e_1, e_2, \ldots, e_r \in \mathbb{Z}_+$. (See Section 1.6.1 for the topic "factorization".)

Although $\mathbb{Z}/m\mathbb{Z}$ and $(\mathbb{Z}/m\mathbb{Z})^*$ can be defined for any integer number m, $\mathbb{Z}/p\mathbb{Z}$, and $(\mathbb{Z}/p\mathbb{Z})^*$ for prime number p are much more important in mathematical cryptography, which are defined as in Equations (1.8) and (1.9)

$$\mathbb{Z}/p\mathbb{Z} = \mathbb{F}_p = \mathbb{Z}_p = \{0, 1, 2, \ldots, p-1\} \tag{1.8}$$

$$(\mathbb{Z}/p\mathbb{Z})^* = \mathbb{F}_p^* = \mathbb{Z}_p^* = \{1, 2, \ldots, p-1\} \tag{1.9}$$

It is clear that $\phi(p) = \#(\mathbb{Z}/p\mathbb{Z})^* = p\left(1 - \frac{1}{p}\right) = p - 1$ always holds, and $\mathbb{Z}/p\mathbb{Z}$ and $(\mathbb{Z}/p\mathbb{Z})^*$ are finite fields (Stein, 2009; Vanstone & van Oorschot, 1989). (In $\mathbb{Z}/p\mathbb{Z}$, although 0 has no multiplicative inverse, $\mathbb{Z}/p\mathbb{Z}$ is still assumed to be a finite field by definition.)

Example 1.8

For $m = 6$, $\mathbb{Z}/6\mathbb{Z} = \{0, 1, 2, 3, 4, 5\}$ and $(\mathbb{Z}/6\mathbb{Z})^* = \{1, 5\}$ hold. Note that $\mathbb{Z}/6\mathbb{Z}$ is a "ring" since it satisfies all the properties of a ring, but not a "finite field", due to the reason that not every element of $\mathbb{Z}/6\mathbb{Z}$ has a "multiplicative inverse" modulo 6. On the other hand, $(\mathbb{Z}/6\mathbb{Z})^*$ is not a "ring" since it is not closed under (+), but it is a "multiplicative group". Note also that 1, 5 are the units modulo 6, since they have the "multiplicative inverses" in $(\mathbb{Z}/6\mathbb{Z})^*$. We can verify that the number of units modulo 6 is 2 according to the "Euler's phi (totient) function" since $\phi(6) = \#(\mathbb{Z}/6\mathbb{Z})^* = 6(1-\frac{1}{2})(1-\frac{1}{3}) = 2$ holds, where $6 = 2 \cdot 3$.

As another example, for $p = 11$, $\mathbb{Z}/11\mathbb{Z} = \{0, 1, 2, 3, \ldots, 10\}$ and $(\mathbb{Z}/11\mathbb{Z})^* = \{1, 2, 3, \ldots, 10\}$ hold. We can also verify that the number of units modulo 11 is 10 according to the "Euler's phi (totient) function" since $\phi(11) = \#(\mathbb{Z}/11\mathbb{Z})^* = 11-1 = 10$ holds.

1.3.2 Primitive root (element) of $\mathbb{F}_p$ (*generator* of $\mathbb{F}_p^*$)

The "primitive root (element)" of $\mathbb{F}_p$ is one of the key concepts in different public key cryptosystems and digital signature algorithms including the basic ElGamal digital signature algorithm to be provided in Chapter 3.

Definition 1.11

$g \in \mathbb{F}_p^*$ is called a "primitive root (element)" of $\mathbb{F}_p$ (generator of $\mathbb{F}_p^*$) if the elements of $\mathbb{F}_p^*$ can be constructed by using $g \in \mathbb{F}_p^*$ as in Equation (1.10) (Hoffstein et al., 2008).

$$\mathbb{F}_p^* = \{1, g^1, g^2, \ldots, g^k, \ldots, g^{p-2}\} \tag{1.10}$$

Please note that a finite field is a multiplicative group which is also cyclic (Kaliski, 2011e). Thus, the definition of the "multiplicative cyclic group" provided in Definition 1.10 can be adapted to Equation (1.10). Please note also that there is no unique primitive root of $\mathbb{F}_p$. $\phi(p-1)$ in Equation (1.11) gives the number of primitive roots of $\mathbb{F}_p$, where $\phi(p-1)$ is again "Euler's phi (totient) function" with $p-1 = p_1^{e1} p_2^{e2} \cdot \ldots \cdot p_r^{e_r}$ (Hoffstein et al., 2008; Kaliski, 2011g).

$$\phi(p-1) = (p-1)\left(1-\frac{1}{p_1}\right)\left(1-\frac{1}{p_2}\right)\ldots\left(1-\frac{1}{p_r}\right) \tag{1.11}$$

Example 1.9

$g = 3$ is a primitive root of $\mathbb{F}_7$ as shown in Table 1.3.

As a result, $\{1, 3, 2, 6, 4, 5\} = \{1, 2, 3, 4, 5, 6\} = \mathbb{F}_7^*$ holds. According to the "Euler's phi (totient) function", there are $\phi(7-1) = \phi(6) = 6(1-\frac{1}{2})(1-\frac{1}{3}) = 2$ primitive roots of $\mathbb{F}_7$. It can be identified that the second primitive root of $\mathbb{F}_7$ is 5.

1.3.3 Ring of convolution polynomials and selected properties

A "ring of convolution polynomials" is a special "polynomial quotient ring" that is used in the NTRU public cryptosystem to be provided in Chapter 5.

Table 1.3 Primitive root $g = 3$ for $\mathbb{F}_7$

	Primitive root $g = 3$ *for* $\mathbb{F}_7$
0	$3^0 \equiv 1 \pmod 7$
1	$3^1 \equiv 3 \pmod 7$
2	$3^2 \equiv 2 \pmod 7$
3	$3^3 \equiv 6 \pmod 7$
4	$3^4 \equiv 4 \pmod 7$
5	$3^5 \equiv 5 \pmod 7$

1.3.3.1 Ring of convolution polynomials (convolution polynomial ring)

The "ring of convolution polynomials" is a special "polynomial quotient ring" that is modulo a fixed polynomial, which is $x^N - 1$ in the standard of IEEE Std 1363.1–2008, where N is a fixed positive integer (Hoffstein et al., 2008). Accordingly, the "ring of convolution polynomials" of degree $N-1$ can be shown as $R = \mathbb{Z}[x]/(x^N - 1)$, where $\mathrm{f}(x) = a_0 + a_1x + a_2x^2 + \cdots + a_{N-1}x^{N-1}$ is an element of R with $(a_0, a_1, \ldots, a_{N-1}) \in \mathbb{Z}^N$ (Hoffstein et al., 2008). On the other hand, the "ring of convolution polynomials modulo p" of degree $N-1$ can be defined as $R_p = (\mathbb{Z}/p\mathbb{Z})[x]/(x^N - 1)$, where $\mathrm{g}(x) = b_0 + b_1x + b_2x^2 + \cdots + b_{N-1}x^{N-1}$ is an element of R_p with $(b_0, b_1, \ldots, b_{N-1}) \in (\mathbb{Z}/p\mathbb{Z})^N$ (Hoffstein et al., 2008).

We need Definition 1.12 for the NTRU public key cryptosystem to be provided in Chapter 5.

Definition 1.12

A "ternary (trinary) polynomial" is a special polynomial whose coefficients, including the constant term, can be −1, +1, or 0 (Hoffstein, Howgrave-Graham, Pipher, & Whyte, 2009). Specifically, a "ternary (trinary) polynomial" $\mathrm{f}(x) \in R$ or $\mathrm{g}(x) \in R_p$ of degree $N-1$, which is denoted as $\tau(d_1, d_2)$, is a polynomial in which the number of the coefficients +1 is d_1 and the number of the coefficients −1 is d_2 (adapted from Hoffstein et al., 2008).

Example 1.10

$\mathrm{f}(x) = -x^6 + x^5 + x^4 - x^2 + x \in R$ of degree 6 is a "ternary polynomial", which can be denoted as $\tau(3, 2)$. Please note that the constant term and the coefficient of x^3 are zero.

In the following sections, we provide some selected properties of the rings of convolution polynomials, which are required to execute the NTRU public key cryptosystem.

1.3.3.2 Polynomial modulo a polynomial

For two polynomials $\mathrm{f}(x)$ and $\mathrm{g}(x)$, $\mathrm{f}(x) \equiv \mathrm{r}(x) (\mathrm{mod}\ \mathrm{g}(x))$ holds if $\mathrm{f}(x) - \mathrm{r}(x)$ can be divided by $\mathrm{g}(x)$, where the result is again a polynomial $\mathrm{h}(x)$, i.e. $\mathrm{f}(x) = \mathrm{r}(x) + \mathrm{g}(x)\mathrm{h}(x)$ holds (Bini & Pan, 1994).

Example 1.11

As given in Example 1.6, $3x^4 + 5x^3 - 6x^2 + x - 2 \equiv -4x + 7 \ (\mathrm{mod}\ (x^2+1))$ holds since $3x^4 + 5x^3 - 6x^2 + x - 2 = (x^2+1)(3x^2+5x-9) + (-4x+7)$ can be written.

1.3.3.3 Addition and multiplication (product) of two polynomials in the ring of convolution polynomials

The addition and multiplication of two polynomials will be illustrated in R_p.

Let $\mathrm{f}(x) = a_0 + a_1x + \cdots + a_ix^i + \cdots + a_{N-1}x^{N-1}$ and $\mathrm{g}(x) = b_0 + b_1x + \cdots + b_jx^j + \cdots + b_{N-1}x^{N-1}$ be two polynomials of degree $N-1$ in R_p. Then, the addition of these two polynomials in R_p will be as in Equation (1.12)

$$\begin{aligned} \mathrm{f}(x) + \mathrm{g}(x) = (a_0 + b_0)(\mathrm{mod}\ p) + (a_1 + b_1)(\mathrm{mod}\ p)x + (a_2 + b_2) \\ (\mathrm{mod}\ p)x^2 + \cdots + (a_{N-1} + b_{N-1})(\mathrm{mod}\ p)x^{N-1} \end{aligned} \tag{1.12}$$

Let $\star$ be the multiplication operator. Then $\mathrm{h}(x) = \mathrm{f}(x) \star \mathrm{g}(x)$ in R_p can be defined as $\mathrm{h}(x) = c_0 + c_1x + c_2x^2 + \cdots + c_{N-1}x^{N-1}$, where each coefficient can be calculated as in Equation (1.13) (Geddes, Czapor, & Labahn, 1992; Hoffstein et al., 2008).

$$c_k = \sum_{i+j \equiv k\ (\mathrm{mod}\ N)} a_ib_j\ (\mathrm{mod}\ p),\ k = 0, 1, 2, \ldots, N-1 \tag{1.13}$$

The addition and multiplication (product) of two polynomials in R are analogous with the difference that mod p is not considered.

Example 1.12

Let $\mathrm{f}(x) = 5 + 3x + 6x^2 + 4x^3 + 5x^4$, $\mathrm{g}(x) = 6 + 5x + 3x^2 + 6x^3 + 4x^4$ be two polynomials in R_7, where $N = 5$. The addition of $\mathrm{f}(x)$ and $\mathrm{g}(x)$ will be $\mathrm{f}(x) + \mathrm{g}(x) = 4 + x + 2x^2 + 3x^3 + 2x^4$. The multiplication of $\mathrm{f}(x)$ and $\mathrm{g}(x)$ will be $\mathrm{h}(x) = \mathrm{f}(x) \star \mathrm{g}(x)$ in R_7 that can be defined as $\mathrm{h}(x) = c_0 + c_1x + c_2x^2 + c_3x^3 + c_4x^4$, where

$$\begin{aligned} c_0 &= (5\cdot6) + (3\cdot4) + (6\cdot6) + (4\cdot3) + (5\cdot5) = 115 \equiv 3\ (\mathrm{mod}\ 7) \\ c_1 &= (5\cdot5) + (3\cdot6) + (6\cdot4) + (4\cdot6) + (5\cdot3) = 106 \equiv 1\ (\mathrm{mod}\ 7) \\ c_2 &= (5\cdot3) + (3\cdot5) + (6\cdot6) + (4\cdot4) + (5\cdot6) = 112 \equiv 0\ (\mathrm{mod}\ 7) \\ c_3 &= (5\cdot6) + (3\cdot3) + (6\cdot5) + (4\cdot6) + (5\cdot4) = 113 \equiv 1\ (\mathrm{mod}\ 7) \\ c_4 &= (5\cdot4) + (3\cdot6) + (6\cdot3) + (4\cdot5) + (5\cdot6) = 106 \equiv 1\ (\mathrm{mod}\ 7) \end{aligned}$$

can be obtained by considering Equation (1.13). Finally, $\mathrm{h}(x) = 3 + x + x^3 + x^4$ in R_7 will hold.

1.3.3.4 Center-lifting (centering lift)

A polynomial $\mathrm{g}(x)$ in R_p can be transformed (so-called center-lifted) to another polynomial $\mathrm{f}(x)$ in R by considering $\mathrm{f}(x) \equiv \mathrm{g}(x) \pmod{p}$, where the coefficients of $\mathrm{f}(x)$ are chosen to be in the interval $\left(-\frac{p}{2}, \frac{p}{2}\right]$ (Hoffstein et al., 2008; Huang, Kueh, & Tan, 2000).

Example 1.13

Let $\mathrm{g}(x) = 6 + 7x^2 - 9x^3 + x^4 + 10x^5$ be chosen in R_{11}. We want to center-lift $\mathrm{g}(x)$ in R_{11} to $\mathrm{f}(x)$ in R. As a result, we find $\mathrm{f}(x) = -5 - 4x^2 + 2x^3 + x^4 - x^5$ in R, where the coefficients are in $\left(-\frac{11}{2}, \frac{11}{2}\right]$.

1.4 DIVISIBILITY, GREATEST COMMON DIVISORS, AND PRIME NUMBERS

For two integer numbers a and b, the notation $b \mid a$ means that b divides a, otherwise the notation $b \nmid a$ means that b does not divide a. For two integer numbers a, b, $\gcd(a,b) = d$ means that the integer number d is the "greatest common divisor (gcd)" that satisfies $d \mid a$ and $d \mid b$. An integer number $p \geq 2$ that satisfies $1 \mid p$, $p \mid p$, but $k \nmid p$ for $k \in \mathbb{Z} \setminus \{1, p\}$ is called a "prime (number)". If an integer number is not a "prime number", then it is called a "composite number". All prime numbers other than 2 are called the "odd prime numbers". If $\gcd(a,b) = 1$, then a and b are called the "relatively prime (coprime) numbers".

Please recall the definition of the "multiplicative inverse" of an integer x modulo m from Section 1.2.2 and recall that not every integer $0 < x < m$ has a multiplicative inverse modulo m. However, if $\gcd(x,m) = 1$ holds, then the integer x has a "multiplicative inverse" modulo m, which is unique, i.e. there is an integer number y that satisfies $x \cdot y \equiv 1 \pmod{m}$ (Delfs & Knebl, 2015; Gregory & Krishnamurthy, 1984; Hoffstein et al., 2008).

Example 1.8 (revisited)

Please recall $(\mathbb{Z}/6\mathbb{Z})^* = \{1, 5\}$ is the "multiplicative group of units" modulo 6, which can be verified since $\gcd(1, 6) = \gcd(5, 6) = 1$ hold. Please recall also $(\mathbb{Z}/11\mathbb{Z})^* = \{1, 2, 3, \ldots, 10\}$ or generally $(\mathbb{Z}/p\mathbb{Z})^* = \{1, 2, 3, \ldots, p-1\}$ holds since for each $a \in (\mathbb{Z}/p\mathbb{Z})^*$ and prime number p, $\gcd(a,p) = 1$ is always true.

1.4.1 Fermat's little theorem

The "Fermat's little theorem" is a fundamental theorem in mathematical cryptography which has different applications including the "primality testing" to be provided in Chapter 2. This theorem is defined for any $a \in \mathbb{Z}$ and any prime number p as in Equation (1.14) (Delfs & Knebl, 2015; Hoffstein et al., 2008; Liskov, 2011):

$$a^{p-1} \equiv \begin{cases} 1 \pmod{p} \text{ if } p \nmid a \\ 0 \pmod{p} \text{ if } p \mid a \end{cases} \tag{1.14}$$

Alternatively, this theorem can be defined as $a^{-1} \equiv a^{p-2} \pmod{p}$ or $a^{p} \equiv a \pmod{p}$ if $p \nmid a$ holds (Hoffstein et al., 2008). Please note that by using $a^{-1} \equiv a^{p-2} \pmod{p}$, the multiplicative inverse of the integer a modulo p can be determined.

Specifically, let g be a "primitive root" of the finite field $\mathbb{F}_{p.}$ Due to the condition $p \nmid g$, $g^{p-1} \equiv 1 \pmod{p}$ or $g^{-1} \equiv g^{p-2} \pmod{p}$ or $g^{p} \equiv g \pmod{p}$ always holds (Hoffstein et al., 2008).

Example 1.14

Let's consider the prime number $p = 176531$. According to the Fermat's little theorem, $2^{176530} \equiv 1 \pmod{176531}$ holds, since 176531 cannot divide 2. However $176531^{176530} \equiv 0 \pmod{176531}$ holds, since 176531 can divide 176531.

Please see Chapter 2, Section 2.9 for more details about the "primality testing".

1.4.2 Euclidean algorithm

Let a, $b \in \mathbb{Z}_{+}$ satisfying $a \geq b$. The "Euclidean algorithm" solves the basic problem $\gcd(a,b)$ in an efficient way. Table 1.4 provides the steps of the "Euclidean algorithm", where we consider q_i as the quotient i and r_i as the remainder i.

Table 1.4 Euclidean algorithm

Euclidean algorithm	$gcd(a,b) = ?$
	$a = r_0,\ b = r_1 \neq 0$
	$r_0 = r_1 \cdot q_1 + r_2 \quad 0 < r_2 < r_1$
	$r_1 = r_2 \cdot q_2 + r_3 \quad 0 < r_3 < r_2$
	$r_2 = r_3 \cdot q_3 + r_4 \quad 0 < r_4 < r_3$
	$r_3 = r_4 \cdot q_4 + r_5 \quad 0 < r_5 < r_4$
	...
	$r_{t-2} = r_{t-1} \cdot q_{t-1} + r_t \quad 0 < r_t < r_{t-1}$
	$r_{t-1} = r_t \cdot q_t$, where $r_t = \gcd(a,b)$

Source: Adapted from Bressoud (1989) and Hoffstein et al. (2008)

Example 1.15

Table 1.5 shows the steps of finding the gcd of 1048 and 246.

Table 1.5 An example for the Euclidean algorithm

Euclidean algorithm	*gcd(1048, 246) = ?*
	$1048 = 246 \cdot 4 + 64$
	$246 = 64 \cdot 3 + 54$
	$64 = 54 \cdot 1 + 10$
	$54 = 10 \cdot 5 + 4$
	$10 = 4 \cdot 2 + 2$
	$4 = \mathbf{2} \cdot 2$, where $\gcd(1048, 246) = 2$

1.4.3 Extended Euclidean algorithm

Let $a, b \in \mathbb{Z}_+$ be given. According to number theory, there are always two integer numbers u, v that satisfy Equation (1.15), where both of u and v do not have to be positive (Delfs & Knebl, 2015; Hoffstein et al., 2008).

$$au + bv = \gcd(a, b) \tag{1.15}$$

When we consider the case $\gcd(a, b) = 1$, it is clear that solving Equation (1.16) for u und v gives $u = a^{-1}$ (mod b) or $v = b^{-1}$ (mod a).

$$au + bv = \gcd(a, b) = 1 \tag{1.16}$$

Please note that as a very special case, the integer number b can replaced by the prime number p, and the solution of $au + pv = \gcd(a, p) = 1$ gives $u = a^{-1} \pmod{p}$.

The extended Euclidean algorithm provided in Table 1.6 is very closely related to the Euclidean algorithm provided in Table 1.4. As given in Table 1.6, the extended Euclidean algorithm works in backward (starting from the last equation given in Table 1.4) to find an equation in the form $au + bv = \gcd(a, b) = 1$ so that the values of u and v can be determined.

Example 1.4 (revisited)

Please recall the problem as: $x \equiv 3 \pmod{17}$, $x \equiv 4 \pmod{19}$, where x is to be found. Please recall also that according to Approach 2, $x = 3 + 17k$, $k \in \mathbb{Z}$, and $17k \equiv 1 \pmod{19}$ hold, where we should compute $17^{-1} \pmod{19}$ to find k so that we can find the solution to $x = 3 + 17k$. Since $p = 19$ is a prime number, there exist two integer numbers u, v such that $17u + 19v = 1$. When we solve for u and v, we find $u = 9, v = -8$ from which we conclude that $u = 9 = 17^{-1} = k \pmod{19}$.

Table 1.6 Extended Euclidean algorithm to find u and v in $au + bv = \gcd(a,b) = 1$

The steps of the Euclidean algorithm (from Table 1.4)	*The steps of the extended Euclidean algorithm*
$r_0 - r_1 \cdot q_1 = r_2$	$r_{t-2} - r_{t-1} \cdot q_{t-1} = 1$
$r_1 - r_2 \cdot q_2 = r_3$	$r_{t-2} - \overbrace{(r_{t-3} - r_{t-2} \cdot q_{t-2})} \cdot q_{t-1} = 1$
$r_2 - r_3 \cdot q_3 = r_4$	$(1 + q_{t-2} \cdot q_{t-1}) r_{t-2} - q_{t-1} r_{t-3} = 1$
	$(1 + q_{t-2} \cdot q_{t-1}) \overbrace{(r_{t-4} - r_{t-3} \cdot q_{t-3})} - q_{t-1} r_{t-3} = 1$
...	...
$r_{t-4} - r_{t-3} \cdot q_{t-3} = r_{t-2}$	
$r_{t-3} - r_{t-2} \cdot q_{t-2} = r_{t-1}$	
$r_{t-2} - r_{t-1} \cdot q_{t-1} = r_t = 1$	$r_0 u + r_1 v = 1$ or $au + bv = 1$, from which u and v can be determined.

Table 1.7 Extended Euclidean algorithm for Example 1.4 (revisited)

Euclidean algorithm for $\gcd(17, 19) = 1$	*Extended Euclidean algorithm* $17u + 19v = 1$
$19 = 17 \cdot 1 + 2$	$17 - 2 \cdot 8 = 1$
$17 = 2 \cdot 8 + 1$	$17 - \overbrace{(19 - 17 \cdot 1)} \cdot 8 = 1$
$2 = 1 \cdot 2$	$17 - (19 \cdot 8 - 17 \cdot 8) = 1$
$\gcd(17,19) = 1$	$17 + 17 \cdot 8 - 19 \cdot 8 = 1$
	$17 \cdot 9 - 19 \cdot 8 = 1$, where $u = 9, v = -8$

Finally, the solution will be $x = 3 + 17k = 3 + 17 \cdot 9 = 156$, which is the same result as in Approach 1. (Please see the steps of the extended Euclidean algorithm in Table 1.7 for the solution of $17u + 19v = 1$.)

1.5 EUCLIDEAN ALGORITHM AND EXTENDED EUCLIDEAN ALGORITHM FOR POLYNOMIALS

The Euclidean algorithm and extended Euclidean algorithm can also be adapted to the polynomials.

1.5.1 Euclidean algorithm for polynomials

The gcd of two polynomials $f(x)$ and $g(x)$ is a monic polynomial with the highest degree that can divide both $f(x)$ and $g(x)$. The "Euclidean algorithm" given in Table 1.4 can be adapted to the polynomials to find the gcd of $f(x)$ and $g(x)$ as given in Table 1.8 (Klein, 2014).

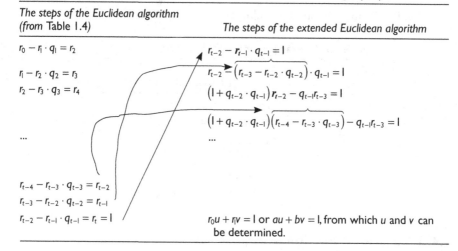

Table 1.8 Euclidean algorithm for polynomials

Euclidean algorithm for polynomials	$\gcd(\mathbf{f}(x),\mathbf{g}(x)) = ?$ $\deg(\mathbf{f}(x)) \geq \deg(\mathbf{g}(x))$ $\mathbf{f}(x) = \mathbf{g}(x)\cdot\mathbf{q}_1(x) + \mathbf{r}_1(x)\ 0 < \deg(\mathbf{r}_1(x)) < \deg(\mathbf{g}(x))$ $\mathbf{g}(x) = \mathbf{r}_1(x)\cdot\mathbf{q}_2(x) + \mathbf{r}_2(x)\ 0 < \deg(\mathbf{r}_2(x)) < \deg(\mathbf{r}_1(x))$ $\mathbf{r}_1(x) = \mathbf{r}_2(x)\cdot\mathbf{q}_3(x) + \mathbf{r}_3(x)\ 0 < \deg(\mathbf{r}_3(x)) < \deg(\mathbf{r}_2(x))$ … $\mathbf{r}_{t-2}(x) = \mathbf{r}_{t-1}(x)\cdot\mathbf{q}_t(x) + \mathbf{r}_t(x)\ 0 < \deg(\mathbf{r}_t(x)) < \deg(\mathbf{r}_{t-1}(x))$ $\mathbf{r}_{t-1}(x) = \mathbf{r}_t(x)\cdot\mathbf{q}_{t+1}(x)$, where $\mathbf{r}_t(x) = \gcd(\mathbf{f}(x),\mathbf{g}(x))$ if $\mathbf{r}_t(x)$ is a monic polynomial.

Source: (adapted from Hoffstein et al., 2008; Toth, 2021)

Example 1.16

Let $\mathrm{f}(x) = x^3 + 3x^2 + 4x + 12$ and $\mathrm{g}(x) = x^2 + x - 6$ be defined. Then we can find $\gcd(\mathrm{f}(x),\mathrm{g}(x))$ by considering the steps given in Table 1.9.

1.5.2 Extended Euclidean algorithm for polynomials

The "multiplicative inverse of a polynomial" will be defined for a polynomial $\mathrm{f}(x)$ in R_p, which is also required for the NTRU public key cryptosystem to be provided in Chapter 5. There exists $\mathrm{f}^{-1}(x)$ in R_p if $\gcd(\mathrm{f}(x),(x^N-1)) = 1$ in $\mathbb{F}_p[x]$ holds (Hoffstein et al., 2008). When we consider $\mathbf{f}(x)\mathbf{u}(x) + (x^N - 1)\mathbf{v}(x) = 1$, where $\mathbf{u}(x), \mathbf{v}(x) \in \mathbb{F}_p[x]$, then $\mathbf{u}(x) = \mathrm{f}^{-1}(x)$ in R_p holds (Hoffstein et al., 2008). The extended Euclidean algorithm's steps for polynomials will be analogous to the steps provided in Table 1.6.

Example 1.17

We consider $\mathrm{f}(x) = x^4 + 3x^2 - x + 5$, $N = 5$, $p = 7$ and would like to find $\mathrm{f}^{-1}(x)$ in R_7. First we should show that $\gcd(x^4 + 3x^2 - x + 5,\ x^5 - 1) = 1$ holds by using the Euclidean algorithm's steps for polynomials as follows:

Table 1.9 Example for Euclidean algorithm for polynomials

Euclidean algorithm for polynomials	$\gcd(\mathbf{f}(x),\mathbf{g}(x)) = ?$ $\mathbf{f}(x)) = x^3 + 3x^2 + 4x + 12$ $\mathbf{g}(x) = x^2 + x - 6$ $(x^3 + 3x^2 + 4x + 12) = (x^2 + x - 6)(x + 2) + (8x + 24)$ $(x^2 + x - 6) = (8x + 24)(\frac{1}{8}x) + (-2x - 6)$ $(8x + 24) = (-2x - 6)(-4) = -2(x + 3)(-4) = (x + 3)8$, where $(x + 3)$ is a monic polynomial that is gcd of $\mathbf{f}(x) = x^3 + 3x^2 + 4x + 12$ and $\mathbf{g}(x) = x^2 + x - 6$.

Please first note that since we work in $\mathbb{F}_7$, we can also write x^5-1 as x^5+6 and x^4+3x^2-x+5 as x^4+3x^2+6x+5. The following steps are made by considering the Euclidean algorithms steps in $\mathbb{F}_7$.

$$x^5+6=\left(x^4+3x^2+6x+5\right)x+4x^3+x^2+2x+6$$

$$x^4+3x^2+6x+5=\left(4x^3+x^2+2x+6\right)(2x+3)+3x^2+2x+1$$

$$4x^3+x^2+2x+6=\left(3x^2+2x+1\right)(6x+1)+x+5$$

$$3x^2+2x+1=(x+5)(3x+1)+3$$

$$x+5=3(5x+4)$$

Since 3 is not a monic polynomial, $\gcd\left(x^4+3x^2-x+5,\ x^5-1\right)=1$.

Next, we perform the following steps for the extended Euclidean algorithm to find $\mathbf{u}(x)=\mathrm{f}^{-1}(x)$ in $(x^4+3x^2+6x+5)\ \mathbf{u}(x)+\left(x^5+6\right)\mathbf{v}(x)=1$ by considering the steps of the Euclidean algorithm in $\mathbb{F}_7$:

$$3x^2+2x+1-(x+5)(3x+1)=3$$

$$4x^3+x^2+2x+6-\left(3x^2+2x+1\right)(6x+1)=x+5$$

$$x^4+3x^2+6x+5-\left(4x^3+x^2+2x+6\right)(2x+3)=3x^2+2x+1$$

$$x^5+6-\left(x^4+3x^2+6x+5\right)x=4x^3+x^2+2x+6$$

As the next step, we replace $x+5$ in $3x^2+2x+1-(x+5)(3x+1)=3$ with $4x^3+x^2+2x+6-\left(3x^2+2x+1\right)(6x+1)$:

$$3x^2+2x+1-\left[4x^3+x^2+2x+6-\left(3x^2+2x+1\right)(6x+1)\right](3x+1)=3.$$

Next, we replace $3x^2+2x+1$ in $3x^2+2x+1-\left[4x^3+x^2+2x+6-\left(3x^2+2x+1\right)(6x+1)\right](3x+1)=3$ with $x^4+3x^2+6x+5-\left(4x^3+x^2+2x+6\right)(2x+3)$, and obtain $x^4+3x^2+6x+5-\left(4x^3+x^2+2x+6\right)(2x+3)-\left[4x^3+x^2+2x+6-\left(x^4+3x^2+6x+5-\left(4x^3+x^2+2x+6\right)(2x+3)\right)(6x+1)\right](3x+1)=3$ as the first main equation.

For the extended Euclidean algorithm, we also consider $x^5+6-\left(x^4+3x^2+6x+5\right)x=4x^3+x^2+2x+6$ as the second main equation.

Since there are various polynomials in the last two main equations, for the sake of clarity, we assume the following replacements for the polynomials:

$$\mathrm{A}=x^4+3x^2+6x+5$$

$$\mathrm{B}=x^5+6$$

$$\mathrm{C}=4x^3+x^2+2x+6$$

$$\mathrm{D}=2x+3$$

$$E = 6x + 1$$

$$F = 3x + 1$$

$$G = x$$

Accordingly, the last two main equations will be formulated as follows:

$$A - CD - [C - (A - CD)E]F = 3$$

$$B - AG = C$$

The first main equation $A - CD - [C - (A - CD)E]F = 3$ will be $A - CD - CF + AEF - CDEF = 3$, and thus $A(1 + EF) - C(D + F + DEF) = 3$ will hold. When we replace C in this equation with $B - AG$, we obtain $A(1 + EF) - (B - AG)(D + F + DEF) = 3$. After further steps, we have the following third main equation:

$$A(1 + EF + GD + GF + GDEF) + B(-D - F - DEF) = 3$$

We calculate $1 + EF + GD + GF + GDEF = 1 + (6x + 1)(3x + 1) + x(2x + 3) + x(3x + 1) + x(2x + 3)(6x + 1)(3x + 1) = 1 + (18x^2 + 9x + 1) + (2x^2 + 3x) + (3x^2 + x) + (2x^2 + 3x)(18x^2 + 9x + 1) = 36x^4 + 72x^3 + 52x^2 + 16x + 2$. Since we work in $\mathbb{F}_7$, $36x^4 + 72x^3 + 52x^2 + 16x + 2$ is equivalent to $x^4 + 2x^3 + 3x^2 + 2x + 2$ in $\mathbb{F}_7$. Please note that the right-hand side of the third main equation is 3, thus we multiply both sides of the third main equation by the multiplicative inverse of 3 in $\mathbb{F}_7$ so that the right-hand side will be 1. The multiplicative inverse of 3 is 5 in $\mathbb{F}_7$ and we multiply each coefficient in $x^4 + 2x^3 + 3x^2 + 2x + 2$ by 5 in $\mathbb{F}_7$, and obtain $5x^4 + 3x^3 + x^2 + 3x + 3$, which is finally the multiplicative inverse of $f(x) = x^4 + 3x^2 - x + 5$ in $\mathbb{F}_7$.

1.6 INTEGER FACTORIZATION RELATED SELECTED MATHEMATICAL FUNDAMENTALS

In this section, only the "fundamental theorem of arithmetic" and the definition of "B-smooth" will be provided regarding the integer factorization-related mathematical fundamentals. For more details about integer factorization, please see Chapter 4, Section 4.4.

1.6.1 Fundamental theorem of arithmetic

There is a unique factorization of an integer $a \geq 2$ into the prime numbers $p_1, p_2, \ldots, p_r$ as $a = p_1^{e_1} \cdot p_2^{e_2} \cdot \ldots \cdot p_r^{e_r}$, where $e_1, e_2, \ldots, e_r \in \mathbb{Z}_+$ are called the exponents or orders (Delfs & Knebl, 2015; Hoffstein et al., 2008)

Example 1.18

1026 can be uniquely factored into the prime numbers as $1026 = 2 \cdot 3^3 \cdot 19$.

1.6.2 B-smooth number

Definition 1.13

An integer number $a = p_1^{e1} \cdot p_2^{e2} \cdot \ldots \cdot p_r^{e_r}$ is "smooth" if all $p_1, p_2, \ldots, p_r$ values are small. Specifically, an integer number $a = p_1^{e1} \cdot p_2^{e2} \cdot \ldots \cdot p_r^{e_r}$ is called B-smooth if $p_1, p_2, \ldots, p_r \leq B$ holds. The "factor base" of a B-smooth integer is the set of the prime factors $p_1, p_2, \ldots, p_r$ (adapted from Hoffstein et al., 2008).

Example 1.19

$20 = 2^2 \cdot 5$ (20 is a 5-smooth integer)

$36 = 2^2 \cdot 3^2$ (36 is a 3-smooth integer)

$42 = 2 \cdot 3 \cdot 7$ (42 is a 7-smooth integer)

1.7 ELLIPTIC CURVES AND RELATED TOPICS

"Elliptic curve cryptography" (ECC) is a distinctive area in mathematical cryptography. Different public key cryptosystems such as the ElGamal public key cryptosystem to be provided in Chapter 3 have also elliptic curve counterparts.

1.7.1 Elliptic curve

Definition 1.14

An "elliptic curve over a field F", E / F, can be defined based on the so-called "generalized Weierstrass equation" given in Equation (1.17), where $a_1, a_2, a_3, a_4, a_6 \in F$ (adapted from Hankerson & Menezes, 2005; Silverman, 2009).

$$E / F : y^2 + a_1xy + a_3y = x^3 + a_2x^2 + a_4x + a_6 \tag{1.17}$$

Δ is the discriminant of E / F, which is defined as in Equation (1.18), where $d_2 = a_1^2 + 4a_2$, $d_4 = 2a_4 + a_1a_3$, $d_6 = a_3^2 + 4a_6$, and $d_8 = a_1^2a_6 + 4a_2a_6 - a_1a_3a_4 + a_2a_3^2 - a_4^2$ (Hankerson & Menezes, 2005; Silverman, 2009).

$$\Delta = -d_2^2d_8 - 8d_4^3 - 27d_6^2 + 9d_2d_4d_6 \tag{1.18}$$

An elliptic curve E / F is generally required to be a "nonsingular curve", which is ensured by $\Delta \neq 0$ so that there exist no repeated roots (Hoffstein et al., 2008).

Rather than Equation (1.17), the "simplified Weierstrass equation" is generally used for ECC, which will be provided next.

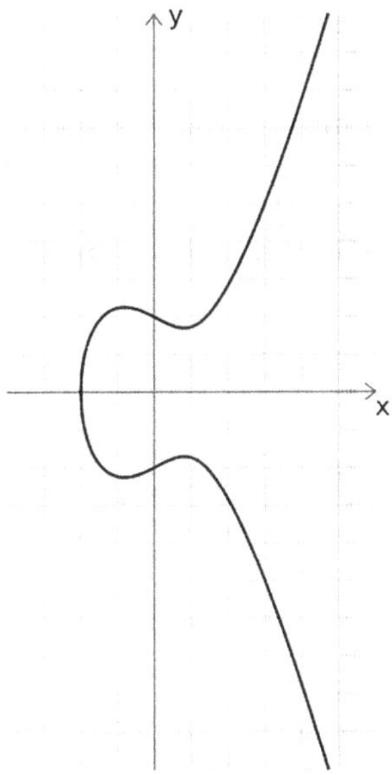

Figure 1.2 A representation of an elliptic curve (elliptic curve has been drawn by using https://cplx.vm.uni-freiburg.de/storage/software/ellipticcurve/wasm/ellipticcurve.html, with permission from Prof. Dr. Stefan Kebekus.)

Simplified Weierstrass equation (adapted from Hankerson & Menezes, 2005; Silverman, 2009*)*

If the "characteristic of F" is not equal to 2 or 3, then the "generalized Weierstrass equation" in Equation (1.17) can be reduced to the "simplified Weierstrass equation" $E/F: y^2 = x^3 + ax + b$; $a, b \in F$ with the non-zero discriminant $\Delta = -16(4a^3 + 27b^2)$.

It should be noted that an "elliptic curve" and an "ellipse" are not the same. Figure 1.2 gives an example of the representation of an elliptic curve. However, several other representations are possible.

1.7.2 An elliptic curve as an Abelian group

An elliptic curve E/F (in the following we will just consider it as E) is an "Abelian group under the operation +" since all the following properties are satisfied (adapted from Ahlswede, 2016; Hoffstein et al., 2008; Silverman, 2006):

Closed under +: For each $P, Q \in E, P + Q \in E$ holds.
Identity: $\mathcal{O}$ is the "identity element". Then $P + \mathcal{O} = \mathcal{O} + P = P$ holds for each $P \in E$.
Inverse: For each $P \in E$, there exists $-P \in E$, which is the inverse of $P \in E$ under the operation +, such that $P + -P = \mathcal{O}$ holds.
Associative: For each $P, Q, R \in E$, $(P + Q) + R = P + (Q + R)$ holds.
Commutative: For each $P, Q \in E$, $P + Q = Q + P$ holds.

1.7.3 Point addition in elliptic curves

The point addition in elliptic curves is a basic operation for ECC. First, we focus on the "geometric definition", then we provide the "elliptic curve addition algorithm".

Geometric definition: Let $P,Q \in E/F$ be two distinctive points. Then the following cases hold (adapted from Hankerson, Vanstone, & Menezes, 2004; Hoffstein et al., 2008):

$$\text{Case 1}: P+Q=Q+P=-T=(x_T,-y_T)$$

In this case, $T=(x_T,y_T)$ is the third point that intersects the elliptic curve E and the line that crosses through P and Q. Then a vertical line is drawn through the point T. The other point on this vertical line that passes through E/F will be $-T$, as shown in Figure 1.3.

$$\text{Case2}: P+P=2P$$

In this case, we consider the tangent line that crosses through P at E to find the second point that intersects the elliptic curve E, and draw a vertical line through this second point as illustrated in Figure 1.4. The other point on the vertical line that crosses through the elliptic curve E will be $2P$.

$$\text{Case3}: P+(-P)=(-P)+P=\mathcal{O}$$

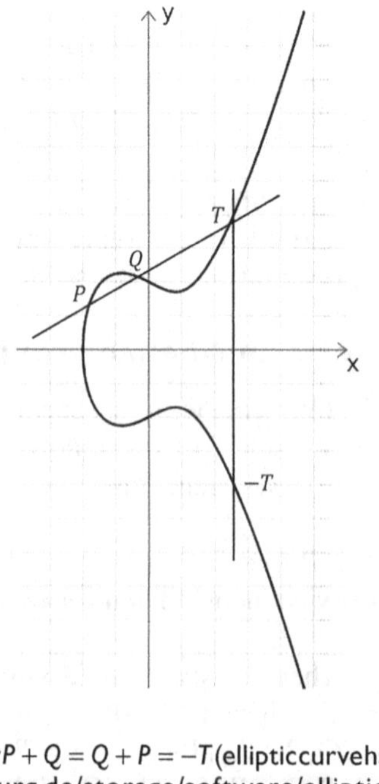

Figure 1.3 Representation for $P+Q=Q+P=-T$ (elliptic curve has been drawn by using https://cplx.vm.uni-freiburg.de/storage/software/ellipticcurve/wasm/ellipticcurve.html, with permission from Prof. Dr. Stefan Kebekus.)

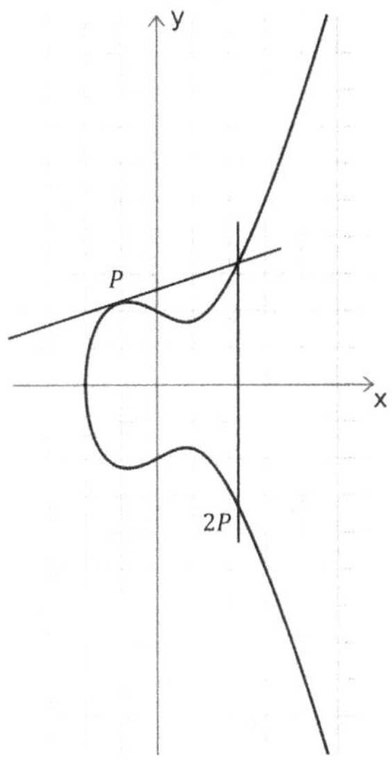

Figure 1.4 Representation for $P + P = 2P$ (elliptic curve has been drawn by using https://cplx.vm.uni-freiburg.de/storage/software/ellipticcurve/wasm/ellipticcurve.html, with permission from Prof. Dr. Stefan Kebekus.)

In this case, there is no third point that intersects the elliptic curve E and the vertical line that passes through P and $-P$ as illustrated in Figure 1.5. Then the total of P and $-P$ will be the point $\mathcal{O}$ that is the "identity element" as introduced in Section 1.7.2. The "identity element" $\mathcal{O}$ is assumed to be on each vertical line of the elliptic curve infinitely, although it actually does not exist (Hoffstein et al., 2008).

Example 1.20

Let $E / F : y^2 = x^3 - 2x + 4$ be an elliptic curve for which $\Delta \neq 0$ holds. Let also $P = (0, 2)$ and $Q = (3, 5)$ be two points of the elliptic curve E. We would like to find $P + Q$. The line that crosses through P and Q is $y = x + 2$. In order to find the third point $T = (x_T, y_T)$ that intersects the elliptic curve E / F and the line $y = x + 2$, we consider the following steps:

$$y^2 = x^3 - 2x + 4$$

$$(x + 2)^2 = x^3 - 2x + 4$$

$$x^2 + 4x + 4 = x^3 - 2x + 4$$

$x^3 - x^2 - 6x = 0$, where $x^3 - x^2 - 6x = x(x - 3)(x + 2) = 0$.

Please note that $x = 0$ is the x-coordinate of $P = (0, 2)$, $x = 3$ is the x-coordinate of $Q = (3, 5)$, thus $x_T = -2$ will be the x-coordinate of the third point, and $T = (-2, 0)$ will be the point which intersects the elliptic curve E and the line $y = x + 2$. Finally, we conclude that $P + Q = -T = (-2, 0)$.

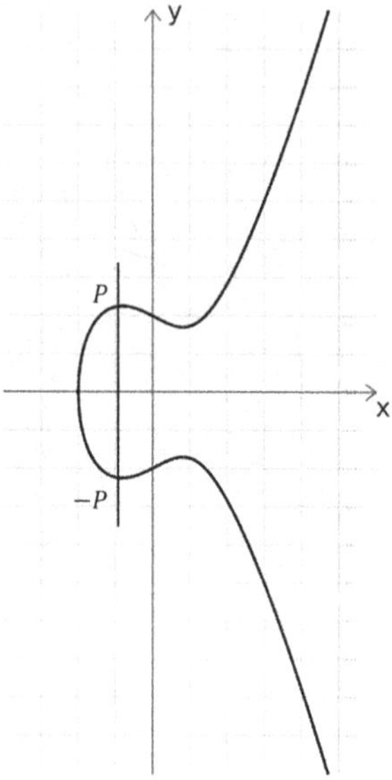

Figure 1.5 Representation for $P+(-P)=(-P)+P=\mathcal{O}$ (elliptic curve has been drawn by using https://cplx.vm.uni-freiburg.de/storage/software/ellipticcurve/wasm/ellipticcurve.html, with permission from Prof. Dr. Stefan Kebekus.)

1.7.3.1 Elliptic curve addition algorithm

Let $P=(x_P,y_P),Q=(x_Q,y_Q)\in E/F$, where $E/F: y^2=x^3+ax+b$ is an elliptic curve. Then the following equations hold (adapted from Hoffstein et al., 2008):

1. $P+Q=Q$, if $P=\mathcal{O}$.
2. $P+Q=P$, if $Q=\mathcal{O}$.
3. If neither of (1) and (2) is satisfied, and if $x_P=x_Q$, $y_P=-y_Q$, then $P+Q=\mathcal{O}$.
4. If none of the conditions (1), (2), (3) hold, then $P+Q=T=(x_T,y_T)\in E/F$ such that $x_T=\lambda^2-x_P-x_Q$, $y_T=\lambda(x_P-x_T)-y_P$, where for $P\neq Q$, $\lambda=\frac{y_Q-y_P}{x_Q-x_P}$ and for $P=Q$, $\lambda=\frac{3x_P^2+a}{2y_P}$.

Example 1.20 (revisited)

Please recall $E/F: y^2=x^3-2x+4$ with the points $P=(0,2)$ and $Q=(3,5)$. We would like to find $P+Q$ by using the "elliptic curve addition algorithm". Accordingly, we assume $P+Q=T=(x_T,y_T)$. It is clear that Condition (4) holds, where $P\neq Q$. Thus, we make the following calculations:

$$\lambda=\frac{5-2}{3-0}=1$$

$$x_T = 1^2 - 0 - 3 = -2$$
$$y_T = 1(0 - (-2)) - 2 = 0$$

Finally, we conclude again that $P + Q = T = (-2, 0)$.

1.7.4 Elliptic curves over finite fields

The application of elliptic curves over finite fields is more important for ECC.

Definition 1.15

A nonsingular elliptic curve $E(\mathbb{F}_p)$ over the finite field $\mathbb{F}_p$ can be defined as in Equation (1.19) (adapted from Enge, 1999; Hoffstein et al., 2008).

$$E(\mathbb{F}_p) = \{(x,y) : y^2 = x^3 + ax + b;\ a,b \in \mathbb{F}_p; p \geq 3; \\ \Delta = -16(4a^3 + 27b^2) \neq 0;\ x,y \in \mathbb{F}_p\} \cup \{\mathcal{O}\} \tag{1.19}$$

When we consider $\mathbb{F}_{p^k}$, then we obtain the elliptic curve $E(\mathbb{F}_{p^k})$ over the field $\mathbb{F}_{p^k}$.

A special theorem, the so-called "Hasse theorem", provides an inequality regarding the number of points on $E(\mathbb{F}_p)$ and $E(\mathbb{F}_{p^k})$.

Theorem 1.1

Hasse theorem (adapted from Crandall & Pomerance, 2001; Enge, 1999; Hoffstein et al., 2008; Washington, 2008)

For a non-singular elliptic curve $E(\mathbb{F}_p)$ over the finite field $\mathbb{F}_p$, $|p + 1 - \#E(\mathbb{F}_p)| \leq 2\sqrt{p}$ holds, where $\#E(\mathbb{F}_p)$ is the order of $E(\mathbb{F}_p)$, which can be assumed as $\#E(\mathbb{F}_p) \approx p + 1$. Generally let $E(\mathbb{F}_{p^k})$ be a nonsingular elliptic curve over the finite field $\mathbb{F}_{p^k}$. Then $|p^k + 1 - \#E(\mathbb{F}_{p^k})| \leq 2\sqrt{p^k}$ holds.

Theorem 1.2 states about the "cyclic" property of the elliptic curves over finite fields.

Theorem 1.2

"Working over a finite field, the group of points $\mathrm{E}(\mathbb{F}_\mathrm{p})$ is always either a cyclic group or the product of two cyclic groups" (Silverman, 2006).

Example 1.21

Let $E(\mathbb{F}_5) : y^2 = x^3 + x + 2$ be defined. The elements of this elliptic curve are given in Table 1.10.

Table 1.10 The elements of $E(\mathbb{F}_5): y^2 = x^3 + x + 2$

x		y	Points of $E(\mathbb{F}_5)$
			$\mathcal{O}$
0	$y^2 \equiv 2 \pmod 5$	No solution	
1	$y^2 \equiv 4 \pmod 5$	$y = 2, 3$	$(1, 2), (1, 3)$
2	$y^2 \equiv 2 \pmod 5$	No solution	
3	$y^2 \equiv 2 \pmod 5$	No solution	
4	$y^2 \equiv 0 \pmod 5$	$y = 0$	$(4, 0)$

As a result, $E(\mathbb{F}_5) = \{\mathcal{O}, (1,2),(1,3), (4,0)\}$. Please note that according to "Hasse theorem", $|5+1-4| = 2 < 2\sqrt{5} \approx 4.47$ holds.

1.7.5 Bilinear pairings, Weil pairings, distortion maps, and modified Weil pairings on elliptic curves

In this section, we provide the fundamental properties of the "bilinear pairings on elliptic curves" and the related concepts including the "modified Weil pairing on elliptic curves". The "pairing-based cryptography" is a distinctive area in cryptography. As one application of pairing-based cryptography, the "modified Weil pairing" is used in the "tripartite Diffie–Hellman key exchange" to be provided in Chapter 3. Moreover, the identity-based public key cryptosystem to be provided in Chapter 6 is mostly called pairing-based cryptography.

1.7.5.1 Bilinear pairings on elliptic curves

In any pairing, two values are taken as the inputs, and one value is obtained as the output. A "bilinear pairing" is a linear transformation (mapping) of two input values to one output value. A "bilinear pairing on an elliptic curve" is a special bilinear pairing, which is a linear transformation of two points of the elliptic curve as the input values to one point of the elliptic curve as the output value (Hoffstein et al., 2008). In the following, we define the "bilinear pairings" for general "cyclic groups", which can also be adapted to the elliptic curves over finite fields.

Definition 1.16

Let G_1, G_2, G_T be the "cylic groups" of the same prime order p, where G_1, G_2 are the additive groups, and G_T is the multiplicative group. If the conditions in Equations (1.20)–(1.23) hold, then a map $e: G_1 \times G_2 \to G_T$ is called a "bilinear pairing" (adapted from Hankerson & Menezes, 2011; Kipkirui, 2018):

$$e(aP, bQ) = e(P, Q)^{ab}, \forall P \in G_1, \forall Q \in G_2, a, b \in \mathbb{Z} \quad (1.20)$$

$$e(P+Q,R)=e(P,R)\cdot e(Q,R),\ \forall P,Q\in G_1,\ \forall R\in G_2 \tag{1.21}$$

$$e(P,Q+R)=e(P,Q)\cdot e(P,R),\ \forall P\in G_1,\ \forall Q,R\in G_2 \tag{1.22}$$

$$e(g_1,g_2)\neq 1, \text{where } g_1 \text{ is the generator of } G_1,\ g_2 \text{ is the generator } of\ G_2 \tag{1.23}$$

The conditions (1.20)–(1.22) refer to bilinearity conditions, while the condition (1.23) refers to non-degeneracy. In addition to the conditions (1.20)–(1.23), there should be an efficient algorithm to compute the bilinear pairing $e: G_1 \times G_2 \to G_T$ easily. Please note that if G_1 and G_2 are the same groups, i.e. if $G_1 = G_2$, then the bilinear pairing is called a "symmetric bilinear pairing", otherwise it is an "asymmetric bilinear pairing" (Hankerson & Menezes, 2011). Note also that G_1, G_2 can also be the multiplicative groups, in this case, Equations (1.20)–(1.22) will be generally replaced with Equation (1.24) (adapted from Hankerson & Menezes, 2011).

$$e(P^a,Q^b)=e(P,Q)^{ab}\quad \forall P\in G_1,\ \forall Q\in G_2, a,b\in\mathbb{Z} \tag{1.24}$$

According to Hoffstein et al. (2008), "it is necessary to work with finite fields $\mathbb{F}_{p^k}$ of prime power order for the application of the bilinear pairings in cryptography".

1.7.5.2 Weil pairings on elliptic curves

The "Weil pairing on elliptic curves" is a special "bilinear pairing" defined on elliptic curves for the so-called "torsion points", which will be defined next:

Definition 1.17

The "order of a point $P \in E/F$" is the smallest $m \in \mathbb{Z}_+$ that satisfies $mP = \mathcal{O}$ (Crandall & Pomerance, 2001). $E[m] = \{P \in E/F : mP = \mathcal{O}\}$ is the "set of points of order m" in E/F, where the points are called the "m-torsion points" (adapted from Hoffstein et al., 2008).

A Weil pairing is a special bilinear pairing which takes two points in $E[m]$ as the inputs, and gives $e_m(\cdot,\cdot)$ as the output. The conditions in Equations (1.25)–(1.30) hold for $P,Q,R \in E[m]$ in case of Weil pairing (adapted from Boneh, Lynn, & Shacham, 2001; Hoffstein et al., 2008; Miller, 2004):

$$e_m(P+Q,R)=e_m(P,R)\cdot e_m(Q,R),\ \forall P,Q,R\in E[m] \tag{1.25}$$

$$e_m(P,Q+R)=e_m(P,Q)\cdot e_m(P,R),\ \forall P,Q,R\in E[m] \tag{1.26}$$

$$e_m(P,Q)^m=1,\ \forall P,Q\in E[m] \tag{1.27}$$

$$e_m(P,P)=1,\ \forall P\in E[m] \tag{1.28}$$

$$\text{If } e_m(P,Q) = 1 \text{ for all } Q \in E[m], \text{ then } P = \mathcal{O}. \quad (1.29)$$

$$e_m(P,Q) = e_m(Q,P)^{-1} \quad (1.30)$$

The Weil pairing can be efficiently calculated by using Miller's algorithm (Miller, 2004).

1.7.5.3 Distortion maps on elliptic curves

The "distortion maps" are also defined for the "torsion points".

Definition 1.18

$P \in E[\ell]$ is assumed to be a "ℓ-torsion point" of prime order $\ell \geq 3$. $\phi : E \rightarrow E$ is called an "ℓ-distortion map" on $E[\ell]$ for P if the conditions in Equations (1.31) and (1.32) hold, where e_ℓ is the Weil pairing on $E[\ell]$ (adapted from Hoffstein et al., 2008):

$$\phi(nP) = n\phi(P) \text{ for all } n \geq 1 \quad (1.31)$$

$$e_\ell(P,\phi(P))^r = 1, r = k\ell,\ k \in \mathbb{Z}_+ \quad (1.32)$$

1.7.5.4 Modified Weil pairings

The "modified Weil pairing" is also defined for the "torsion points". $P \in E[\ell]$, $\phi : E \rightarrow E$, and e_ℓ are defined as in Section 1.7.5.3. The "modified Weil pairing" $\hat{e}_\ell$ on $E[\ell]$ has the properties in Equations (1.33) and (1.34) for $Q = sP, Q' = tP$, where $s \in \mathbb{Z}, t \in \mathbb{Z}$ (adapted from Hoffstein et al., 2008; Jao, 2010; Park, Kim, & Yung, 2005):

$$\hat{e}_\ell(Q,Q') = e_\ell(Q,\phi(Q')) = e_\ell(sP,\phi(tP)) = e_\ell(sP,t\phi(P)) = e_\ell(P,\phi(P))^{st} \quad (1.33)$$

$$\hat{e}_\ell(Q,Q') = 1 \text{ if and only if } Q = \mathcal{O} \text{ or } Q' = \mathcal{O} \quad (1.34)$$

Please note that we consider $Q = sP, Q' = tP$ in Equation (1.33) since they are used in cryptographic applications including the modified Weil pairing. For more details regarding bilinear pairings, Weil pairings, distortion maps, and modified Weil pairings on elliptic curves, please see Hoffstein et al. (2008).

1.8 VECTOR SPACES AND LATTICES

Vector spaces and lattices are interrelated concepts in linear algebra. Like the "elliptic curve cryptography", the "lattice-based cryptography" is also a distinctive area in cryptography with hard problems. As an example, the lattice-based "GGH public key cryptosystem" will be provided in Chapter 5.

1.8.1 Vector spaces

In this part, we provide the basic properties of the vector spaces. For more information, the reader is recommended to read linear algebra books such as the book by Strang (2016).

A vector space $V \subset \mathbb{R}^m$ consists of the vectors $\mathbf{v}_i$, $i = 1, 2, 3, \ldots$ with m components (coordinates) that take real numbers. For any $k \in \mathbb{Z}_+$, $\alpha_1\mathbf{v}_1 + \alpha_2\mathbf{v}_2 + \cdots + \alpha_k\mathbf{v}_k \in V$ holds, where $\mathbf{v}_1, \mathbf{v}_2, \ldots, \mathbf{v}_k \in V \subset \mathbb{R}^m, \alpha_1, \alpha_2, \ldots, \alpha_k \in \mathbb{R}$ hold, and $\alpha_1\mathbf{v}_1 + \alpha_2\mathbf{v}_2 + \cdots + \alpha_k\mathbf{v}_k$ is called the "linear combination" of $\mathbf{v}_1, \mathbf{v}_2, \ldots, \mathbf{v}_k$. If $\alpha_1\mathbf{v}_1 + \alpha_2\mathbf{v}_2 + \cdots + \alpha_k\mathbf{v}_k = 0$ holds only in case of $\alpha_1 = \alpha_2 = \cdots = \alpha_k = 0$, then $\mathbf{v}_1, \mathbf{v}_2, \ldots, \mathbf{v}_k$ are "linearly independent", otherwise they are "linearly dependent". If every vector $\mathbf{w} \in V$ can be written as $\mathbf{w} = \alpha_1\mathbf{b}_1 + \alpha_2\mathbf{b}_2 + \cdots + \alpha_n\mathbf{b}_n$ by using the "linearly independent" vectors $\mathbf{b}_1, \mathbf{b}_2, \ldots, \mathbf{b}_n \in V \subset \mathbb{R}^m$ for a unique choice of $\alpha_1, \alpha_2, \ldots, \alpha_n \in \mathbb{R}$, then $\mathcal{B} = \{\mathbf{b}_1, \mathbf{b}_2, \ldots, \mathbf{b}_n\}$ is called a "basis of the vector space" $V \subset \mathbb{R}^m$, which is a matrix with columns $\{\mathbf{b}_1, \mathbf{b}_2, \ldots, \mathbf{b}_n\}$. A vector space possesses multiple bases and each basis has the same number of vectors n, where n is called the "rank of the basis" or "dimension" of the vector space $V \subset \mathbb{R}^m$.

For any vectors $\mathbf{u}, \mathbf{v}, \mathbf{w} \in V$, and any scalar $\alpha \in \mathbb{R}$, the "inner product of two vectors" $< \cdot, \cdot >$, has the properties of nonnegativity and commutativity. The additional properties of the inner product of two vectors are given in Equations (1.35)–(1.37) (Anton & Rorres, 2010; Larson, 2013)

$$< \mathbf{u}, \mathbf{u} > = 0 \text{ for any } \mathbf{u} = 0 \tag{1.35}$$

$$< \mathbf{u} + \mathbf{v}, \mathbf{w} > = < \mathbf{u}, \mathbf{w} > + < \mathbf{v}, \mathbf{w} > \tag{1.36}$$

$$< \alpha\mathbf{u}, \mathbf{v} > = \alpha < \mathbf{u}, \mathbf{v} > \tag{1.37}$$

Please note that the "inner product of two vectors" is a "bilinear pairing" on the vector space $V \subset \mathbb{R}^m$, where two vectors are mapped to a real number. The "dot product (Euclidean inner product)" is a special case of the inner product. Let $\mathbf{u} = (x_1, x_2, \ldots, x_m)$, $\mathbf{v} = (y_1, y_2, \ldots, y_m)$ be two vectors in the vector space $V \subset \mathbb{R}^m$. Then, the "dot product" of $\mathbf{u}$ and $\mathbf{v}$ can be defined as $\mathbf{u} \cdot \mathbf{v} = x_1y_1 + x_2y_2 + \cdots + x_my_m$. The "length" of $\mathbf{u} = (x_1, x_2, \ldots, x_m)$ can be measured by using the so-called "Euclidean norm" which is defined as $\|\mathbf{u}\| = \sqrt{x_1^2 + x_2^2 + \cdots + x_m^2}$. The Euclidean distance between $\mathbf{u}$ and $\mathbf{v}$ can be calculated as $\|\mathbf{u} - \mathbf{v}\| = \sqrt{(x_1 - y_1)^2 + (x_2 - y_2)^2 + \cdots + (x_m - y_m)^2}$. It should be noted that $\sqrt{\mathbf{u} \cdot \mathbf{u}} = \|\mathbf{u}\|$ also holds. An important inequality related to the vector spaces is the "Cauchy-Schwartz inequality" defined as $|\mathbf{u} \cdot \mathbf{v}| \le \|\mathbf{u}\| \cdot \|\mathbf{v}\|$. If for any $\mathbf{u}, \mathbf{v} \in V \subset \mathbb{R}^m$, $\mathbf{u} \cdot \mathbf{v} = 0$ holds, then $\mathbf{u}$ and $\mathbf{v}$ are said to be "orthogonal" to one another. Additionally if $\|\mathbf{u}\| = 1$ and $\|\mathbf{v}\| = 1$ hold, i.e. if $\mathbf{u}$ and $\mathbf{v}$ are unit vectors, then $\mathbf{u}$ and $\mathbf{v}$ are "orthonormal" to one another.

1.8.2 Lattices

As mentioned before, the lattices and vector spaces are interrelated. However in a lattice, the vectors can only be multiplied by the integer numbers, not the real numbers as in the vector spaces, i.e. a lattice $L \subset \mathbb{R}^m$ consists of the vectors $\mathbf{v}_j$, $j = 1, 2, 3, \ldots$ with m components (coordinates) that take real numbers, and the lattice will be $L = L(\mathcal{B}) = \left\{\mathbf{v}_j : \mathbf{v}_j = \Sigma_{i=1}^{n} z_i \mathbf{b}_i : z_i \in \mathbb{Z}\right\}$, where $z_1, z_2, \ldots, z_n \in \mathbb{Z}$ are unique for any $\mathbf{v}_j \in L$, and the "linearly independent" vectors $\{\mathbf{b}_1, \mathbf{b}_2, \ldots, \mathbf{b}_n\}$ form a "basis" $\mathcal{B} = \{\mathbf{b}_1, \mathbf{b}_2, \ldots, \mathbf{b}_n\}$, which is again a matrix with the columns $\{\mathbf{b}_1, \mathbf{b}_2, \ldots, \mathbf{b}_n\}$. As for the vector spaces, there is no unique basis of a lattice, and all bases of a lattice have the same number of vectors n, where n is again the dimension of L (Nguyen, 2011). The definitions for the "dot product" of two vectors in a lattice, "orthogonal", "orthonormal" vectors, the "length" (Euclidean norm) of a vector in a lattice, and the "Euclidean distance" between two vectors in a lattice are the same as the definitions for the vectors in a vector space. The "orthogonality" of two vectors in a basis of a lattice is very crucial in "lattice-based cryptography".

1.8.2.1 Fundamental domain, Hadamard's inequality, and Hadamard ratio

The fundamental domain, Hadamard's inequality, and Hadamard ratio are significant concepts in "lattice-based cryptography", which will be considered in the "GGH public key cryptosystem" to be provided in Chapter 5.

Definition 1.19

The "fundamental domain" (fundamental parallelepiped) corresponding to the basis $\mathcal{B} = \{\mathbf{b}_1, \mathbf{b}_2, \ldots, \mathbf{b}_n\}$ of a lattice L is the set given in Equation (1.38) (Hoffstein et al., 2008).

$$\mathcal{F}(\mathcal{B}) = \mathcal{F}(\mathbf{b}_1, \mathbf{b}_2, \ldots, \mathbf{b}_n) = \{t_1\mathbf{b}_1 + t_2\mathbf{b}_2 + \cdots + t_n\mathbf{b}_n : 0 \le t_i < 1,\ i = 1, 2, 3, \ldots, n\} \tag{1.38}$$

According to Nguyen and Regev (2009), in Equation (1.38), $-\frac{1}{2} \le t_i \le \frac{1}{2}$ holds.

Definition 1.20

$\mathrm{Vol}(\mathcal{F}(\mathcal{B}))$ is the "n-dimensional volume of the fundamental domain $\mathcal{F}(\mathcal{B})$" and it can be shown that Equation (1.39) holds (adapted from Hoffstein et al., 2008; Nguyen & Regev, 2009).

$$\det(L) = \det(L(\mathcal{B})) = |\det(\mathcal{B})| = |\det\mathcal{F}(\mathcal{B})| = \mathrm{Vol}(\mathcal{F}(\mathcal{B})) \tag{1.39}$$

As clear from Equation (1.39), $\det(L)$ is independent of the basis $\mathcal{B}$.

Definition 1.21

The "Hadamard's inequality" corresponding to the basis $\mathcal{B} = \{\mathbf{b}_1, \mathbf{b}_2, \ldots, \mathbf{b}_n\}$ is defined as in Equation (1.40) (adapted from Hoffstein et al., 2008).

$$\begin{aligned}\det(L)=\det(L(\mathcal{B}))=|\det(\mathcal{B})|=|\det\mathcal{F}(\mathcal{B})|=\\ \operatorname{Vol}(\mathcal{F}(\mathcal{B}))\le\|\mathbf{b}_1\|\cdot\|\mathbf{b}_2\|\cdot\cdots\cdot\|\mathbf{b}_n\|\end{aligned} \tag{1.40}$$

Definition 1.22

The "Hadamard ratio" corresponding to the basis $\mathcal{B}=\{\mathbf{b}_1,\mathbf{b}_2,\ldots,\mathbf{b}_n\}$ is defined as in Equation (1.41) (adapted from Hoffstein et al., 2008):

$$\begin{aligned}\mathcal{H}(\mathcal{B})&=\left(\frac{\det(L)}{\|\mathbf{b}_1\|\cdot\|\mathbf{b}_2\|\cdot\cdots\cdot\|\mathbf{b}_n\|}\right)^{1/n}=\left(\frac{\det(L(\mathcal{B}))}{\|\mathbf{b}_1\|\cdot\|\mathbf{b}_2\|\cdot\cdots\cdot\|\mathbf{b}_n\|}\right)^{1/n}\\ &=\left(\frac{|\det(\mathcal{B})|}{\|\mathbf{b}_1\|\cdot\|\mathbf{b}_2\|\cdot\cdots\cdot\|\mathbf{b}_n\|}\right)^{1/n}\end{aligned} \tag{1.41}$$

Please note that $0<\mathcal{H}(\mathcal{B})\le 1$ holds and a Hadamard ratio value closer to 1 shows a higher degree of orthogonality of the basis vectors (Hoffstein et al., 2008).

1.8.2.2 Fundamental lattice problems

There are some fundamental lattice problems with different applications in mathematics and "lattice-based cryptography" (IEEE Std 1363.1-2008, 2009). In the following, we provide the "shortest vector problem", the "closest vector problem", "approximate closest vector problem", and "Babai's closest vertex algorithm" very briefly.

Shortest vector problem (SVP): SVP is related to finding $\mathbf{u}_{\text{shortest}}\in L(\mathcal{B})\subset\mathbb{R}^m$ with the minimum length $\|\mathbf{u}_{\text{shortest}}\|$ (Micciancio, 2016; Micciancio & Regev, 2009). It should be noted that there may be multiple shortest vectors. The "LLL algorithm" proposed by Lenstra, Lenstra, and Lovász (1982) is a very well-known polynomial time algorithm for finding an approximate solution to the SVP (Hoffstein et al., 2009).

Closest vector problem (CVP) (Nearest vector problem): Let $\mathbf{v}\in\mathbb{R}^m$ be a vector not in $L(\mathcal{B})$. The CVP is related to finding a vector $\mathbf{u}_{\text{closest}}\in L(\mathcal{B})\subset\mathbb{R}^m$ that minimizes $\|\mathbf{v}-\mathbf{u}\|$ (Micciancio, 2011).

Approximate closest vector problem (apprCVP): apprCVP is related to finding the approximate solution to CVP as $\mathbf{u}_{\text{apprclosest}}$ (Hoffstein et al., 2008). The "Babai's closest vertex (round-off) algorithm" is an algorithm to solve the apprCVP, which is used in the "GGH public key cryptosystem" to be provided in Chapter 5.

Babai's closest vertex (round-off) algorithm for solving the apprCVP: If the basis vectors $\mathcal{B}=\{\mathbf{b}_1,\mathbf{b}_2,\ldots,\mathbf{b}_n\}$ of $L(\mathcal{B})\subset\mathbb{R}^m$ are "pairwise sufficiently orthogonal" to one another, then the following steps of the

Babai's algorithm can be used for the solution of the apprCVP (adapted from Babai, 1986; Hoffstein et al., 2008):

We write $\mathbf{v} = x_1\mathbf{b}_1 + x_2\mathbf{b}_2 + \cdots + x_n\mathbf{b}_n$ with $x_1, x_2, \ldots, x_n \in \mathbb{R}$, where $\mathbf{v} \in \mathbb{R}^m$ is a vector not in $L(\mathcal{B}) \subset \mathbb{R}^m$.

We solve for x_i for $i = 1, 2, 3, \ldots, n$.

We find $y_i = \lfloor x_i \rceil$, for $i = 1, 2, 3, \ldots, n$, where $\lfloor x_i \rceil$ means rounding of x_i.

Finally we find $\mathbf{u}_{\text{apprclosest}} = y_1\mathbf{b}_1 + y_2\mathbf{b}_2 + \cdots + y_n\mathbf{b}_n \in L \subset \mathbb{R}^m$.

Example 1.22

Let's consider a lattice L in $\mathbb{R}^3$ with dimension $n = 3$ such that one basis is $\mathcal{B} = \{\mathbf{b}_1, \mathbf{b}_2, \mathbf{b}_3\}$, where $\mathbf{b}_1 = \begin{bmatrix} 3 \\ 4 \\ 7 \end{bmatrix}$, $\mathbf{b}_2 = \begin{bmatrix} 4 \\ 5 \\ 6 \end{bmatrix}$, $\mathbf{b}_3 = \begin{bmatrix} 3 \\ 8 \\ 11 \end{bmatrix}$ are linearly independent basis vectors. Let $\mathbf{v} = \begin{bmatrix} 10 \\ 3 \\ 5 \end{bmatrix}$ be a vector not in lattice L.

We consider the following steps to find $\mathbf{u}_{\text{apprclosest}} \in L(\mathcal{B})$:

- We write $\mathbf{v} = x_1\mathbf{b}_1 + x_2\mathbf{b}_2 + x_3\mathbf{b}_3$, i.e. $\begin{bmatrix} 10 \\ 3 \\ 5 \end{bmatrix} = x_1\begin{bmatrix} 3 \\ 4 \\ 7 \end{bmatrix} + x_2\begin{bmatrix} 4 \\ 5 \\ 6 \end{bmatrix} + x_3\begin{bmatrix} 3 \\ 8 \\ 11 \end{bmatrix}$

from which the following equations will follow:

$$3x_1 + 4x_2 + 3x_3 = 10$$

$$4x_1 + 5x_2 + 8x_3 = 3$$

$$7x_1 + 6x_2 + 11x_3 = 5$$

In matrix notation, the above equations can be written as $\begin{bmatrix} 3 & 4 & 3 \\ 4 & 5 & 8 \\ 7 & 6 & 11 \end{bmatrix} \cdot \begin{bmatrix} x_1 \\ x_2 \\ x_3 \end{bmatrix} = \begin{bmatrix} 10 \\ 3 \\ 5 \end{bmatrix}$.

- We solve $\begin{bmatrix} x_1 \\ x_2 \\ x_3 \end{bmatrix} = \begin{bmatrix} 3 & 4 & 3 \\ 4 & 5 & 8 \\ 7 & 6 & 11 \end{bmatrix}^{-1} \cdot \begin{bmatrix} 10 \\ 3 \\ 5 \end{bmatrix} = \begin{bmatrix} 7/36 & -13/18 & 17/36 \\ 1/3 & 1/3 & -1/3 \\ -11/36 & 5/18 & -1/36 \end{bmatrix} \cdot \begin{bmatrix} 10 \\ 3 \\ 5 \end{bmatrix} = \begin{bmatrix} 77/36 \\ 8/3 \\ -85/36 \end{bmatrix}$.

- We find $\begin{bmatrix} y_1 \\ y_2 \\ y_3 \end{bmatrix} = \begin{bmatrix} \lfloor x_1 \rceil \\ \lfloor x_2 \rceil \\ \lfloor x_3 \rceil \end{bmatrix} = \begin{bmatrix} 2 \\ 3 \\ -2 \end{bmatrix}$.

- We determine $\mathbf{u}_{\text{apprclosest}} = 2\mathbf{b}_1 + 3\mathbf{b}_2 - 2\mathbf{b}_3 = 2\begin{bmatrix} 3 \\ 4 \\ 7 \end{bmatrix} + 3\begin{bmatrix} 4 \\ 5 \\ 6 \end{bmatrix} - 2\begin{bmatrix} 3 \\ 8 \\ 11 \end{bmatrix} =$

$\begin{bmatrix} 12 \\ 7 \\ 10 \end{bmatrix}$, which is expected to be close to $\mathbf{v} = \begin{bmatrix} 10 \\ 3 \\ 5 \end{bmatrix}$.

When we check $\|\mathbf{v} - \mathbf{u}\| = \sqrt{(12-10)^2 + (7-3)^2 + (10-5)^2} = 6.708$, we can conclude that **u** and **v** are rather close to each other. If we apply the Hadamard ratio $\mathcal{H}(\mathcal{B}) = \left(\frac{\det(L)}{\|\mathbf{b}_1\| \cdot \|\mathbf{b}_2\| \cdot \|\mathbf{b}_3\|}\right)^{1/3} = \left(\frac{|\det(B)|}{\|\mathbf{b}_1\| \cdot \|\mathbf{b}_2\| \cdot \|\mathbf{b}_3\|}\right)^{1/3}$, where $B = \begin{bmatrix} 3 & 4 & 3 \\ 4 & 5 & 8 \\ 7 & 6 & 11 \end{bmatrix}$, $\det(B) = 36$, $\|\mathbf{b}_1\| = 8.60$, $\|\mathbf{b}_2\| = 8.78$, $\|\mathbf{b}_3\| = 13.93$, we find $\mathcal{H}(\mathcal{B}) = \left(\frac{|36|}{(8.60) \cdot (8.78) \cdot (13.93)}\right)^{1/3} = 0.325$.

Please note that although the "Hadamard ratio" is not fairly high in this example, the "Babai's algorithm" succeeded to yield a good result.

1.9 SELECTED BASICS OF PROBABILITY

Since the randomness is part of mathematical cryptography, some selected basics of probability will be provided in this section based on Bas (2019) and Ross (2014). Two basic concepts of probability are "random experiments" and "random variables", which will be provided next.

1.9.1 Random experiment and the basic principle of counting

A "random experiment" is a process with well-defined possible results, but the real result cannot be predicted before each realization of the experiment. The "sample space" S is the set of the possible results of a random experiment, while an event E is a subset of a sample space. Two well-known random experiments are flipping a coin and tossing a die, whose sample spaces are $S = \{H, T\}$ and $S = \{1, 2, 3, 4, 5, 6\}$, respectively, where H stands for Head, and T stands for Tail.

The "basic principle of counting" describes the number of possible results of executing more than one random experiment simultaneously, which can be computed by multiplying the number of the possible results of all considered random experiments.

Example 1.23

A fair coin is flipped and also a fair die is tossed. The total number of possible results will be $2 \cdot 6 = 12$ due to the basic principle of counting.

Example 1.24

A byte includes eight bits. Each bit takes the value of either 0 or 1. Then, there are $2^8 = 256$ different bytes.

1.9.2 Random variables

A random variable (r.v.) X is a function with the domain of the sample space and the range of real values. As an example, if we flip two fair coins, then the sample space will be $S = \{(H,H),(H,T),(T,H),(T,T)\}$, and if we define X as the number of heads, then $X = \{0, 1, 2\}$ will be a random variable.

If the number of elements of a random variable is countable or the elements are discrete-valued, then it is a "discrete random variable", otherwise it is a "continuous random variable". In the example of flipping two coins, the number of heads is a discrete r.v. The discrete r.v.s. are identified by means of the "probability mass function (pmf)", while the continuous r.v.s. are characterized with the (continuous) "probability density function" (pdf) $f(x)$. In the example of flipping two fair coins, the pmf of X will be $P(X=0) = P(X=2) = \frac{1}{4}, P(X=1) = \frac{2}{4}$, where $\Sigma_{x \in X} P(X=x) = 1$ always holds.

The probability of a continuous r.v. can only be considered in an interval (a,b) as $\int_a^b f(x)dx$, where $f(x)$ is pdf of the continuous r.v. $F(a) = P(X \le a)$ is the general formula for the "cumulative distribution function" (cdf) for both discrete and continuous r.v.s. The "expected value" $E(X)$ is defined as $E(X) = \Sigma_{x \in X} x \cdot P(X=x)$ and $E(X) = \int_{x_{\min}}^{x_{\max}} xf(x)dx$ for the discrete and continuous r.v.s., respectively. The "variance" $Var(X)$ and "standard deviation" $SD(X)$ can generally be defined as $Var(X) = E(X^2) - (E(X))^2$ and $SD(X) = \sqrt{Var(X)}$ for both r.v.s. A very special continuous r.v. that is important in cryptography is uniform r.v., which is defined for an interval (a,b) with $f(x) = \frac{1}{b-a}$.

1.10 CONCLUSIONS

The basic structure of the public key cryptosystems is based on the mathematical fundamentals and the security of the public key cryptosystems depends on the hardness of solving some mathematical problems. Thus, this chapter covered selected fundamental mathematical concepts in cryptography including modular arithmetic, rings, groups, fields, divisibility, greatest common divisors and prime numbers, Euclidean algorithm and extended Euclidean algorithm for polynomials, integer factorization related selected mathematical fundamentals, elliptic curves, vector spaces and lattices, and the selected basics of probability. Several examples were provided in this chapter to illustrate the applicability of the concepts and algorithms. It should be noted that simple examples with small values were considered in this chapter, however in real-life cryptographic applications the values should be much larger.

REFERENCES

Ahlswede, R. (2016). Elliptic curve cryptosystems. In A. Ahlswede, I. Althöfer, C. Deppe, & U. Tamm (Eds.), *Hiding data-selected topics. Foundations in signal processing, communications and networking*, 12. Cham: Springer. https://doi.org/10.1007/978-3-319-31515-7_4

Anton, H., & Rorres, C. (2010). *Elementary linear algebra. Applications version.* River Street, Hoboken: Wiley.

Babai, L. (1986). On Lovász' lattice reduction and the nearest lattice point problem. *Combinatorica*, 6, 1–13. https://doi.org/10.1007/BF02579403

Bas, E. (2019). *Basics of probability and stochastic processes.* Cham: Springer.

Becker, T., & Weispfenning, V. (1993). Polynomial rings. *Gröbner bases. Graduate texts in mathematics*, 141. New York, NY: Springer. https://doi.org/10.1007/978-1-4612-0913-3_3

Bini, D., & Pan, V. Y. (1994). Fundamental computations with polynomials. *Polynomial and matrix computations. Progress in theoretical computer science.* Boston, MA: Birkhäuser. https://doi.org/10.1007/978-1-4612-0265-3_1.

Boneh, D., Lynn, B., & Shacham, H. (2001). Short signatures from the Weil pairing. In C. Boyd (Ed.), *Advances in cryptology-ASIACRYPT 2001.* Lecture Notes in Computer Science, 2248. Berlin, Heidelberg: Springer. https://doi.org/10.1007/3-540-45682-1_30

Bressoud, D. M. (1989). Unique factorization and the euclidean algorithm. In *Factorization and primality testing.* Undergraduate Texts in Mathematics. New York, NY: Springer. https://doi.org/10.1007/978-1-4612-4544-5_1

Charpin, P. (2011). Cyclic codes. In H. C. A. van Tilborg & S. Jajodia (Eds.), *Encyclopedia of cryptography and security.* Boston, MA: Springer. https://doi.org/10.1007/978-1-4419-5906-5_343

Childs, L. N. (1995). Cyclic groups and primitive roots. *A concrete introduction to higher algebra.* Undergraduate Texts in Mathematics. New York, NY: Springer. https://doi.org/10.1007/978-1-4419-8702-0_24

Childs, L. N. (Ed.), (2009). Rings and fields. *A concrete introduction to higher algebra.* Undergraduate Texts in Mathematics. New York, NY: Springer. https://doi.org/10.1007/978-0-387-74725-5_7.

Contini, S., Kaya Koç, Ç, & Walter, C. D. (2011). Modular arithmetic. In H. C. A. van Tilborg & S. Jajodia (Eds.), *Encyclopedia of cryptography and security.* Boston, MA: Springer. https://doi.org/10.1007/978-1-4419-5906-5_49

Crandall, R., & Pomerance, C. (2001). Elliptic curve arithmetic. *Prime numbers.* New York, NY: Springer. https://doi.org/10.1007/978-1-4684-9316-0_7.

Delfs, H., & Knebl, H. (2015). *Introduction to cryptography. Principles and applications.* Berlin, Heidelberg: Springer.

Earl, R. (2018). A3 Rings and modules. https://www.maths.ox.ac.uk/system/files/attachments/lectures%20rings%20and%20modules.pdf.

Enge, A. (1999). Elliptic curves over finite fields. *Elliptic curves and their applications to cryptography.* Boston, MA: Springer. https://doi.org/10.1007/978-1-4615-5207-9_3.

Forman, S., & Rash, A. M. (2015). Congruences. *The whole truth about whole numbers*. Cham: Springer. https://doi.org/10.1007/978-3-319-11035-6_6

Geddes, K. O., Czapor, S. R., & Labahn, G. (1992). Algebra of polynomials, rational functions, and power series. *Algorithms for computer algebra*. Boston, MA: Springer. https://doi.org/10.1007/978-0-585-33247-5_2

Golan, J. S. (2012). Fields. *The linear algebra a beginning graduate student ought to know*. Dordrecht: Springer. https://doi.org/10.1007/978-94-007-2636-9_2.

Gómez Pardo, J. L. (2013). Basic concepts from probability, complexity, algebra and number theory. *Introduction to cryptography with maple*. Berlin, Heidelberg: Springer. https://doi.org/10.1007/978-3-642-32166-5_2

Gouvêa, F. Q. (2012). *A guide to groups, rings and fields*. Washington: The Mathematical Association of America.

Gregory, R. T., & Krishnamurthy, E. V. (1984). Residue or modular arithmetic. *Methods and applications of error-free computation*. Texts and Monographs in Computer Science. New York, NY: Springer. https://doi.org/10.1007/978-1-4612-5242-9_1

Hall, M. (1999). *The theory of groups*. Providence, Rhode Island: AMS Chelsea Publishing.

Hankerson, D., Vanstone, S., & Menezes, A. (2004). Elliptic curve arithmetic. *Guide to elliptic curve cryptography*. New York, NY: Springer Professional Computing. Springer=. https://doi.org/10.1007/0-387-21846-7_3

Hankerson, D., & Menezes, A. (2005). Elliptic curve. In H. C. A. van Tilborg (Ed.), *Encyclopedia of cryptography and security*. Boston, MA: Springer. https://doi.org/10.1007/0-387-23483-7_130.

Hankerson, D., & Menezes, A. (2011). Pairings. In H. C. A. van Tilborg & S. Jajodia (Eds.), *Encyclopedia of cryptography and security*. Boston, MA: Springer. https://doi.org/10.1007/978-1-4419-5906-5_254

Hibbard, A. C., & Levasseur, K. M. (1999). Polynomial rings. *Exploring abstract algebra with mathematica*. New York, NY: Springer. https://doi.org/10.1007/978-1-4612-1530-1_20

Hoffstein, J., Pipher, J., & Silverman, J. H. (2008). *An introduction to mathematical cryptography*. New York, NY: Springer Science + Business Media.

Hoffstein, J., Howgrave-Graham, N., Pipher, J., & Whyte, W. (2009). Practical lattice-based cryptography: NTRUEncrypt and NTRUSign. In P. Nguyen & B. Vallée (Eds.), *The LLL algorithm. Information security and cryptography*. Berlin, Heidelberg: Springer. https://doi.org/10.1007/978-3-642-02295-1_11

Huang, M. D. A., Kueh, K. L., & Tan, K. S. (2000) Lifting elliptic curves and solving the elliptic curve discrete logarithm problem. In W. Bosma (Ed.), *Algorithmic number theory. ANTS 2000*. Lecture Notes in Computer Science, 1838. Berlin, Heidelberg: Springer. https://doi.org/10.1007/10722028_22

IEEE Std 1363.1-2008. (2009). IEEE standard specification for public key cryptographic techniques based on hard problems over lattices, 1–81.

Jao, D. (2010). Elliptic curve cryptography. In P. Stavroulakis & M. Stamp (Eds.), *Handbook of information and communication security*. Berlin, Heidelberg: Springer. https://doi.org/10.1007/978-3-642-04117-4_3

Kaliski, B. (2005). Homomorphism. In H. C. A. van Tilborg (Ed.), *Encyclopedia of cryptography and security*. Boston, MA: Springer. https://doi.org/10.1007/0-387-23483-7_188

Kaliski, B. (2011a). Quadratic residue. In H. C. A. van Tilborg, & S. Jajodia (Eds.), *Encyclopedia of cryptography and security*. Boston, MA: Springer. https://doi.org/10.1007/978-1-4419-5906-5_428

Kaliski, B. (2011b). Legendre symbol. In H. C. A. van Tilborg & S. Jajodia (Eds.), *Encyclopedia of cryptography and security*. Boston, MA: Springer. https://doi.org/10.1007/978-1-4419-5906-5_418

Kaliski, B. (2011c). Quadratic residuosity problem. In H. C. A. van Tilborg & S. Jajodia (Eds.), *Encyclopedia of cryptography and security.* Boston, MA: Springer. https://doi.org/10.1007/978-1-4419-5906-5_429.

Kaliski, B., (2011d). Finite field. In H. C. A. van Tilborg & S. Jajodia (Eds.), *Encyclopedia of cryptography and security.* Boston, MA: Springer,. https://doi.org/10.1007/978-1-4419-5906-5_409

Kaliski, B. (2011e). Group. In H. C. A. van Tilborg & S. Jajodia (Eds.), *Encyclopedia of cryptography and security.* Boston, MA: Springer. https://doi.org/10.1007/978-1-4419-5906-5_411.

Kaliski, B. (2011f). Ring. In H. C. A. van Tilborg & S. Jajodia (Eds.), *Encyclopedia of cryptography and security.* Boston, MA: Springer. https://doi.org/10.1007/978-1-4419-5906-5_431.

Kaliski, B. (2011g). Euler's totient function. In H. C. A. van Tilborg & S. Jajodia (Eds.), *Encyclopedia of cryptography and security.* Boston, MA: Springer. https://doi.org/10.1007/978-1-4419-5906-5_403.

Kebekus, S. (2024). Elliptic Curve Software. https://cplx.vm.uni-freiburg.de/storage/software/ellipticcurve/wasm/ellipticcurve.html

Khattar, D., & Agrawal, N. (2023). Integral domains and fields. *Ring theory.* Cham: Springer. https://doi.org/10.1007/978-3-031-29440-2_2

Kipkirui, K. (2018). Fundamental aspects of pairing based cryptography. *International Journal of Computational and Applied Mathematics, 13*(1), 9–18

Klein, A. (2014). Matrix algebraic properties of the fisher information matrix of stationary processes. *Entropy, 16*, 2023–2055.

Knuth, D. E. (1998). *The art of computer programming. Volume 2. Seminumerical algorithms.* Reading, MA: Pearson Education.

Larson, R. (2013). *Elementary linear algebra.* Boston, MA: Cengage Learning.

Lenstra, A. K., Lenstra, H. W., & Lovász, L. (1982). Factoring polynomials with rational coefficients. *Mathematische Annalen, 261*, 515–534. https://doi.org/10.1007/BF01457454

Liskov, M. (2011). Fermat's little theorem. In H. C. A. van Tilborg & S. Jajodia (Eds.), *Encyclopedia of cryptography and security.* Boston, MA: Springer. https://doi.org/10.1007/978-1-4419-5906-5_449

Meijer, A. R. (2016). Basic properties of the integers. *Algebra for cryptologists.* Springer Undergraduate Texts in Mathematics and Technology. Cham: Springer. https://doi.org/10.1007/978-3-319-30396-3_2

Micciancio, D., & Regev, O. (2009). Lattice-based cryptography. In D. J. Bernstein, J. Buchmann, & E. Dahmen (Eds.), *Post-quantum cryptography.* Berlin, Heidelberg: Springer. https://doi.org/10.1007/978-3-540-88702-7_5.

Micciancio, D. (2011). Closest vector problem. In H. C. A. van Tilborg & S. Jajodia (Eds.), *Encyclopedia of cryptography and security.* Boston, MA: Springer. https://doi.org/10.1007/978-1-4419-5906-5_399

Micciancio, D. (2016). Shortest vector problem. In M Y. Kao (Ed.), *Encyclopedia of algorithms.* New York, NY: Springer. https://doi.org/10.1007/978-1-4939-2864-4_374

Miller, V. (2004). The Weil pairing, and its efficient calculation. *Journal of Cryptology, 17*, 235–261. https://doi.org/10.1007/s00145-004-0315-8.

Nguyen, P. (2011). Lattice. In H. C. A. van Tilborg & S. Jajodia (Eds.), *Encyclopedia of cryptography and security.* Boston, MA: Springer. https://doi.org/10.1007/978-1-4419-5906-5_456

Nguyen, P. Q., & Regev, O. (2009). Learning a parallelepiped: Cryptanalysis of GGH and NTRU signatures. *Journal of Cryptology, 22*, 139–160. https://doi.org/10.1007/s00145-008-9031-0

Norman, C. (2012). The polynomial ring f[x] and matrices over f[x]. *Finitely generated abelian groups and similarity of matrices over a field.* Springer Undergraduate

Mathematics Series. London: Springer. https://doi.org/10.1007/978-1-4471-2730-7_4
Park, C. M., Kim, M. H., & Yung, M. (2005). A remark on implementing the Weill pairing. In D. Feng, D. Lin, & M. Yung (Eds.), *Information security and cryptology. CISC 2005*. Lecture Notes in Computer Science, 3822. Berlin, Heidelberg: Springer. https://doi.org/10.1007/11599548_27
Rosenthal, D., Rosenthal, D., & Rosenthal, P. (2014). Modular arithmetic. *A readable introduction to real mathematics*. Undergraduate Texts in Mathematics. Cham: Springer. https://doi.org/10.1007/978-3-319-05654-8_3.
Ross, S. M. (2014). *A first course in probability*. New York: Pearson Education.
Schroeder, M. (2009). The Chinese remainder theorem and simultaneous congruences. *Number theory in science and communication*. Berlin, Heidelberg: Springer. https://doi.org/10.1007/978-3-540-85298-8_17
Silverman, J. H. (2006). *An introduction to the theory of elliptic curves. Summer school on computational number theory and applications to cryptography*. https://www.math.brown.edu/johsilve/Presentations/WyomingEllipticCurve.pdf.
Silverman, J. H. (2009). Elliptic curves over global fields. *The arithmetic of elliptic curves*. Graduate Texts in Mathematics, 106. New York, NY: Springer. https://doi.org/10.1007/978-0-387-09494-6_8
Stein, W. (2009). The ring of integers modulo n. In *Elementary number theory: Primes, congruences, and secrets*. Undergraduate Texts in Mathematics. New York, NY: Springer. https://doi.org/10.1007/978-0-387-85525-7_2
Strang, G. (2016). *Introduction to linear algebra*. Wellesley.
Tilborg, H. C. A. (2011). Chinese Remainder theorem. In H. C. A. van Tilborg & S. Jajodia (Eds.), *Encyclopedia of cryptography and security*. Boston, MA: Springer. https://doi.org/10.1007/978-1-4419-5906-5_2
Toth, G. (2021). Polynomial functions. *Elements of mathematics*. Undergraduate Texts in Mathematics. Cham: Springer. https://doi.org/10.1007/978-3-030-75051-0_7.
Vanstone, S. A., & van Oorschot, P. C. (1989). Finite fields. *An introduction to error correcting codes with applications*. The Springer International Series in Engineering and Computer Science, 71. Boston, MA: Springer. https://doi.org/10.1007/978-1-4757-2032-7_2
Washington, L. C. (2008). Elliptic curves over finite fields. *Elliptic curves number theory and cryptography*. Boca Raton, London, New York: Taylor & Francis Group, CRC Press.

Chapter 2

Fundamental concepts related to cryptography and public key cryptosystems

2.1 INTRODUCTION

This chapter is an introduction to the basic concepts and terms in public key cryptosystems. We start with very simple concepts such as plaintext and ciphertext as provided in Section 2.2. We continue with the basic properties of the encryption function and decryption function as given in Section 2.3. The concepts provided in Sections 2.2 and 2.3 are not only applicable for public key cryptosystems but also for all types of cryptosystems. However, Section 2.4 is about the distinction between public key and private key, both of which are used only in public key cryptosystems. Since the security of any cryptosystem, specifically public key cryptosystems, is of utmost importance, increasing the security by means of randomness has been a generally accepted approach, with this aim probabilistic encryption has been implemented in different public key cryptosystems. Thus, Section 2.5 provides deterministic encryption and probabilistic encryption in comparison to each other. Although they seem to be similar, encoding/decoding and encryption/decryption are not the same; thus, Section 2.6 is devoted to the explanation of the basic differences between these concepts.

Section 2.7 is one of the fundamental sections in this chapter since the basic features of public key cryptosystems are explained in comparison to private key cryptosystems in this section. Homomorphic encryption has been a well-known encryption method since the calculations on the ciphertext can be made as if the calculations were made on the plaintext. Section 2.8 provides the basic definition and basic requirements of homomorphic encryption that can be adapted to both private key cryptosystems and public key cryptosystems. In many public key cryptosystems, large prime numbers are used, thus determining whether a large number is a prime number is very crucial. Section 2.9 is devoted to the topic "primality testing" and subtopics "Fermat's little theorem", "Miller-Rabin probabilistic primality testing", and "Agrawal-Kayal-Saxena (AKS) primality testing". The hash function is generally used for the uniform storage of data. The cryptographic hash functions that can be used both in public key cryptosystems and digital signature algorithms are given in Section 2.10. In this section, basic terms regarding

DOI: 10.1201/9781003514190-2

hash functions, basic properties of cryptographic hash functions, and random oracle model are briefly explained. Digital signatures, which are analogous to the public key cryptosystems, are part of the book. Section 2.11 is devoted to digital signatures, and the basic parameters and basic structure of a digital signature algorithm are introduced in this section. Cryptanalysis is also part of the book. In Section 2.12, several definitions of cryptanalysis from the literature, basic types of cryptanalysis, classification of cryptographic attacks based on the knowledge of ciphertexts or plaintext/ciphertext pairs, and the basic terms regarding the attacks to the digital signature algorithms are provided as the fundamentals of cryptanalysis. Like Chapter 1, this chapter is also intended to provide some background for the remaining chapters of the book.

2.2 PLAINTEXT VS. CIPHERTEXT

A plaintext $p \in \mathcal{P}$ is the "original text" or message, whereas the corresponding ciphertext $c \in \mathcal{C}$ is the "hidden (scrambled)" form of the plaintext $p \in \mathcal{P}$ that is actually transmitted from the sender to the receiver(s) so that the plaintext can be recovered from the ciphertext by the receivers (allowed party or parties) who has (have) the "private (secret) key". In this definition, $\mathcal{P}$ refers to the set of the possible plaintexts or plaintext space, and $\mathcal{C}$ refers to the set of the possible ciphertexts or ciphertext space.

2.3 ENCRYPTION FUNCTION VS. DECRYPTION FUNCTION

A plaintext should be encrypted (enciphered) into a ciphertext by one party by using an "encryption key", whereas the ciphertext can be decrypted (deciphered) into the plaintext by the allowed party (parties) who has (have) the "private (secret) key" called the "decryption key". Let $\mathcal{K}$ be the set of the possible keys (key space) defined with $\mathcal{K} = (\mathcal{K}_{enc}, \mathcal{K}_{dec})$, where $\mathcal{K}_{enc}$ is the set of the encryption keys and $\mathcal{K}_{dec}$ is the set of the decryption keys. Accordingly, Table 2.1 depicts the distinction between the "encryption function" and the "decryption function" very basically.

Table 2.1 Encryption function vs. decryption function

Encryption function	*Decryption function*
e: $\mathcal{K}_{enc} \times \mathcal{P} \to \mathcal{C}$ is an encryption function or $e_{k_{enc}}(p) = c, k_{enc} \in \mathcal{K}_{enc}, p \in \mathcal{P}, c \in \mathcal{C}$	d: $\mathcal{K}_{dec} \times \mathcal{C} \to \mathcal{P}$ is a decryption function or $d_{k_{dec}}(c) = p, k_{dec} \in \mathcal{K}_{dec}, c \in \mathcal{C}, p \in \mathcal{P}$

2.4 PUBLIC KEY VS. PRIVATE (SECRET) KEY

The distinction between the public key k_{pub} and the private (secret) key k_{priv} is crucial for the "public key cryptosystems" (public key encryption, asymmetric key cryptosystem, asymmetric key cipher, and asymmetric cryptography). In a "public key cryptosystem", the public key k_{pub} is made publicly available and used for the encryption function, that is, $k_{pub} = k_{enc}$, while the private (secret) key k_{priv} is known by the allowed party or parties and used for the decryption function, that is, $k_{priv} = k_{dec}$. On the other hand, in a "private key cryptosystem" (symmetric key cryptosystem, symmetric key cipher, and symmetric cryptography), $k_{priv} = k_{enc} = k_{dec}$ holds. (See Section 2.7 for more details regarding the distinction between private key cryptosystems and public key cryptosystems.)

The *Kerckhoff's principle* is a fundamental assumption in mathematical cryptography. According to Kerckhoff's principle, the security of a cryptosystem should only depend on the knowledge of the private (secret) key, not on the encryption/decryption algorithm or any other public information (Paar & Pelzl, 2010; Petitcolas, 2011).

2.5 DETERMINISTIC ENCRYPTION VS. PROBABILISTIC ENCRYPTION

The deterministic encryption works basically as shown in Table 2.1. In probabilistic encryption, a "random string of data" $r \in \mathcal{R}$ is considered, which is called the "number used once (nonce)" that is used only for one execution of the algorithm, where $\mathcal{R}$ is the set of the random string of data (Barker & Barker, 2019; Fuchsbauer, 2006; Smart, 2016). If the nonce is short-lived, then it is called an "ephemeral key". Note that a nonce in other contexts does not have to be randomly generated (Smart, 2016). Table 2.2 provides the basic distinction between the encryption function and the decryption function in case of the probabilistic encryption.

As evident from Table 2.2, the random string of data is needed only for the encryption function. The "ElGamal public key cryptosystem" provided in

Table 2.2 Encryption function vs. decryption function in case of the probabilistic encryption

Encryption function for the probabilistic encryption	*Decryption function corresponding to the probabilistic encryption*
e: $\mathcal{K}_{enc} \times \mathcal{R} \times \mathcal{P} \rightarrow \mathcal{C}$	d: $\mathcal{K}_{dec} \times \mathcal{C} \rightarrow \mathcal{P}$
or	or
$e_{k_{enc},r}(p) = c, k_{enc} \in \mathcal{K}_{enc}, r \in \mathcal{R}, p \in \mathcal{P}, c \in \mathcal{C}$	$d_{k_{dec}}(c) = p, k_{dec} \in \mathcal{K}_{dec}, c \in \mathcal{C}, p \in \mathcal{P}$

Source: Adapted from Fuchsbauer (2006).

Chapter 3 and the "Goldwasser-Micali probabilistic public key cryptosystem" provided in Chapter 6 are two examples of public key cryptosystems based on the probabilistic encryption. Note that for any $r_1 \in \mathcal{R}, r_2 \in \mathcal{R}$, $r_1 \neq r_2$ and for any $p \in \mathcal{P}$, $e_{k_{enc},r_1}(p) = c_1$ and $e_{k_{enc},r_2}(p) = c_2$ hold, where $c_1 \neq c_2$, although the same plaintext will be recovered during the decryption process.

2.6 ENCODING/DECODING VS. ENCRYPTION/DECRYPTION

Although they seem very similar, encoding/decoding and encryption/decryption have different purposes as explained very briefly in Table 2.3.

There are different types of "text encoding" schemes. American Standard Code for Information Interchange (ASCII) is a text encoding scheme for the English alphabet and it is used to map each of the 94 characters to any of $2^7 = 128$ different values ranging from 0 to 127 (Fortner, 1995; Nugues, 2014). Note that in ASCII each character is actually encoded as a block of seven bits, although a block of eight bits (byte) is considered, where the initial (top) bit is not used (Fortner, 1995). Since ASCII is restricted to the English alphabet, another text coding scheme, the so-called Unicode was developed by the Unicode Consortium to be the universal standard for text encoding. It considers all the characters of the languages of the world and also the technical symbols, punctuations, and many other characters (Nugues, 2014; Piotrowski, 2012; Unicode, 2024).

2.7 PRIVATE KEY CRYPTOSYSTEMS VS. PUBLIC KEY CRYPTOSYSTEMS

Although this book is dedicated to the public key cryptosystems, a basic distinction between the private key cryptosystems and public key cryptosystems will be given in this section. It has been a convention to use "Alice" and "Bob" as the names of two individuals who want to communicate through

Table 2.3 Encoding/decoding vs. encryption/decryption

Encoding/decoding	*Encryption/decryption*
The encoding is a method of "converting" one sort of data into another sort of data. A typical example of encoding is "text encoding" (character encoding) which includes converting the text characters into a sequence of numbers.	The encryption is a method of "hiding (concealing)" information from anyone who is not allowed, that is, who does not possess the private decryption key.
The decoding can be done by anyone.	The decryption can only be made by the allowed party (parties) who has (have) the private decryption key.

Source: Adapted from Jo (2019).

Table 2.4 Private key cryptosystems vs. public key cryptosystems

Private key cryptosystems	*Public key cryptosystems*
Alice and Bob should share the common private (secret) key $k \in \mathcal{K}$, where $k = k_{enc} = k_{dec}$.	Alice creates $k_{priv} \in \mathcal{K}_{priv}$, computes $k_{pub} \in \mathcal{K}_{pub}$ from $k_{priv} \in \mathcal{K}_{priv}$, and sends $k_{pub} \in \mathcal{K}_{pub}$ to Bob.
Encryption function (used by Bob)	Encryption function (used by Bob)
e: $\mathcal{K} \times \mathcal{P} \to \mathcal{C}$	e: $\mathcal{K}_{pub} \times \mathcal{P} \to \mathcal{C}$
or	or
$e_k(p) = c;\ k \in \mathcal{K}, p \in \mathcal{P}, c \in \mathcal{C}$	$e_{k_{pub}}(p) = c;\ k_{pub} \in \mathcal{K}_{pub},\ p \in \mathcal{P}, c \in \mathcal{C}$
Decryption function (used by Alice)	Decryption function (used by Alice)
$d: \mathcal{K} \times \mathcal{C} \to \mathcal{P}$	$d: \mathcal{K}_{priv} \times \mathcal{C} \to \mathcal{P}$
or	or
$d_k(c) = p;\ k \in \mathcal{K},\ c \in \mathcal{C}, p \in \mathcal{P}$	$d_{k_{priv}}(c) = p;\ k_{priv} \in \mathcal{K}_{priv}, c \in \mathcal{C},\ p \in \mathcal{P}$

a network by means of encryption/decryption, and "Eve" as the name of the "adversary (eavesdropper)" who tries to monitor the communication, intervene with the communication, or recover some secret information such as the plaintext or secret key during the communication between "Alice" and "Bob". The "eavesdropping" is a term used for the unauthorized monitoring or intervention of a communication session. In "passive eavesdropping", there is only monitoring of communication without any intervention, but in "active eavesdropping", there is also the intervention to the communication contents (Sherr, 2011). We will also keep the "Alice-Bob-Eve setting" throughout the book. Table 2.4 provides the basic distinction between the private key cryptosystems and public key cryptosystems by considering this convention without the involvement of Eve.

Shannon was the first to give a formal definition of the private key cryptosystems in 1949 and defined $e_k(p)$ as a one-to-one mapping (Shannon, 1949; van Tilborg, 2011). In a private key cryptosystem, a "key generation algorithm" is needed. A secure network is also required to share the common private key. The stream ciphers, block ciphers, and message authentication codes (MACs) are three examples of private key cryptosystems.

As provided in Table 2.4, in a public key cryptosystem, $k_{pub} \in \mathcal{K}_{pub}$ is computed from $k_{priv} \in \mathcal{K}_{priv}$ and shared through an "insecure network". Many public key cryptosystem algorithms use the following structure, which can also be adapted to the private key cryptosystems (adapted from Gómez Pardo, 2013a):

Let ε = (*KeyGen*, *Enc*, *Dec*) be a set of polynomial-time algorithms, where

KeyGen: Probabilistic algorithm with the security parameter k as the input, the private key, and the public key as the outputs.

Enc: Possibly probabilistic algorithm with the public key, plaintext as the inputs, and the ciphertext as the output.

Dec: Deterministic algorithm with the ciphertext, private key as the inputs, and the plaintext as the output.

There is also the so-called "hybrid cryptosystem" (hybrid cipher), which is a combination of the public key cryptosystem and private key cryptosystem. In a hybrid cryptosystem, a public key cryptosystem is used to share a private key, while a private key cryptosystem is used to encrypt the plaintext (and decrypt the ciphertext) with the shared private key (Kurosawa, 2011; Smart, 2016).

2.8 HOMOMORPHIC ENCRYPTION

Homomorphic encryption is a special type of encryption which allows a third party to make some computations on the ciphertext without knowing the plaintext, where the computations made on the ciphertext correspond to the similar computations on the plaintext (Gómez Pardo, 2013a; Li, 2009). Thus, in addition to the encryption and decryption, there is the so-called "evaluation procedure" in a homomorphic encryption, where the evaluation function $f(c)$ with an "evaluation key" corresponds to $f(p)$ (Albrecht et al., 2021; Halevi, 2017). Analogous to the structure considered for public key cryptosystems given in Section 2.7, the basic structure of a homomorphic encryption can be defined as $\varepsilon = (KeyGen, Enc, Dec, Evaluate)$ (Halevi, 2017).

Note that the homomorphic encryption can be adapted to both public key cryptosystems and private key cryptosystems. The basic requirements of the homomorphic encryption are listed as follows (adapted from Hoffstein, 2015):

1. Given the plaintexts $p_1, p_2, \ldots$ and the encryption key k_{enc}, it should be easy to compute the ciphertexts $e_{k_{enc}}(p_1) = c_1, e_{k_{enc}}(p_2) = c_2, \ldots$
2. Given the ciphertexts $e_{k_{enc}}(p_1) = c_1, e_{k_{enc}}(p_2) = c_2, \ldots$, and the decryption key k_{dec}, it should be easy to compute the plaintexts $d_{k_{dec}}(c_1) = p_1, d_{k_{dec}}(c_2) = p_2, \ldots$
3. Without k_{dec}, it must be hard to recover the plaintexts $d_{k_{dec}}(c_1) = p_1, d_{k_{dec}}(c_2) = p_2, \ldots$
4. Given an arbitrarily long sequence $(p_1, e_{k_{enc}}(p_1))$, $(p_2, e_{k_{enc}}(p_2))$, $(p_3, e_{k_{enc}}(p_3))$,...it must be very hard to obtain information about a new p, given $e_{k_{enc}}(p)$.
5. In case of the "fully homomorphic encryption", for all $p_1, p_2 \in \mathcal{P}$, Equations (2.1) and (2.2) should hold:

$$e_{k_{enc}}(p_1 + p_2) = e_{k_{enc}}(p_1) + e_{k_{enc}}(p_2) \tag{2.1}$$

$$e_{k_{enc}}(p_1 \cdot p_2) = e_{k_{enc}}(p_1) \cdot e_{k_{enc}}(p_2) \tag{2.2}$$

In a "fully homomorphic function", the plaintext lies in the ring R, and the ciphertext lies in the ring S such that $e : R \rightarrow S$ and $d : S \rightarrow R$ must be the "ring homomorphisms", that is, both Equations (2.1) and (2.2) should hold for all $p_1, p_2 \in \mathcal{P}$. In a "partially homomorphic encryption", either the addition or multiplication is satisfied, that is, either Equation (2.1) or Equation (2.2) is possible (Li, 2009).

Regarding the public key cryptosystems, the ElGamal public key cryptosystem provided in Chapter 3, the Rivest, Shamir, Adleman (RSA) public key cryptosystem provided in Chapter 4, and the Goldwasser-Micali probabilistic public key cryptosystem provided in Chapter 6 are the examples of "partially homomorphic encryption" (see Tekin, 2023 for the details).

2.9 PRIMALITY TESTING

Since some public key cryptosystems such as the ElGamal public key cryptosystem provided in Chapter 3 and the RSA public key cryptosystem provided in Chapter 4 work by using very large prime numbers, it is of great importance to determine whether a very large number is a prime number. Before we explain some selected primality testing methods, we provide the following theorems.

Theorem 2.1 (Primality test by trial division)

Let $n > 1$ be an integer number. If n has no prime factors less than or equal to $\sqrt{n}$, then n is a prime number (adapted from Koç, Özdemir, & Ödemiş Özger, 2021; Yan, 2009).

Theorem 2.2 (Prime number theorem)

Let $n > 1$ be a real number. According to the prime number theorem, the expected number of prime numbers in $[2, n]$ is approximately $\frac{n}{\ln(n)}$, and the probability of a randomly chosen number a to be a prime number is approximately $1/\ln(a)$ (adapted from Hoffstein, Pipher, & Silverman, 2008; Smart, 2016).

Example 2.1

As an example, the expected number of the prime numbers between 1000 and 100000 is $\frac{100000}{\ln(100000)} - \frac{1000}{\ln(1000)} = 8541$. As another example, the probability of 21456789342335 to be a prime number is $1/\ln(21456789342335) = 0.0326$ according to the prime number theorem.

2.9.1 Primality testing based on the *Fermat's* little theorem

Recall from Section 1.4.1 in Chapter 1, according to the Fermat's little theorem, if p is a prime number, then $a^p \equiv a \pmod{p}$ holds for every integer a. However, this leads to the following conclusion for an integer number n (Fine & Rosenberger, 2016; Hoffstein et al., 2008; Koç et al., 2021):

It is possible that $a^n \equiv a \pmod{n}$ does not hold for some integers a, thus it is possible that n is not a prime number, that is, n is a composite number.

Based on this conclusion, the "witness for the compositeness of an odd number n" can be defined based on the Fermat's little theorem as in Definition 2.1 (adapted from Hoffstein et al., 2008; Koç et al., 2021).

Definition 2.1

An integer a is called a "witness for the compositeness of an odd number n" based on the Fermat's little theorem if $a^n \not\equiv a \pmod{n}$ holds.

Note that one witness a is sufficient to conclude that n is a composite number.

Example 2.2

We would like to find a witness for the compositeness of 247 based on the Fermat's little theorem. Let's try for $a = 2$. It is clear that $2^{247} \equiv 193 \not\equiv 2 \pmod{247}$. Thus, 2 is a witness for the compositeness of the odd number 247 based on the Fermat's little theorem.

We would also like to find a witness for the compositeness of 725 based on the Fermat's little theorem. Let's try for $a = 3$. Since $3^{725} \equiv 43 \not\equiv 3 \pmod{725}$ holds, 3 is a witness for the compositeness of 725 based on the Fermat's little theorem.

Although some positive odd numbers are composite numbers, they satisfy the Fermat's little theorem. These numbers are called the "Fermat pseudoprime numbers" or "Carmichael numbers". 561 is the smallest Carmichael number. We provide Definition 2.2 and Theorem 2.3 related to the Carmichael numbers.

Definition 2.2

A composite number n is a "Carmichael number" if it satisfies $a^n \equiv a \pmod{n}$ for every positive integer a such that $\gcd(a, n) = 1$ holds (adapted from Gómez Pardo, 2013b; Yan, 2009).

Theorem 2.3

A composite number $n > 2$ is a "Carmichael number" if and only if $n = \prod_{i=1}^{k} p_i$, $k \geq 3$ holds for distinct odd prime numbers p_i such that $p_i - 1 \mid n - 1$ for all $i = 1, 2, \ldots, k$ hold (adapted from Yan, 2009).

Note that the smallest Carmichael number 561 can be written as $561 = 3 \cdot 11 \cdot 17$. Note also that $2 \mid 560$, $10 \mid 560$, and $16 \mid 560$ hold.

2.9.2 Miller-Rabin probabilistic primality testing

There is another witness for the compositeness of an odd number n that is called the "Miller-Rabin witness", which will be defined next.

Definition 2.3

Let n be an odd number, which can be written as $n = 1 + 2^k q$, where $k \in \mathbb{Z}_+$ and q is an odd integer number. A positive integer a satisfying $\gcd(a, n) = 1$ is called a "Miller-Rabin witness" for the compositeness of the odd number n if both of the following conditions hold (adapted from Gómez Pardo, 2013b; Hoffstein et al., 2008):

i. $a^q \not\equiv 1 \pmod{n}$
ii. $a^{2^i q} \not\equiv -1 \pmod{n}$ for all $i = 0, 1, 2, \ldots, k-1$

Again, one witness a is sufficient to conclude that n is a composite number.

Example 2.2 (revisited)

We would like to find a "Miller-Rabin witness" for the compositeness of 247. We write 247 as $247 = 1 + 2^1 \cdot 123$, where $k = 1$ and $q = 123$ is an odd number. As an example, we check for $a = 2$ as follows:

i. $2^{123} \equiv 164 \neq 1 \pmod{247}$
Note that since $k = 1$, we consider only $i = 0$.
ii. $2^{2^0 \cdot 123} \equiv 2^{123} \equiv 164 \neq -1 \pmod{247}$

Accordingly, 2 is a Miller-Rabin witness for the compositeness of 247.

We would also like to find a Miller-Rabin witness for the compositeness of 725. We write 725 as $725 = 1 + 2^2 \cdot 181$, where $k = 2$ and $q = 181$ is an odd number. As an example, we check for $a = 3$ as follows:

i. $3^{181} \equiv 628 \neq 1 \pmod{725}$

Note that since $k = 2$, we consider $i = 0, 1$ as follows:

i. $3^{2^0 \cdot 181} \equiv 3^{181} \equiv 628 \neq -1 \pmod{725}$
ii. $3^{2^1 \cdot 181} \equiv 3^{362} \equiv 709 \neq -1 \pmod{725}$

As a result, 3 is a Miller-Rabin witness for the compositeness of 725.

The Miller-Rabin primality test (Miller-Selfridge-Rabin test, strong pseudoprimality test) is a "probabilistic primality test", which was developed based on the Miller-Rabin witness with the steps as follows (adapted from Liskov, 2011; Pun, 2024; Yan, 2009):

1. If $n = 2$, then n is prime, and if $n > 2$ and even, then n is composite. Otherwise, write
   $n = 1 + 2^k q$, where q is an odd number for the possible maximum value of $k \in \mathbb{Z}_+$.
2. Select $2 \le a \le n-1$ randomly that satisfies $\gcd(a,n) = 1$.
3. For $i = 0$ do $b = a^q \pmod{n}$
   If $b = 1$ or $b = n-1$, then output "n is probably prime".
4. For $i = 1, 2, \ldots, k-1$ do

$b = b^2 \pmod{n}$
If $b = n-1$, then output "n is probably prime".
Otherwise output "n is definitely composite".

Example 2.3

We would like to apply the Miller-Rabin probabilistic primality test for the odd number 787. We write 787 as $787 = 1 + 2 \cdot 393$, where $k = 1$ and $q = 393$ is an odd number. We select $a = 2$ randomly. We set $i = 0$ and calculate $b = 2^{393} \equiv 786 \pmod{787}$. Since $i = 0$ and $b = 786 = 787 - 1$ hold, we output "787 is probably prime". Indeed 787 is a prime number.

Example 2.4

Let's also consider the application of the Miller-Rabin test for the odd number 27553. We write $27553 = 1 + 2^5 \cdot 861$, where $k = 5, q = 861$. We select $a = 7$ randomly. We set $i = 0$ and calculate $b = 7^{861} \equiv 14539 \pmod{27553}$. Since $14539 \ne 1$ or $14539 \ne 27552$, we go on with $i = 1$, and calculate $b = 14539^2 \equiv 23458 \pmod{27553}$. Since $23458 \ne 27552$, we go on with $i = 2$, and calculate $b = 23458^2 \equiv 16801 \pmod{27553}$. In the same manner, we set $i = 3$ and $b = 16801^2 \equiv 20669 \pmod{27553}$. Finally, we set $i = 4$ and find $b = 20669^2 \equiv 25849 \pmod{27553}$. Since none of the results yield 27552, then we output "27553 is definitely composite". Indeed 27553 is a composite number.

2.9.3 Agrawal-Kayal-Saxena (AKS) primality testing

The AKS primality testing is a deterministic, polynomial-time algorithm, which has been developed based on Lemma 2.1 (adapted from Agrawal, Kayal, & Saxena, 2004; Yan, 2009):

Lemma 2.1:

Let $a \in \mathbb{Z}$, $n \in \mathbb{Z}_+$, $n \ge 2$, where $\gcd(a,n) = 1$. Then n is a prime number if and only if the polynomial equation
$(x+a)^n \equiv x^n + a \pmod{n}$ over the polynomial ring $\mathbb{Z}[x]$ or
$(x-a)^n \equiv x^n - a \pmod{n}$ over the polynomial ring $\mathbb{Z}[x]$
can be solved, which is equivalent to
$(x+a)^n \equiv x^n + a \pmod{x^r - 1, n}$ or
$(x-a)^n \equiv x^n - a \pmod{x^r - 1, n}$.

In Lemma 2.1, x is an indeterminate and $\left(\text{mod } x^r - 1, n\right)$ means that both sides of the congruences are evaluated modulo $x^r - 1$ over the polynomial ring $(\mathbb{Z}/n\mathbb{Z})[x]$ for an appropriately chosen small value of r (Agrawal et al., 2004).

In the following we provide the original algorithm for the AKS primality testing (Agrawal et al., 2004):

Input: Integer $n > 1$

1. If $n = a^b$ for some $a \in \mathbb{N}$ and $b > 1$, then output "n is composite".
2. Find the smallest r such that $d > \log^2 n$ holds, where d is the smallest integer that satisfies $a^d \equiv 1 \pmod{r}$.
3. If $1 < \gcd(a, n) < n$ for some $a \leq r$, then output "n is composite".
4. If $n \leq r$, then output "n is prime".
5. For $a = 1$ to $\left\lfloor \sqrt{\phi(r)} \log n \right\rfloor$ do

if $(x+a)^n \not\equiv x^n + a \bmod (x^r - 1, n)$, then output "$n$ is composite".

Otherwise, output "n is prime".

Note that $\phi(r)$ is Euler's phi (totient) function as defined in Section 1.3.1 of Chapter 1, and $\lfloor x \rfloor$ is the floor function which gives the greatest integer less than or equal to x.

Example 2.5

We would like to apply the AKS primality testing for the odd number 19.

1. Since there are no $a \in \mathbb{N}$ and $b > 1$ values that satisfy $19 = a^b$, we cannot output "n is composite".
2. Since $d > log^2 19 = 1.63521$, holds, we set $d = 2$. We also set $a = 2$. Then $2^2 \equiv 1 \pmod{r}$ holds and we find $r = 3$.
3. Since $\gcd(1, 19) = \gcd(2, 19) = \gcd(3, 19) = 1$ holds, we cannot output "19 is composite".
4. Since $19 > 3$, we cannot also output "19 is prime".
5. For $a = 1$ to $\left\lfloor \sqrt{\phi(3)}\ log 19 \right\rfloor = \lfloor 1.8084 \rfloor = 1$, that is, for $a = 1$, we expand the polynomial equation $(x+1)^{19} - \left(x^{19} + 1\right)$ as follows:

$$(x+1)^{19} - \left(x^{19}+1\right) = 19x^{18} + 171x^{17} + 969x^{16} + 3876x^{15} + 11628x^{14} + 27132x^{13} + 50388x^{12} + 75582x^{11} + 92378x^{10} + 92378x^9 + 75582x^8 + 50388x^7 + 27132x^6 + 11628x^5 + 3876x^4 + 969x^3 + 171x^2 + 19x$$

Since all the coefficients of the expansion are divided by 19, we output "19 is prime".

2.10 CRYPTOGRAPHIC HASH FUNCTIONS

The cryptographic hash function is an important term in cryptography that allows the uniform storage of the data. They have implementations in various public key cryptosystems and digital signature algorithms.

2.10.1 Basic terms regarding hash functions

In the following, we provide some basic definitions related to hash functions:

Definition 2.4

A "one-way function (irreversible function)" is a function which is easy to compute in one direction but hard to compute in the reverse direction, that is, hard to invert. In other words, in a "one-way function" $f(x)$, it is easy to find $y = f(x)$ for all x values but hard to compute $f^{-1}(y) = x$ for all y values (adapted from Antunes, Matos, Pinto, Souto, & Teixeira, 2012; Robshaw, 2011a).

Definition 2.5

A "trapdoor one-way function" is a special "one-way function" which is easy to invert if an additional secret value called the "trapdoor" is available (adapted from Robshaw, 2011b; Rompel, 1990).

Definition 2.6

A "compression function" is defined as h: $\{0,1\}^m \to \{0,1\}^n$; $m, n \in \mathbb{Z}_+$, $m > n$, where m is the number of the bits of the input string, and n is the number of the bits of the output string (adapted from Buchmann, 2004). It can be usually assumed that $m \geq 2n$ holds (Stinson, 2006).

Definition 2.7

A "hash function" is a function defined as h: $\{0,1\}^* \to \{0,1\}^n$ $n \in \mathbb{Z}_+$, where * is the number of the bits of the input string with arbitrary length, while n is the number of the bits of the output string with fixed length (adapted from Blanton, 2018; Buchmann, 2004; Preneel, 2011).

The output of the hash function, that is, $\{0,1\}^n$ is called the hash value (hash, digest). There are various ways of generating the hash functions such as generating from the compression functions (Buchmann, 2004). Note that a generic hash function does not have to be a "one-way function" or a "trapdoor one-way function", although a hash function can be a "one-way function" or a "trapdoor one-way function".

Cryptographic hash functions are special hash functions, which will be provided in the next section.

2.10.2 Basic properties of cryptographic hash functions

A cryptographic hash function is a special hash function that should be easy-and-efficient-to-compute, in which a finite and sequential series of the substitutions and transformations of the input message may be required to produce the hash value (Buchmann, 2004; Garewal, 2020). The basic properties of the cryptographic hash functions are provided in Table 2.5.

Table 2.5 Basic properties of the cryptographic hash functions

Preimage resistance	*Second preimage resistance*	*Collision resistance*
It is computationally infeasible to find x value that satisfies $h(x) = y$.	It is computationally infeasible to find for any x value, an x' value such that $x' \neq x, h(x') = h(x)$ holds.	It is computationally infeasible to find two values x, x' such that $x' \neq x, h(x') = h(x)$ holds.

Source: Adapted from Gauravaram & Knudsen (2010) and Stinson (2006).

If $h(x) = y = 0$ holds, then the "preimage resistance" provided in the first column of Table 2.5 is called the "zero preimage" (Stinson, 2006).

Definition 2.8

A "one-way hash function (OWHF)" is a hash function with the properties "preimage resistance" and "second preimage resistance" (Preneel, 2011).

Definition 2.9

A "collision-resistant hash function (CRHF)" is a hash function with the properties "preimage resistance", "second preimage resistance", and "collision resistance" (Preneel, 2011).

One of the most common applications of the cryptographic hash functions is digital signature algorithms (Preneel, 2011). There are different cryptographic hash functions. As an example, secure hash algorithm (SHA) is a family of cryptographic hash functions published by the American National Institute of Standards and Technology (NIST). There were basically three versions of SHA including SHA-0, SHA-1, and SHA-2 (Handschuh, 2011). However, since they have been vulnerable to attacks, NIST announced a competition for SHA-3 in 2007, ended the competition in 2012, and announced KECCAK as the "winning algorithm to be standardized as the new SHA-3" (National Institute of Standards and Technology, 2024a). Some other selected cryptographic hash functions are MD (message digest), BLAKE, and RACE Integrity Primitives Evaluation Message Digest (RIPEMD) (see Aumasson, Meier, Phan, & Henzen, 2014; Bosselaers & Preneel, 1995; Furht, 2008).

2.10.3 Random oracle model

The random oracle model is an idealized model. In a random oracle model, it is assumed that there exists a "public function" managed by an "oracle", which can be generally a "hash function" that outputs a "truly random output" for each input. The private queries are sent to the oracle. As the first step, the oracle checks from the memory whether the queried input and the corresponding output exist. If they exist, the oracle returns the output corresponding to that input. Otherwise, the oracle generates a random string of the appropriate length as the output, returns the result, and stores it in the memory as the output of the corresponding input to be used later (see Bleumer, 2011a; Katz, 2010; Preneel, 2011).

2.11 DIGITAL SIGNATURES

A digital signature is the substitute for a conventional signature, and it is always accompanied by a digital document which is digitally signed. Digital signatures are in the scope of this book since they can also be considered under the topic "public key cryptosystems" due to the fact that there is a "private signing key" and a "public verification key" in a digital signature algorithm. Analogous to the names "Alice", "Bob", and "Eve" for the public key cryptosystems, the names "Samantha", "Victor", and "Eve" can be used for the digital signature algorithms due to Hoffstein et al. (2008). In this setting, "Samantha" is responsible for signing the digital documents by using her "private signing key", "Victor" is responsible for verifying the digital signature of the digital document signed by Samantha by using the "public verification key", and "Eve" is the adversary who can perform passive or active eavesdropping. We will also keep "Samantha-Victor-Eve setting" while explaining the digital signature algorithms in Chapters 3–6.

In the following, we merely provide the basic parameters and basic structure of a digital signature algorithm.

Basic parameters of a digital signature algorithm (*adapted from* Hoffstein et al., 2008):

D: Digital document of Samantha
$h(D)$: Hash value of the digital document D
D^{sig}: Digital signature of the digital document D signed by Samantha
s: Private signing key of Samantha
v: Public verification key to be used by Victor

Basic structure of a digital signature algorithm (adapted from Hoffstein et al., 2008)

As mentioned previously, a digital signature is always accompanied by the corresponding digital document (message) similar to a conventional signature. In a digital signature algorithm, there are two basic parts: (1) Signing algorithm (Sign) and (2) Verification algorithm (Verify), which can be briefly explained as follows:

Sign: Samantha takes as the inputs D (or $h(D)$) and s, and returns D^{sig} for D (or $h(D)$).
Verify: Victor takes D (or $h(D)$), D^{sig} and v as the inputs, and checks if D^{sig} is a digital signature for D (or $h(D)$) associated to s.

2.12 CRYPTANALYSIS

The basic cryptanalysis approaches to the public key cryptosystems and digital signature algorithms are also in the scope of this book. There are several definitions of cryptanalysis in the literature, some of which will be provided directly as follows:

Cryptanalysis is the discipline of deciphering a ciphertext without having access to the keytext usually by recovering more or less directly the plaintext or even the keytext used, in cases favorable for the attacker by reconstructing the whole cryptosystem used. This being the worst case possible for the attacked side, an acceptable level of security should rest completely in the key.

(*Bauer, 2005*)

Cryptanalysis is the study of secret code systems in order to obtain secret information.

(*Cambridge Dictionary, 2024*)

Cryptanalysis is the analysis of information systems in order to gain information about potential hidden sets of data in these systems.

(*Ciesla, 2020*)

Cryptanalysis is a formal process whereby one applies specific techniques in an attempt to crack cryptography.

(*Easttom, 2021*)

Cryptanalysis is the process of studying cryptographic systems to look for weaknesses or leaks of information.

(*Edgar & Manz, 2017*)

Cryptanalysis is the art of decrypting messages without previous knowledge of the key.

(*Hoffstein et al., 2008*)

Cryptanalysis is the study of mathematical techniques for attempting to defeat cryptographic techniques and/or information systems security. This includes the process of looking for errors or weaknesses in the implementation of an algorithm or of the algorithm itself.

(*National Institute of Standards and Technology, 2024b*)

Cryptanalysis is the science and sometimes art of breaking cryptosystems.

(*Paar & Pelzl, 2010*)

Cryptanalysis is breaking of secret codes. It implies an attack of some sort to read the messages.

(*Stamp & Low, 2007*)

> Cryptanalysis is the opposite of cryptography. The field deals with the uncovering of encrypted messages without initial knowledge of the key used in the encryption process.
>
> *(Z'aba & Maarof, 2006)*

As a summary of the provided definitions, cryptanalysis is used to deduce some secret (hidden) information such as the private key, plaintext, or some other secret information by searching for the weaknesses and information leakages in the cryptographic system with the help of different techniques including mathematical techniques.

In the following, we also provide the definition of "semantically secure cryptosystem", which is a crucial term in cryptanalysis.

Definition 2.10

"An encryption scheme is semantically secure, if an adversary cannot guess with better probability than 1 / 2 whether the given ciphertext is an encryption of one of the two messages" (Sako, 2011).

There is a special area in cryptography called "post-quantum cryptography" which includes the cryptographic algorithms that are resistant to attacks made by using the quantum computers, which are believed to be able to solve various problems in cryptography including integer factoring. Some examples of the "post-quantum cryptography" are code-based cryptography, lattice-based cryptography, multivariate cryptography, and DNA biological cryptography (Bernstein, 2011; Yan, 2019). In Chapter 5, the Goldreich, Goldwasser, Halevi (GGH) public key cryptosystem and Nth Degree Truncated Polynomial Ring Units (NTRU) public key cryptosystem, which are two examples of the lattice-based cryptography, will be provided. For more information regarding the post-quantum cryptography, see references including Easttom (2022) and Yan (2019).

2.12.1 Basic types of cryptanalysis

According to Paar and Pelzl (2010), there are three basic types of cryptanalysis:

1. Classical cryptanalysis: It is the science of recovering the plaintext or private key from the ciphertext by using different techniques including mathematical techniques.
2. Implementation attacks: Implementation attacks are related to the physical attacks applied to the system. There are two basic subclassifications of implementation attacks which are "side-channel attacks" and "fault attacks" (Krämer, 2015).
3. Social engineering: This type of cryptanalysis is different from "classical cryptanalysis" and "implementation attacks". It is the use of some psychological tricks to get computer users to assist attackers in their attack, which

means that it is totally related to the techniques based on human behavior to deduce some secret information (Abraham & Chengalur-Smith, 2010).

As part of the "implementation attacks", the "side-channel attack" is an attack against the physical system without making any modification. It includes the measurement of the physical leakages during the actual implementation, such as the measurement of the "timing" and "power consumption". More specifically, a "timing attack" is a type of side-channel attack by considering the variations in the running times of the algorithms. The "power analysis attack" is a special side-channel attack based on the analysis of power consumption. There are two subtypes of "power analysis attack": in the "simple power analysis (SPA) attack", the power consumption of the device is merely interpreted, while in the "differential power analysis (DPA) attack", the differences and variations in the power consumption are considered to be used for the statistical analysis (Caddy, 2011; Standaert, 2010).

The "fault attack" is an "implementation attack" applied by making modifications to the physical electronic device. The fault attack has two main steps: (1) "Fault injection", which is physical perturbation such as electrical perturbation applied to the physical system. (2) "Fault exploitation", which is exploiting the erroneous result obtained as a result of "fault injection". The targets of the fault attack can be several including the operating system and cryptographic algorithm (Benot, 2011).

2.12.2 Classification of cryptographic attacks based on the knowledge of ciphertexts or plaintext/ciphertext pairs

In this section, we provide the basic classification of cryptographic attacks based on the knowledge of only ciphertext or plaintext/ciphertext pairs:

Ciphertext-only attack: It is an attack in which the attacker only knows the ciphertexts, but not the corresponding plaintexts (Biryukov, 2011a; Ciesla, 2020).

Known plaintext attack (Known message attack): It is an attack in which the attacker knows some plaintexts and their corresponding ciphertexts or at least some parts of some plaintexts, and their corresponding ciphertexts (Biryukov, 2011b; Ciesla, 2020). The "*meet-in-the-middle attack*" is a special "known plaintext attack" to estimate the private key in which the attacker proceeds from both ends of a cryptosystem to meet in the middle. If the calculations made from both sides do not match in the middle, then the key to be considered as the private key estimate can be discarded (Biryukov, 2005).

Chosen plaintext attack (Chosen message attack): It is an attack in which the attacker can choose (randomly) some plaintexts and view their corresponding ciphertexts (Biryukov, 2011c; Ciesla, 2020).

Chosen ciphertext attack: It is an attack in which the attacker can choose (randomly) some ciphertexts and view their corresponding plaintexts (Biryukov, 2011d; Ciesla, 2020).

Chosen plaintext and chosen ciphertext attack: It is an attack in which the attacker is allowed to apply the "chosen plaintext attack" and the "chosen ciphertext attack" simultaneously (Biryukov, 2011e; Ciesla, 2020).

Adaptive chosen plaintext attack (Adaptively chosen plaintext attack): It is a special "chosen plaintext attack" in which the attacker can choose the plaintexts by considering the previously chosen plaintexts and view their corresponding ciphertexts (Biryukov, 2011f; Ciesla, 2020).

Adaptive chosen ciphertext attack (Adaptively chosen ciphertext attack): It is a special "chosen ciphertext attack" in which the attacker can choose the ciphertexts by considering the previously chosen ciphertexts and view their corresponding plaintexts (Biryukov, 2011g; Ciesla, 2020).

Adaptive chosen plaintext and chosen ciphertext attack: It is a special attack in which the attacker can apply the "adaptive chosen plaintext attack" and "adaptive chosen ciphertext attack" simultaneously (Biryukov, 2011h; Ciesla, 2020).

2.12.3 Basic terms regarding the attacks on digital signature algorithms

There are several terms regarding the attacks on the digital signature algorithms, some of which will be explained in this section.

The *forgery* usually describes a document-related attack against a digital signature algorithm by generating the digital signature without knowing the private signing key. The following forgery types against the digital signature algorithms have been defined in the literature (Bleumer, 2011b; Paar & Pelzl, 2010; Pointcheval & Stern, 1996; Vaudenay, 2006):

Total break: It is the most serious attack which involves recovering the private signing key from the public verification key. This private signing key can be used to forge all digital signatures.

Universal forgery: This is also a serious attack in which the attacker derives an efficient signing algorithm from the public verification key. By using this signing algorithm, the attacker can again forge all digital signatures.

Selective forgery: It is a document-related forgery. First, the attacker selects a document D, and then (s)he gets the knowledge of the public verification key. Finally, the attacker forges the signature D^{sig} for D with respect to the public verification key.

Existential forgery: The attacker forges a valid signature D^{sig} for at least one new document D such that D^{sig} is valid for D with respect to the public verification key.

The existential forgery, which is the weakest attack, is used to define formally the security requirements of the digital signature algorithms (Bleumer, 2011b; Vaudenay, 2006).

There are also some other classifications of attacks defined for the digital signature algorithms in the literature such as active vs. passive attacks, sequential vs. concurrent attacks, no-document vs. known-document attacks, and generic chosen-document attacks (see Bleumer, 2011b; Goldwasser, Micali, & Rivest, 1985; Pointcheval & Stern, 1996).

2.13 CONCLUSIONS

This chapter provided fundamental concepts related to cryptography and public key cryptosystems including plaintext and ciphertext, encryption function and decryption function, public key and private key, deterministic encryption and probabilistic encryption, the distinction between encoding/decoding and encryption/decryption, the distinction between private key cryptosystems and public key cryptosystems, homomorphic encryption, primality testing, cryptographic hash functions, digital signatures, and cryptanalysis. The basic objective of this chapter was to provide the fundamental concepts related to cryptography and public key cryptosystems in comparison to each other. The primality testing approaches and algorithms were also provided in this chapter and illustrated with simple examples. As discussed in Section 1.10 of Chapter 1, the values should be actually much larger since the public key cryptosystems work with large prime numbers.

REFERENCES

Abraham, S., & Chengalur-Smith, I. (2010). An overview of social engineering malware: Trends, tactics, and implications. *Technology in Society*, *32*(3), 183–196.

Agrawal, M., Kayal, N., & Saxena, N. (2004). PRIMES is in p. *Annals of Mathematics*, *160*(2), 781–793. https://doi.org/10.4007/annals.2004.160.781

Albrecht, M. et al. (2021). Homomorphic encryption standard. In K. Lauter, W. Dai, & K. Laine (Eds.), *Protecting privacy through homomorphic encryption*. Cham: Springer. https://doi.org/10.1007/978-3-030-77287-1_2

Antunes, L., Matos, A., Pinto, A., Souto, A., & Teixeira, A. (2012). One-way functions using algorithmic and classical information theories. *Theory of Computing Systems*, *52*, 346–356. https://doi.org/10.1007/s00224-012-9418-z

Aumasson, J.-P., Meier, W., Phan, R. C.-W., & Henzen, L. (2014). *The hash function BLAKE*. Berlin, Heidelberg: Springer.

Barker, E., & Barker, W. C. (2019). *Recommendation for key management: Part 2 – Best practices for key management organizations*. NIST Special Publication 800-57 Part 2 Revision 1. https://nvlpubs.nist.gov/nistpubs/SpecialPublications/NIST.SP.800-57pt2r1.pdf.

Bauer, F. L. (2005). Cryptanalysis. In H. C. A. van Tilborg, (Eds.), *Encyclopedia of cryptography and security*. Boston, MA: Springer. https://doi.org/10.1007/0-387-23483-7_87

Benot, O. (2011). Fault attack. In H. C. A. van Tilborg & S. Jajodia (Eds.), *Encyclopedia of cryptography and security*. Boston, MA: Springer. https://doi.org/10.1007/978-1-4419-5906-5_505
Bernstein, D. J. (2011). Post-quantum cryptography. In H. C. A. van Tilborg & S. Jajodia (Eds.), *Encyclopedia of cryptography and security*. Boston, MA: Springer. https://doi.org/10.1007/978-1-4419-5906-5_386
Biryukov, A. (2011a). Ciphertext-only attack. In H. C. A. van Tilborg & S. Jajodia (Eds.), *Encyclopedia of cryptography and security*. Boston, MA: Springer. https://doi.org/10.1007/978-1-4419-5906-5_560
Biryukov, A. (2011c). Chosen plaintext attack. In H. C. A. van Tilborg & S. Jajodia (Eds.), *Encyclopedia of cryptography and security*. Boston, MA: Springer. https://doi.org/10.1007/978-1-4419-5906-5_557
Biryukov, A. (2011d). Chosen ciphertext attack. In H. C. A. van Tilborg & S. Jajodia (Eds.), *Encyclopedia of cryptography and security*. Springer, Boston, MA. https://doi.org/10.1007/978-1-4419-5906-5_556.
Biryukov, A. (2011e). Chosen plaintext and chosen ciphertext attack. In H. C. A. van Tilborg, S. Jajodia (Eds.), *Encyclopedia of cryptography and security*. Boston, MA: Springer. https://doi.org/10.1007/978-1-4419-5906-5_558
Biryukov, A. (2011f). Adaptive chosen plaintext attack. In H. C. A. van Tilborg, S. Jajodia (Eds.), *Encyclopedia of cryptography and security*. Boston, MA: Springer. https://doi.org/10.1007/978-1-4419-5906-5_545
Biryukov, A. (2011g). Adaptive chosen ciphertext attack. In H. C. A. van Tilborg & S. Jajodia (Eds.), *Encyclopedia of cryptography and security*. Boston, MA: Springer. https://doi.org/10.1007/978-1-4419-5906-5_543
Biryukov, A. (2011h). Adaptive chosen plaintext and chosen ciphertext attack. In H. C. A. van Tilborg & S. Jajodia (Eds.), *Encyclopedia of cryptography and security*. Boston, MA: Springer. https://doi.org/10.1007/978-1-4419-5906-5_544.
Biryukov, A. (2005). Meet-in-the-middle attack. In H. C. A. van Tilborg (Ed.), *Encyclopedia of cryptography and security*. Boston, MA: Springer. https://doi.org/10.1007/0-387-23483-7_251
Biryukov, A. (2011b). Known plaintext attack. In H. C. A. van Tilborg & S. Jajodia (Eds.), *Encyclopedia of cryptography and security*. Boston, MA: Springer. https://doi.org/10.1007/978-1-4419-5906-5_588
Blanton, M. (2018). Hash functions. In L. Liu & M. T. Özsu (Eds.), *Encyclopedia of database systems*. New York, NY: Springer. https://doi.org/10.1007/978-1-4614-8265-9_1482
Bleumer, G. (2011a). Random oracle model. In H. C. A van Tilborg & S. Jajodia (Eds.), *Encyclopedia of cryptography and security*. Boston, MA: Springer. https://doi.org/10.1007/978-1-4419-5906-5_220
Bleumer, G. (2011b). Forgery. In H. C. A. van Tilborg & S. Jajodia (Eds.), *Encyclopedia of cryptography and security*. Boston, MA: Springer. https://doi.org/10.1007/978-1-4419-5906-5_206
Bosselaers, A., & Preneel, B. (Ed.). (1995). RIPEMD. In *Integrity primitives for secure information systems*. Lecture Notes in Computer Science, 1007. Berlin, Heidelberg: Springer. https://doi.org/10.1007/3-540-60640-8_5
Buchmann, J. A. (2004). *Introduction to cryptography*. Springer Science + Business Media: New York.
Caddy, T. (2011). Differential power analysis. In H. C. A. van Tilborg & S. Jajodia (Eds.), *Encyclopedia of cryptography and security*. Boston, MA: Springer. https://doi.org/10.1007/978-1-4419-5906-5_196
Cambridge Dictionary (2024). *Cryptanalysis*. https://dictionary.cambridge.org/dictionary/english/cryptanalysis
Ciesla, R. (Ed.). (2020). Common attacks against cryptographic systems. In *Encryption for organizations and individuals*. Berkeley, CA: Apress. https://doi.org/10.1007/978-1-4842-6056-2.

Easttom, C. (Ed.). (2022). More approaches to quantum-resistant cryptography. In *Modern cryptography*. Cham: Springer. https://doi.org/10.1007/978-3-031-12304-7_21

Easttom, W. (2021). Cryptanalysis. In *Modern cryptography*. Cham: Springer. https://doi.org/10.1007/978-3-030-63115-4_17

Edgar, T. W., & Manz, D. O. (2017). *Research methods for cyber security*. Cambridge, MA: Elsevier. Syngress.

Fine, B., & Rosenberger, G. (Ed.). (2016). Primality testing-an overview. In *Number theory*. Cham: Birkhäuser. https://doi.org/10.1007/978-3-319-43875-7_5

Fortner, B. (1995). ASCII text numbers. In *The data handbook*. New York, NY: Springer. https://doi.org/10.1007/978-1-4612-2538-6_6

Fuchsbauer, G. J. (2006). An introduction to probabilistic encryption. *Osjeˇcki Matematiˇcki List*, *6*, 37–44.

Furht, B. (Eds.) (2008). Message digest (MD5) algorithm and secure hash algorithm (SHA). *Encyclopedia of multimedia*. Boston, MA: Springer. https://doi.org/10.1007/978-0-387-78414-4_110

Garewal, K. S. (2020). *Practical blockchains and cryptocurrencies. Speed up your application development process and develop distributed applications with confidence*. New York: Apress.

Gauravaram, P., & Knudsen, L. (2010). Cryptographic hash functions. In P. Stavroulakis & M. Stamp (Eds.), *Handbook of information and communication security*. Berlin, Heidelberg: Springer. https://doi.org/10.1007/978-3-642-04117-4_4

Goldwasser, S., Micali, S., & Rivest, R. L. (1985). A "paradoxical" solution to the signature problem. In G. R. Blakley & D. Chaum (Eds.), *Advances in cryptology. CRYPTO 1984*. Lecture Notes in Computer Science, 196. Berlin, Heidelberg: Springer. https://doi.org/10.1007/3-540-39568-7_37

Gómez Pardo, J. L. (Ed.). (2013a). Public-key encryption. In *Introduction to cryptography with maple*. Berlin, Heidelberg: Springer. https://doi.org/10.1007/978-3-642-32166-5_8

Gómez Pardo, J. L. (Ed.). (2013b). Algorithmic number theory for cryptography and cryptanalysis: Primality, factoring and discrete logarithms. In *Introduction to cryptography with maple*. Berlin, Heidelberg: Springer. https://doi.org/10.1007/978-3-642-32166-5_6

Halevi, S. (2017). Homomorphic encryption. In Y. Lindell (Ed.), *Tutorials on the foundations of cryptography. Information security and cryptography*. Cham: Springer. https://doi.org/10.1007/978-3-319-57048-8_5

Handschuh, H. (2011). SHA-0, SHA-1, SHA-2 (secure hash algorithm). In H. C. A. van Tilborg & S. Jajodia (Eds.), *Encyclopedia of cryptography and security*. Boston, MA: Springer. https://doi.org/10.1007/978-1-4419-5906-5_615

Hoffstein, J. (2015). *An introduction to homomorphic encryption. 20 years of cryptography and security at WPI*. https://web.wpi.edu/Images/CMS/Cybersecurity/HomomorphicEncryption.pdf

Hoffstein, J., Pipher, J., & Silverman, J. H. (2008). *An introduction to mathematical cryptography*. New York, NY: Springer Science + Business Media, LLC.

Jo, T. (Ed.). (2019). Text encoding. In *Text mining. Concepts, implementation, and big data challenge*, 45. Cham: Springer. https://doi.org/10.1007/978-3-319-91815-0_3

Katz, J. (Ed.). (2010). The random oracle model. In *Digital signatures*. Boston, MA: Springer. https://doi.org/10.1007/978-0-387-27712-7_6

Koç, Ç. K., Özdemir, F., & Ödemiş Özger, Z. (2021). Mathematical background. In Ç. K. Koç, F. Özdemir, Z. Ödemiş Özger, *Partially homomorphic encryption*. Cham: Springer. https://doi.org/10.1007/978-3-030-87629-6_2

Krämer, J. (Ed.). (2015). Introduction. In *Why cryptography should not rely on physical attack complexity*. T-Labs Series in Telecommunication Services. Singapore: Springer. https://doi.org/10.1007/978-981-287-787-1_1

Kurosawa, K. (2011). Hybrid encryption. In H. C. A. van Tilborg & S. Jajodia (Eds.), *Encyclopedia of cryptography and security*. Boston, MA: Springer. https://doi.org/10.1007/978-1-4419-5906-5_321

Li, N. (2009). Homomorphic encryption. In L. Liu, M. T. Özsu (Eds.), *Encyclopedia of database systems*. Boston, MA: Springer. https://doi.org/10.1007/978-0-387-39940-9_1486

Liskov, M. (2011). Miller–Rabin probabilistic primality test. In H. C. A. van Tilborg & S. Jajodia (Eds.), *Encyclopedia of cryptography and security*. Boston, MA: Springer. https://doi.org/10.1007/978-1-4419-5906-5_461

National Institute of Standards and Technology. (2024b). *Cryptanalysis*. https://csrc.nist.gov/glossary/term/cryptanalysis

National Institute of Standards and Technology. (2024a). *Hash functions. SHA-3 project*. https://csrc.nist.gov/projects/hash-functions/sha-3-project

Nugues, P. M. (2014). Encoding and annotation schemes. In *Language processing with perl and prolog. Cognitive technologies*. Berlin, Heidelberg: Springer. https://doi.org/10.1007/978-3-642-41464-0_3

Paar, C., & Pelzl, J. (2010). *Understanding cryptography. A textbook for students and practitioners*. Heidelberg, Dordrecht, London, New York: Springer.

Petitcolas, F. A. P. (2011). Kerckhoffs' principle. In H. C. A. van Tilborg & S. Jajodia (Eds.), *Encyclopedia of cryptography and security*. Boston, MA: Springer. https://doi.org/10.1007/978-1-4419-5906-5_487

Piotrowski, M. (2012). Text encoding and annotation schemes. In M. Piotrowski, *Natural language processing for historical texts*. Synthesis Lectures on Human Language Technologies. Cham: Springer. https://doi.org/10.1007/978-3-031-02146-6_5

Pointcheval, D., & Stern, J. (1996). Security proofs for signature schemes. In U. Maurer (Ed.), *Advances in cryptology – EUROCRYPT'96*. Lecture Notes in Computer Science, 1070. Berlin, Heidelberg: Springer. https://doi.org/10.1007/3-540-68339-9_33

Preneel, B. (2011). Hash functions. In H. C. A. van Tilborg & S. Jajodia (Eds.), *Encyclopedia of cryptography and security*. Boston, MA: Springer. https://doi.org/978-1-4419-5906-5_580

Pun, N. (2024). *Survey of primality testing methods*. https://nicholaspun.github.io/primality_testing_survey.pdf

Robshaw, M. J. B. (2011a). One-way function. In H. C. A. van Tilborg & S. Jajodia (Eds.), *Encyclopedia of cryptography and security*. Boston, MA: Springer. https://doi.org/10.1007/978-1-4419-5906-5_467

Robshaw, M. J. B. (2011b). Trapdoor one-way function. In H. C. A. van Tilborg & S. Jajodia (Eds.), *Encyclopedia of cryptography and security*. Boston, MA: Springer. https://doi.org/10.1007/978-1-4419-5906-5_482

Rompel, J. (1990). One-way functions are necessary and sufficient for secure signatures. *STOC '90: Proceedings of the twenty-second annual ACM symposium on theory of computing*, 387–394. https://doi.org/10.1145/100216.100269

Sako, K. (2011). Semantic security. In H. C. A. van Tilborg & S. Jajodia (Eds.), *Encyclopedia of cryptography and security*. Boston, MA: Springer. https://doi.org/10.1007/978-1-4419-5906-5_23

Shannon, C. E. (1949). Communication theory of secrecy systems. *Bell System Technical Journal*, *28*(4), 656–715.

Sherr, M. (2011). Eavesdropping. In H. C. A. van Tilborg & S. Jajodia S. (Eds.), *Encyclopedia of cryptography and security*. Boston, MA: Springer. https://doi.org/10.1007/978-1-4419-5906-5_109

Smart, N. P. (2016). *Cryptography made simple. information security and cryptography*. Cham: Springer.

Stamp, M., & Low, R. M. (2007). *Applied cryptanalysis. Breaking ciphers in the real world.* Hoboken, NJ: Wiley.
Standaert, F. X. (2010). Introduction to side-channel attacks. In I. Verbauwhede (Ed.), *Secure integrated circuits and systems. Integrated circuits and systems.* Boston, MA: Springer. https://doi.org/10.1007/978-0-387-71829-3_2
Stinson, D. R. (2006). Some observations on the theory of cryptographic hash functions. *Designs, Codes and Cryptography*, *38*, 259–277. https://doi.org/10.1007/s10623-005-6344-y
Tekin, E. N.. (2023). *Homomorphic encryption. A comprehensive study of types, techniques, and real-world applications.* A thesis submitted to the graduate school of applied mathematics of Middle East Technical University. https://open.metu.edu.tr/bitstream/handle/11511/105506/Thesis_ENTekin.pdf
Unicode (2024). *Unicode.* https://home.unicode.org
van Tilborg, H. C. (2011). Shannon's model. In H. C. A. van Tilborg & S. Jajodia (Eds.), *Encyclopedia of cryptography and security.* Boston, MA: Springer. https://doi.org/10.1007/978-1-4419-5906-5_3
Vaudenay, S. (Ed.). (2006) Digital signature. In *A classical introduction to cryptography.* Boston, MA: Springer. https://doi.org/10.1007/0-387-25880-9_10
Yan, S. Y. (2009). *Primality testing and integer factorization in public-key cryptography. advances in information security.* New York, NY: Springer.
Yan, S. Y. (Ed.). (2019). Quantum safe cryptography. In *Cybercryptography: applicable cryptography for cyberspace security.* Cham: Springer. https://doi.org/10.1007/978-3-319-72536-9_8
Z'aba, M. R., & Maarof, M. A. (2006). A survey on the cryptanalysis of the advanced encryption standard. *Proceedings of the postgraduate annual research seminar 2006*, 97–102.

Chapter 3

Discrete logarithm problem, elliptic curve discrete logarithm problem, and the related public key cryptosystems and digital signature algorithms

3.1 INTRODUCTION

All public key cryptosystems are based on the hardness of some mathematical problems. This chapter is devoted to the discrete logarithm problem (DLP), elliptic curve DLP (ECDLP), and the related public key cryptosystems including digital signature algorithms. The DLP and ECDLP are hard in case of appropriate selection of parameters and the security of the related public key cryptosystems, including digital signature algorithms is fundamentally based on the hardness of solving DLP and ECDLP. Section 3.2 provides the basic protocols, while Section 3.3 gives the elliptic curve analogs of the protocols provided in Section 3.2. In Section 3.2.1, we define the DLP by considering three versions, illustrate it with an example, and introduce the Diffie-Hellman key exchange in Section 3.2.2, which is the first protocol based on the DLP. The Diffie-Hellman key exchange has been a breakthrough in the history of public key cryptosystems, and the basic objective of the basic Diffie-Hellman key exchange is the mutual creation of a common private key by considering the public values communicated in an insecure network. We also provide the "decisional Diffie-Hellman problem", "computational Diffie-Hellman problem", and some cryptanalysis approaches proposed for the basic Diffie-Hellman key exchange in Section 3.2.2. In Section 3.2.3, we introduce the basic ElGamal public key cryptosystem, which is the first public key cryptosystem based on DLP. We also provide the basic ElGamal digital signature algorithm which is analogous to the ElGamal public key cryptosystem and DSA which is an extension of the ElGamal digital signature algorithm, although DSA is no longer approved in the Federal Information Processing Standard (FIPS) 186-5, which is published in 2023. In this section, some selected cryptanalysis approaches are also provided briefly for the ElGamal public key cryptosystem, ElGamal digital signature algorithm, and DSA.

In Section 3.3.1, the ECDLP is defined analogous to the definition of the DLP. Afterward, the elliptic curve Diffie-Hellman key exchange is introduced in Section 3.3.2. In this section, the "tripartite Diffie-Hellman key exchange developed based on the modified Weil pairing" is also provided as an extension of the elliptic curve Diffie-Hellman key exchange with two parties. The

DOI: 10.1201/9781003514190-3

remaining subtopics of Section 3.3 are the elliptic curve ElGamal public key cryptosystem, ECDSA, and some selected cryptanalysis approaches for the elliptic curve Diffie-Hellman key exchange, elliptic curve ElGamal public key cryptosystem, and ECDSA. Since the security of the DLP-based and ECDLP-based public key cryptosystems and digital signature algorithms is based on the solution of the DLP and ECDLP, Section 3.4 is devoted to some selected basic algorithms for the solution of the DLP and ECDLP including Shanks' baby-step giant-step algorithm for the basic DLP and ECDLP, Pohlig-Hellman algorithm for the basic DLP, and index calculus method for the basic DLP. All public key cryptosystems, digital signature algorithms, and the basic algorithms for the solution of DLP are illustrated with examples to show their practicality.

3.2 BASIC DISCRETE LOGARITHM PROBLEM AND THE RELATED PUBLIC KEY CRYPTOSYSTEMS

The DLP (also called "index problem") and the related algorithms are of immense importance in the public key cryptosystems. Note that by using the word "basic", we mean "not elliptic" in all subsections of Section 3.2.

3.2.1 Basic discrete logarithm problem (DLP)

As provided in Table 3.1, there are three versions of the basic DLP.

For the basic DLP (Version 1) and the basic DLP (Version 2), if there is one solution x, it can be shown that there are infinitely many solutions in the form of $x+k(p-1)$ for every $k \in \mathbb{Z}$ due to the Fermat's little theorem provided in Section 1.4.1 of Chapter 1. Thus, the basic DLP provided in the first two columns of Table 3.1 is actually equivalent to Equation (3.1) (Hoffstein et al., 2008).

$$g^x \equiv h \pmod{(p-1)} \tag{3.1}$$

Example 3.1

We consider the values $p = 347$, $g = 2 \in \mathbb{F}_{347}^*$, $h = 270$, and the basic DLP $2^x \equiv 270 \pmod{347}$, $x = ?$ Table 3.2 provides the steps of the solution for this simple example by using the "trial-and-error method".

Table 3.1 Three versions of the basic DLP

Basic DLP (Version 1)	*Basic DLP (Version 2)*	*Basic DLP (Version 3)*
g is a primitive root of $\mathbb{F}_p$, where p is a large prime number, and $h \in \mathbb{F}_p^*$.	$g \in \mathbb{F}_p^*$, where p is a large prime number, and $h \in \mathbb{F}_p^*$.	$g \in G$, where g is the generator of the cyclic group $(G, \star)$, and $h \in G$.
$g^x \equiv h \pmod{p}$ or	$g^x \equiv h \pmod{p}$ or	$\underbrace{g \star g \star g \star \ldots \star g}_{x \text{ times}} = h$
$x \equiv \log_g(h) \pmod{p}$	$x \equiv \log_g(h) \pmod{p}$	
$x = ?$	$x = ?$	$x = ?$

Source: Adapted from Gordon (2011), Hoffstein, Pipher, & Silverman (2008), and van Tilborg (1988).

Table 3.2 An example for the basic DLP

x	$2^x \pmod{347}$
0	1
1	2
2	4
3	8
...	...
16	300
17	253
...	...
42	270

As a result of the "trial-and-error method" given in Table 3.2, we find the solution $x = 42$. Note that in Example 3.1, small numbers are used for illustrating the solution of the DLP by using the "trial-and-error method". The values should actually be much larger in real-life cryptographic applications.

3.2.2 Basic Diffie-Hellman key exchange and its cryptanalysis

3.2.2.1 *Basic Diffie-Hellman key exchange*

The basic Diffie-Hellman key exchange has been a breakthrough in the history of the public key cryptography. It was defined by Whitfield Diffie and Martin Hellman in 1976 for "two parties" to create their "common private (secret) key" by communicating through an "insecure network" (Diffie & Hellman, 1976). First, we provide the basic steps of the basic Diffie-Hellman key exchange in Table 3.3 and then the basic parameters.

Table 3.3 Basic Diffie-Hellman key exchange

	Alice	*Bob*
Private: a, b	- Chooses a.	- Chooses b.
Public: $p, g \in \mathbb{F}_p^*, A, B$	- Computes	- Computes
	$A \equiv g^a \pmod{p}$.	$B \equiv g^b \pmod{p}$.
	- Sends A to Bob.	- Sends B to Alice.
	- Computes	- Computes
	$B^a \equiv (g^b)^a \pmod{p}$	$A^b \equiv (g^a)^b \pmod{p}$
	$\equiv g^{ba} \pmod{p}$.	$\equiv g^{ab} \pmod{p}$.
Result: Common private (secret) key	$g^{ab} \pmod{p}$	

Source: Adapted from Hoffstein et al. (2008).

Basic parameters for the basic Diffie-Hellman key exchange (adapted from Diffie & Hellman, 1976; Hoffstein et al., 2008):

- p: A large prime number ($p \cong 2^{1000}$) (chosen by Alice or Bob or a trusted third party)
- $g \in \mathbb{F}_p^*$ such that N is the prime order of $g \in \mathbb{F}_p^*$ satisfying $N \approx p/2$ (chosen by Alice or Bob or a trusted third party)
- a,b: Private (secret) integers of Alice and Bob, respectively that satisfy $1 \le a \le p-1$ and $1 \le b \le p-1$

Note that Alice and Bob exchange the values A and B through an insecure network; thus, A and B are the public values. Note also that the private (secret) integers a and b do not have to be prime numbers. If Eve can solve either the basic DLP $A \equiv g^a \pmod{p}$ to find the private (secret) integer a of Alice or the basic DLP $B \equiv g^b \pmod{p}$ to find the private (secret) integer b of Bob, then she can recover the common private (secret) key by making either the calculation $B^a \pmod{p}$ or the calculation $A^b \pmod{p}$. Eve can also consider the "decisional Diffie-Hellman problem" and "computational Diffie-Hellman problem" to be provided following Example 3.2.

Example 3.2

We use again small numbers to illustrate the Diffie-Hellman key exchange. Let $p = 347$ and $g = 2$ be chosen by Alice or Bob or a trusted third party. We assume that Alice and Bob choose $a = 25$ and $b = 18$ as the private (secret) integers, respectively. Table 3.4 shows the steps of the basic Diffie-Hellman key exchange for this simple example.

3.2.2.1.1 *Decisional Diffie-Hellman problem vs. computational Diffie-Hellman problem*

Related to the security of the basic Diffie-Hellman key exchange, the "decisional Diffie-Hellman problem" and the "computational Diffie-Hellman problem" have been defined in the literature. Table 3.5 provides these problems for the DLP (Version 3).

Table 3.4 An example for the basic Diffie-Hellman key exchange

	Alice	*Bob*
Public: $p = 347, g = 2$	- Chooses $a = 25$. - Computes $A \equiv 2^{25} \equiv 226 \pmod{347}$. - Sends $A = 226$ to Bob. - Computes $159^{25} \equiv 342 \pmod{347}$.	- Chooses $b = 18$. - Computes $B \equiv 2^{18} \equiv 159 \pmod{347}$. - Sends $B = 159$ to Alice. - Computes $226^{18} \equiv 342 \pmod{347}$.
Result: Common private (secret) key	342	

Table 3.5 Decisional vs. computational Diffie-Hellman problem

Decisional Diffie-Hellman problem (DDHP)	*Computational Diffie-Hellman problem (CDHP)*
g: Generator of the finite cyclic group G Decide whether a, b exist such that $g^a \in G, g^b \in G, g^{ab} \in G$ hold.	g: Generator of the finite cyclic group G Compute $g^{ab} \in G$ given $g^a \in G, g^b \in G$.

Source: Adapted from Canetti & Varia (2011) and Shparlinski (2011).

The decisional and computational Diffie-Hellman problems defined in Table 3.5 can also be extended to the basic DLP (Version 1) and the basic DLP (Version 2). Regarding the "computational Diffie-Hellman problem", the finite cyclic group G should be chosen such that it is hard to compute $g^{ab} \in G$ only by considering $g^a \in G$ and $g^b \in G$. In the DLP (Version 1) and (Version 2), the prime number p should be chosen so large that it will be hard to compute $g^{ab} \pmod{p}$ only by considering $g^a \pmod{p}$ and $g^b \pmod{p}$.

3.2.2.2 *Cryptanalysis of the basic Diffie-Hellman exchange*

Raymond and Stiglic (2002) provided a list of the basic attacks targeted at the Diffie-Hellman key exchange. One important attack is called the "man (woman)-in-the-middle attack", which is briefly explained in Table 3.6. Accordingly, Alice and Bob do not actually exchange A and B values with each other, but take the value $E = g^e$ computed by Eve, thus the algorithm results in two different keys.

Another attack mentioned in Raymond and Stiglic (2002) is the so-called "degenerate message attack", which considers some degenerate cases in which the Diffie-Hellman key can be broken very easily. One such case is $A = g^a \equiv 1 \pmod{p}$ or $B = g^b \equiv 1 \pmod{p}$ if $a = p-1$ or $b = p-1$ holds. However, this attack can be prevented when a, b are chosen in $[1, 2, \ldots, p-2]$.

Table 3.6 Woman in-the-middle attack for the Diffie-Hellman key exchange

	Alice	*Eve*	*Bob*
Private: a, e, b	- Chooses a. - Computes $A \equiv g^a \pmod{p}$.	- Chooses e. - Computes $E = g^e \pmod{p}$.	- Chooses b. - Computes $B \equiv g^b \pmod{p}$.
Public: $p, g \in F_p^*, A, E, B$	- Intends to send A to Bob; however, A cannot be sent. - Computes $E^a = (g^e)^a \equiv g^{ea} \pmod{p}$.	- Succeeds to send E to both Alice and Bob.	- Intends to send B to Alice; however, B cannot be sent. - Computes $E^b = (g^e)^b \equiv g^{eb} \pmod{p}$.
Result: Two different private keys	$g^{ea} \pmod{p} \neq g^{eb} \pmod{p}$		

Source: Adapted from Raymond & Stiglic (2002).

Some other attacks against the Diffie-Hellman key exchange are the so-called "insider attacks", "outsider attacks", "message replay attacks", "message redirection attacks", and "timing attacks" whose details can be found in Raymond and Stiglic (2002). As per selected security guidelines, the Diffie-Hellman secret key should be modified before using for the respective cryptographic algorithm, and it should be changed frequently. Moreover, different Diffie-Hellman secret keys should be independent of each other (Raymond & Stiglic, 2002).

Two more examples from the literature about the cryptanalysis of the basic Diffie-Hellman key exchange are Phan and Goi (2006) and Sharma and Purushothama (2023) in which the cryptanalysis of the group key agreement Diffie-Hellman key exchange was considered (see Phan and Goi (2006) and Sharma and Purushothama (2023) for more details).

3.2.3 Basic ElGamal public key cryptosystem, basic ElGamal digital signature algorithm, basic digital signature algorithm (DSA), and their cryptanalysis

3.2.3.1 Basic ElGamal public key cryptosystem

The basic ElGamal public key cryptosystem is the first public key cryptosystem developed based on the basic DLP. It was proposed by Taher ElGamal in 1985 as the adaptation of the Diffie-Hellman key exchange to a public key cryptosystem (ElGamal, 1985). In the following, we define the basic parameters for the basic ElGamal public key cryptosystem by considering the case of the finite field. The ElGamal public key cryptosystem can also be defined for the case of the finite group as provided in Gómez Pardo (2013).

Basic parameters for the basic ElGamal public key cryptosystem (adapted from ElGamal, 1985; Hoffstein et al., 2008):

p: A large prime number (chosen by Alice or Bob or a trusted third party)
$g \in \mathbb{F}_p^*$ (chosen by Alice or Bob or a trusted third party)
a: Private (secret) key of Alice satisfying $1 \le a \le p-1$ (or $0 \le a \le p-1$ according to ElGamal, 1985)
$r \in \mathbb{F}_p^*$: Ephemeral key (chosen by Bob)
m: Plaintext chosen by Bob satisfying $2 \le m \le p-1$ (or $0 \le m \le p-1$ according to ElGamal, 1985)

We assume that Bob makes the encryption, whereas Alice makes the decryption. Accordingly, the basic ElGamal public key cryptosystem is outlined in Table 3.7.

As provided in Section 2.5 of Chapter 2, the ephemeral key r is a short-lived random private key to be used just for one encryption. Since r is random, the ElGamal public key cryptosystem can be interpreted as a probabilistic encryption that is provided in Section 2.5 of Chapter 2. As provided in Section 2.7 of Chapter 2, the public key is computed from the private key as clear from

Table 3.7 Basic ElGamal public key cryptosystem

	Alice	Bob
Private: a	- Chooses a.	
Public: A, g, p	- Computes $A \equiv g^a \pmod{p}$. - Sends A to Bob.	
Encryption Private: m, r		- Chooses m. - Chooses (randomly) $r \in \mathbb{F}_p^*$. - Computes
Public: (c_1, c_2)		$c_1 \equiv g^r \pmod{p}$ and $c_2 \equiv m \cdot A^r \pmod{p}$. - Sends (c_1, c_2) to Alice.
Decryption	- Recovers m from $(c_1^a)^{-1} \cdot c_2 \equiv m \pmod{p}$.	

Source: Adapted from ElGamal (1985) and Hoffstein et al. (2008).

Table 3.7; that is, the public key A is computed from the private key a of Alice. Note that the ciphertext in the basic ElGamal public key cryptosystem is not a single value, but rather a vector with the values c_1 and c_2. As in the Diffie-Hellman key exchange, if Eve can solve the hard DLP $A \equiv g^a \pmod{p}$ to find the private (secret) key a, then she can recover the plaintext m.

Example 3.3

Let $p = 347$ and $g = 2$ be chosen by Alice or Bob or a trusted third party. We assume that Alice chooses $a = 25$, Bob chooses $r = 16$ and $m = 9$. Then, the steps of the basic ElGamal public key cryptosystem for this example are provided in Table 3.8.

3.2.3.2 *Basic ElGamal digital signature algorithm*

The ElGamal digital signature algorithm has been developed analogous to the ElGamal public key cryptosystem. Next, we provide the basic parameters of the ElGamal digital signature algorithm.

Basic parameters of the ElGamal digital signature algorithm (adapted from Hoffstein et al., 2008):

- p: Large prime number (chosen by Samantha or Victor or a trusted third party)
- g: A primitive root of $\mathbb{F}_p$ (chosen by Samantha or Victor or a trusted third party)
- s: Private signing key of Samantha satisfying $1 \le s \le p-1$ (or $1 \le s \le p-2$ according to Buchmann (2004))

Table 3.8 An example of the basic ElGamal public key cryptosystem

	Alice	Bob
$p = 347, g = 2$	- Chooses $a = 25$. - Computes $A \equiv 2^{25} \equiv 226 \pmod{347}$. - Sends $A = 226$ to Bob.	
Encryption		- Chooses $m = 9$. - Chooses (randomly) $r = 16$. - Computes $c_1 \equiv 2^{16} \equiv 300 \pmod{347}$, $c_2 \equiv 9 \cdot 226^{16} \equiv 279 \pmod{347}$. - Sends $(300,\ 279)$ to Alice.
Decryption	- Recovers m from $(300^{25})^{-1} \cdot 279 \pmod{347}$ $\equiv 31^{-1} \cdot 279 \pmod{347}$ $\equiv 56 \cdot 279 \pmod{347}$ $\equiv 9 \equiv m \pmod{347}$.	

v: Public verification key to be used by Victor

D: Digital document of Samantha satisfying $1 < D \leq p-1$ (or $0 \leq D \leq p-1$ according to ElGamal (1985))

r: Ephemeral key chosen by Samantha satisfying $1 < r \leq p-1$ and $\gcd(r, p-1)) = 1$ (or $0 \leq r \leq p-1$ according to ElGamal (1985) or $1 < r \leq p-2$ according to Buchmann (2004))

$D^{sig} = (S_1, S_2)$: Digital signature of the digital document D signed by Samantha

In Table 3.9, the basic steps of the ElGamal digital signature algorithm are given.

Instead of D, the hash value $h(D)$ can also be considered during signing and verification. Analogous to the ElGamal public key cryptosystem, if Eve can solve the basic DLP $v \equiv g^s \pmod{p}$, then she can recover the private signing key s of Samantha and forge all digital signatures of Samantha. Note the similarities (and dissimilarities) between the ElGamal public key cryptosystem and the ElGamal digital signature algorithm, as provided in Table 3.10.

Example 3.4

Let $p = 347$ be chosen and let $g = 2$ be a primitive root of $\mathbb{F}_{347}$. We assume that Samantha selects $s = 25$, $D = 9$, and $r = 17$. Accordingly, the steps of the ElGamal digital signature algorithm can be viewed in Table 3.11.

Table 3.9 ElGamal digital signature algorithm

	Samantha	*Victor*
Private: s	- Chooses s.	
Public: $g,\ p, v$	- Computes $v \equiv g^s \pmod{p}$.	
Signing	- Chooses D.	
	- Chooses (randomly) r.	
Private: r	- Computes $S_1 \equiv g^r \pmod{p}$ and $S_2 \equiv (D - s \cdot S_1) \cdot r^{-1} \pmod{(p-1)}$.	
Public: $D, D^{sig} = (S_1, S_2)$	- Sends D and $D^{sig} = (S_1, S_2)$ to Victor.	
Verification		- Checks $1 \le S_1 \le p-1$.
		- Computes and verifies $v^{S_1} \cdot S_1^{S_2} \equiv g^D \pmod{p}$.

Source: Adapted from Hoffstein et al. (2008).

3.2.3.3 *Basic digital signature algorithm (DSA)*

The basic DSA, which is an extension of the ElGamal digital signature algorithm, was an FIPS 186-4 (National Institute of Standards and Technology, 2013). As provided on the web page of the American National Institute of Standards and Technology, "FIPS 186-4 has been superseded with the publication of FIPS 186-5 (February 3, 2023)" (National Institute of Standards and Technology, 2023a). FIPS 186-5 "no longer approves the DSA for digital signature generation. However, the DSA may be used to verify signatures generated prior to the implementation date of this standard" (National Institute of Standards and Technology, 2023b). Nevertheless, we will provide the basic parameters for the DSA in the following and the basic steps of the DSA in Table 3.12.

Table 3.10 Comparison of the basic ElGamal public key cryptosystem and the basic ElGamal digital signature algorithm

Basic ElGamal public key cryptosystem	*Basic ElGamal digital signature algorithm*
$A \equiv g^a \pmod{p}$	$v \equiv g^s \pmod{p}$
$g \in \mathbb{F}_p^*$	g is a primitive root of $\mathbb{F}_p$.
a: Private decryption key	s: Private signing key
A: Public encryption key	v: Public verification key
$c_1 \equiv g^r \pmod{p}$	$S_1 \equiv g^r \pmod{p}$
r: Ephemeral key	r: Ephemeral key
$c_2 \equiv m \cdot A^r \pmod{p}$	$S_2 \equiv (D - s \cdot S_1) \cdot r^{-1} \pmod{(p-1)}$
(c_1, c_2): Ciphertext	(S_1, S_2): Digital signature

Table 3.11 An example for the ElGamal digital signature algorithm

	Samantha	*Victor*
$p = 347, g = 2$	- Chooses $s = 25$. - Computes $v \equiv 2^{25} \equiv 226 \pmod{347}$.	
Signing	- Chooses $D = 9$. - Chooses (randomly) $r = 17$. - Computes $S_1 \equiv 2^{17} \equiv 253 \pmod{347}$ and $S_2 \equiv (9 - 25 \cdot 253) \cdot 17^{-1} \pmod{346} \equiv (9 - 25 \cdot 253) \cdot 285 \pmod{346} \equiv 178 \pmod{346}$. - Sends $D = 9$ and $D^{sig} = (253, 178)$ to Victor.	
Verification		- Checks $1 < 253 < 346$. - Computes and verifies $226^{253} \cdot 253^{178} \equiv 165 \equiv 2^9 \pmod{347}$, where $D = 9$.

Table 3.12 DSA

	Samantha	*Victor*
Private: s Public: p, g, v	- Chooses $1 \le s \le q - 1$. - Computes $v \equiv g^s \pmod{p}$. - Sends v to Victor.	
Signing Private: r Public: q, D, $D^{sig} = (S_1, S_2)$	- Chooses $1 \le D \le q - 1$. - Chooses (randomly) $1 \le r \le q - 1$. - Computes $S_1 \equiv (g^r \pmod{p}) \pmod{q}$ and $S_2 \equiv (D + s \cdot S_1) \cdot r^{-1} \pmod{q}$. - Sends D and $D^{sig} = (S_1, S_2)$ to Victor.	
Verification		- Checks $1 \le S_1 \le q - 1$ and $1 \le S_2 \le q - 1$. - Computes $V_1 \equiv D \cdot S_2^{-1} \pmod{q}$ and $V_2 \equiv S_1 \cdot S_2^{-1} \pmod{q}$. - Computes and verifies $(g^{V_1} \cdot v^{V_2} \pmod{p}) \pmod{q} \equiv S_1$.

Source: Adapted from Buchmann (2004), Hoffstein et al. (2008), and National Institute of Standards and Technology (2013).

Basic parameters for DSA (adapted from Hoffstein et al., 2008):

p,q: Large prime numbers satisfying $p \equiv 1 \pmod{q}$, $2^{1000} < p < 2^{2000}$ and $2^{160} < q < 2^{320}$ (chosen by Samantha or Victor or a trusted third party)
$g \in \mathbb{F}_p^*$ of order q (chosen by Samantha or Victor or a trusted third party)
s: Private signing key of Samantha satisfying $1 \le s \le q-1$
v: Public verification key to be used by Victor
D: Digital document of Samantha satisfying $1 \le D \le q-1$
r: Ephemeral key chosen by Samantha satisfying $1 \le r \le q-1$
$D^{\text{sig}} = (S_1, S_2)$: Digital signature of the digital document D signed by Samantha

Other conditions for p,q have also been proposed in the literature as follows:

$2^{511+64t} < p < 2^{512+64t}$ $t = 0, 1, 2, \ldots, 8$ (Buchmann, 2004)
$2^{L-1} < p < 2^{L}$, where L is the bit length of p (National Institute of Standards and Technology, 2013)
$2^{159} < q < 2^{160}$ (Buchmann, 2004)
$2^{N-1} < q < 2^{N}$, where N is the bit length of q (National Institute of Standards and Technology, 2013)

As in the ElGamal digital signature algorithm, instead of D, the hash value $h(D)$ can also be considered during signing and verification. As in the ElGamal digital signature algorithm, Eve must solve the basic DLP $v \equiv g^s \pmod{p}$ to recover the private signing key s of Samantha. Note the high similarity between the ElGamal digital signature algorithm and the DSA during some steps with a basic exception that the DSA involves additional modulo q to increase security.

Example 3.5

We consider the values $p = 59$ and $q = 29$ such that $p = 59 \equiv 1 \pmod{29}$ holds. Let $g = 36 \in \mathbb{F}_{59}^*$ be chosen of order $q = 29$, that is, $q = 29$ is the smallest integer satisfying $36^{29} \equiv 1 \pmod{59}$. We assume that Samantha chooses $s = 25$, $D = 9$, and $r = 17$, which are smaller than $q - 1 = 28$. Accordingly, the steps of the DSA for this simple example are given in Table 3.13.

Note that rather small values were considered in Example 3.5 for the illustration of the steps of the DSA. Actually, the conditions given before should be satisfied for real- life cryptographic applications.

3.2.3.4 *Cryptanalysis of the basic ElGamal public key cryptosystem, basic ElGamal digital signature algorithm, and basic DSA*

3.2.3.4.1 *Cryptanalysis of the basic ElGamal public key cryptosystem*

In this section, some selected parts of the well-known approach by Boneh, Joux, and Nguyen (2000) will be explained very briefly. For more details, the reader is strongly recommended to read all the details in Boneh et al. (2000).

Table 3.13 An example for the DSA

	Samantha	*Victor*
Public: $p = 59, g = 36$	- Chooses $s = 25$. - Computes $v \equiv 36^{25} \equiv 15 \pmod{59}$. - Sends $v = 15$ to Victor.	
Signing	- Chooses $D = 9$.	
Public: $q = 29$	- Chooses (randomly) $r = 17$. - Computes $S_1 \equiv \left(36^{17} \bmod 59\right) \pmod{29} \equiv 12$ and $S_2 \equiv (9 + 25 \cdot 12) \cdot 17^{-1} \pmod{29}$ $\equiv (9 + 25 \cdot 12) \cdot 12 \pmod{29}$ $\equiv 25 \pmod{29}$. - Sends $D = 9$ and $D^{sig} = (12, 25)$ to Victor.	
Verification		- Checks $1 < S_1 = 12 < 28$ $1 < S_2 = 25 < 28$. - Computes $V_1 \equiv 9 \cdot 25^{-1} \pmod{29} \equiv$ $9 \cdot 7 \equiv 5 \pmod{29}$ and $V_2 \equiv 12 \cdot 25^{-1} \equiv$ $12 \cdot 7 \equiv 26 \pmod{29}$. - Computes and verifies $\left(36^5 \cdot 15^{26} \pmod{59}\right)$ $\pmod{29} \equiv 12 = S_1$.

Boneh et al. (2000) proposed a modified version of the ElGamal public key cryptosystem, in which there existed the so-called "blinding process". Table 3.14 provides the encryption steps of the original and modified ElGamal public key cryptosystem.

As evident from Table 3.14, in the encryption of the original ElGamal public key cryptosystem, the calculation of c_2 includes multiplication, whereas it includes addition in the modified ElGamal public key cryptosystem. Boneh et al. (2000) proposed an attack based on the so-called "subgroup rounding problems", which is described very briefly in Table 3.15.

When n is sufficiently small, z is uniquely determined in the "additive subgroup rounding problem" and "multiplicative subgroup rounding problem" (Boneh et al., 2000). According to Boneh et al. (2000), "an efficient solution to additive or multiplicative subgroup rounding problem would imply that the corresponding plain ElGamal encryption scheme is insecure". As an example, based on the multiplicative subgroup rounding problem, the so-called "meet-in-the-middle attack" can be developed, as given in Table 3.16.

Boneh et al. (2000) proposed to build a table of size 2^{n_1} containing the values $(\Delta_1)^q \pmod{p}$ for all $\Delta_1 = 0, 1, 2, \ldots, 2^{n_1}$. They proposed to check whether

Table 3.14 Encryption in the original and modified ElGamal public key cryptosystem

Encryption in the original ElGamal public key cryptosystem	*Encryption in the modified ElGamal public key cryptosystem*
Let $g \in \mathbb{F}_p^*$ be of order q, where $q \ll p$.	Let $g \in \mathbb{F}_p^*$ be of order q, where $q \ll p$.
- Bob chooses a plaintext m.	- Bob chooses a short plaintext m of bit length n, which is smaller than $log_2(p/q)$-bits
- Chooses (randomly) r.	- Chooses (randomly) r.
- Computes	- Computes
$c_1 \equiv g^r \pmod{p}$ and	$c_1 \equiv g^r \pmod{p}$ and
$c_2 \equiv m \cdot A^r \pmod{p}$.	$c_2 \equiv m + A^r \pmod{p}$ (Blinding process).
(c_1, c_2): Ciphertext	(c_1, c_2): Ciphertext

Source: Adapted from Boneh et al. (2000).

Table 3.15 Additive vs. multiplicative subgroup rounding problem

Additive subgroup rounding problem	*Multiplicative subgroup rounding problem*
Modified ElGamal public key cryptosystem	Original ElGamal public key cryptosystem
Finding z satisfying $c_2 = z + \Delta \pmod{p}$, where $\Delta < 2^n$ is an integer number, n is the bit length of the plaintext m that is sufficiently small, and $z \in \mathbb{G}_q$, where $\mathbb{G}_q$, generated by g, is the subgroup of $\mathbb{F}_p^*$.	Finding z satisfying $c_2 = z \cdot \Delta \pmod{p}$, where $\Delta < 2^n$ is an integer number, n is the bit length of the plaintext m that is sufficiently small, and $z \in \mathbb{G}_q$, where $\mathbb{G}_q$, generated by g, is the subgroup of $\mathbb{F}_p^*$.

Source: Adapted from Boneh et al. (2000).

Table 3.16 Meet-in-the-middle attack based in the multiplicative subgroup rounding problem

Meet-in-the-middle attack
$\Delta = \Delta_1 \cdot \Delta_2$ is assumed where $\Delta_1 \le 2^{n_1}, \Delta_2 \le 2^{n_2}$ are not necessarily prime numbers.
(As an example, $n_1 = n_2 = n/2$ holds.)
Then $c_2 = z \cdot \Delta = z \cdot \Delta_1 \cdot \Delta_2 \pmod{p}$ and $(c_2/\Delta_2)^q = z^q \cdot (\Delta_1)^q = (\Delta_1)^q \pmod{p}$ hold.

Source: Adapted from Boneh et al. (2000).

$(c_2/\Delta_2)^q$ is present for any $\Delta_2 = 0, 1, 2, \ldots, 2^{n_2}$ in this table. If so, $\Delta = \Delta_1 \cdot \Delta_2$ would be a candidate value for Δ. Boneh et al. (2000) proposed also an attack for the ElGamal public key cryptosystem by using a generator of $\mathbb{F}_p^*$. The basic recommendation given by Boneh et al. (2000) for increasing the security of the basic ElGamal public key cryptosystem is to make preprocessing to the plaintext before the encryption.

As two examples from the recent literature regarding the cryptanalysis of the basic ElGamal public key cryptosystem, Das and Chakraborty (2022) applied statistical cryptanalysis including entropy analysis, floating frequency analysis, histogram, N-gram, autocorrelation, and periodicity analysis for the

ElGamal public key cryptosystem. Jia, Wang, Zhang, Wang, and Liu (2019) proposed the cryptanalysis of the ElGamal-like cryptosystem proposed by Inam and Ali (2018) that is based on matrices over group ring.

3.2.3.4.2 Cryptanalysis of the basic ElGamal digital signature algorithm

Pointcheval and Stern (1996) discussed that the basic ElGamal digital signature algorithm is existentially forgeable; that is, the attacker can forge a valid ElGamal signature D^{sig} for at least one new document D such that D^{sig} is valid for D with respect to the public verification key. There have been some basic attacks and cryptanalysis approaches against the ElGamal digital signature algorithm. In this section, we provide some selected approaches from the literature.

Vaudenay (2006) presented a forgery against the ElGamal digital signature algorithm, which can be described very briefly with the following steps (adapted from Vaudenay, 2006):

- The attacker's goal is to find S_1, S_2 that satisfy $v^{S_1} \cdot S_1^{S_2} \equiv g^D \pmod{p}$ for given p, g, D, v, which is the verification step in Table 3.9.
- The attacker selects the values $\alpha \in \mathbb{F}_{p-1}$, $\beta \in \mathbb{F}^*_{p-1}$ randomly.
- The attacker defines $S_{1,p} \equiv v^{\alpha} \cdot g^{\beta} \pmod{p}$, $S_2 \equiv D / \beta \pmod{(p-1)}$, and $S_{1,p-1} \equiv -S_2 \cdot \alpha \pmod{(\mathrm{p}-1)}$.
- Finally, the attacker solves $S_1 \equiv S_{1,p} \pmod{p}$ and $S_1 \equiv S_{1,p-1} \pmod{(p-1)}$ by using the Chinese Remainder Theorem (CRT) to generate S_1.

Bleichenbacher (1996) proposed to forge the ElGamal signatures without knowing the secret key based on the idea of the weak generator g. According to Bleichenbacher (1996), if some information about the generator g is available, then the ElGamal signatures can be forged based on Theorem 1 provided inBleichenbacher (1996). Accordingly, if the following conditions hold, then a valid ElGamal signature $D^{sig} = (S_1, S_2)$ for the digital document $h(D)$ can be generated (adapted from Bleichenbacher, 1996):

Condition 1

$p - 1 = bw$ is assumed, where b is smooth.

Condition 2

g^* is a primitive root of $\mathbb{F}_p^*$ that satisfies $g^* = cw$, $0 < c < b$. (Note that the primitive root g^* in this condition is different from the primitive root g to be used in the ElGamal digital signature algorithm.)

Condition 3

k is an integer such that $g^{*k} \equiv g \pmod{p}$ holds.

For more details regarding the proof of Theorem 1, as well as regarding the cryptanalysis, and some countermeasures for the basic ElGamal digital signature algorithm, see Bleichenbacher (1996).

As another selected example regarding the cryptanalysis of the ElGamal digital signature algorithm, Giraud and Knudsen (2004) proposed the extension of the "bit-fault attacks" proposed by Bao et al. (1997) applied for the digital signature algorithms including the ElGamal digital signature algorithm. Specifically, Giraud and Knudsen (2004) applied the "byte-fault attack" to the private signing key of the ElGamal digital signature algorithm. Recall from Section 2.12.1 of Chapter 1 that "fault attack" is a type of "implementation attack" applied by making modifications to the physical electronic device. The details are available in Giraud and Knudsen (2004).

3.2.3.4.3 Cryptanalysis of the basic DSA

According to Gómez Pardo (2013), the security concerns of the basic DSA are mainly related to the parameter size, especially the size of the prime number p. According to Johnson, Menezes, and Vanstone (2001), two primary security parameters of the DSA are the prime numbers p and q, whose sizes should be simultaneously increased for more DSA security. The attacks on the hash functions are also possible for the DSA according to Gómez Pardo (2013).

Vaudenay (2003) analyzed the security of the DSA and ECDSA, specifically providing the "Bleichenbacher attack against the pseudorandom generator" for the random ephemeral key r, and "restart attack" for the DSA. As an example, in the "restart attack", the ephemeral key r created for the digital document D_1 is assumed to be reused for the digital document D_2. Thus, the digital signatures for D_1 and D_2 will be $\left(S_1, S_2^1\right)$ and $\left(S_1, S_2^2\right)$, respectively. Finally, it can be shown that the common private signing key s can be recovered as $s = -\frac{S_2^2 D_1 - S_2^1 D_2}{S_1\left(S_2^2 - S_2^1\right)} \pmod{q}$ (Vaudenay, 2003). In the "restart attack", the hashed documents can also be considered. The details of the "Bleichenbacher attack against the pseudorandom generator" for r are available in Vaudenay (2003).

As another cryptanalysis approach for the DSA, Naccache, Nguyen, Tunstall, and Whelan (2005) applied the so-called "glitch attack" against the DSA, which is a type of "fault attack" that causes transient fault. After the attack, the system becomes functional again. The basic objective of this approach is to recover the private signing key (for details, see Naccache et al. (2005)).

3.3 ELLIPTIC CURVE DISCRETE LOGARITHM PROBLEM (ECDLP) AND THE RELATED PUBLIC KEY CRYPTOSYSTEMS

The ECDLP and the related algorithms are the extensions to the basic DLP and algorithms provided in Section 3.2.

3.3.1 ECDLP

Let $E(\mathbb{F}_p)$ be an elliptic curve over the finite field $\mathbb{F}_p$, and let $P \in E(\mathbb{F}_p)$ be a point of order n. The ECDLP is the problem of finding l that satisfies $Q = \underbrace{P + P + P + \cdots + P}_{l \text{ times}} = lP$, $0 \le l \le n-1$ in $E(\mathbb{F}_p)$ (Hankerson & Menezes, 2011; Hoffstein et al., 2008).

3.3.2 Elliptic curve Diffie-Hellman key exchange

Analogous to the basic Diffie-Hellman key exchange, the elliptic curve Diffie-Hellman key exchange has been developed with the following basic parameters and the basic steps provided in Table 3.17.

Basic parameters for the elliptic curve Diffie-Hellman key exchange (adapted from Hankerson & Menezes, 2011; Hoffstein et al., 2008):

p: A large prime number (chosen by Alice or Bob or a trusted third party)
$E(\mathbb{F}_p)$: Elliptic curve over the finite field $\mathbb{F}_p$ (chosen by Alice or Bob or a trusted third party)
$P \in E(\mathbb{F}_p)$ of order n (chosen by Alice or Bob or a trusted third party)
a,b: Private (secret) integers of Alice and Bob, respectively, that satisfy $1 \le a \le n-1, 1 \le b \le n-1$

Normally, Alice and Bob should send two coordinates of P_a and P_b to each other. But since $E(\mathbb{F}_p)$ is known publicly, it is sufficient for Alice and Bob to send only the x-coordinate of P_a and P_b to each other. Although they may compute y or $-y$ value corresponding to the x-value, in the end, they can use only the x-value to find the common secret key (Hoffstein et al., 2008; Paar & Pelzl, 2010). The "decisional elliptic curve Diffie-Hellman key exchange" and "computational elliptic curve Diffie-Hellman key exchange" can be defined as analogous to those of the basic Diffie-Hellman key exchange provided in Table 3.5.

Note that the computations $P_a = aP, P_b = bP$, aP_b, bP_a must be made efficiently. Analogous to the "fast-powering algorithm" given in Section 1.2.3 of

Table 3.17 Elliptic curve Diffie-Hellman key exchange

	Alice	*Bob*
Private: a, b	- Chooses a.	- Chooses b.
Public: $p, E(\mathbb{F}_p), P, P_a, P_b$	- Computes $P_a = aP$ in $E(\mathbb{F}_p)$. - Sends P_a to Bob.	- Computes $P_b = bP$ in $E(\mathbb{F}_p)$. - Sends P_b to Alice.
	- Computes $aP_b = abP$ in $E(\mathbb{F}_p)$.	- Computes $bP_a = baP$ in $E(\mathbb{F}_p)$.
Result: Common private (secret) key	abP in $E(\mathbb{F}_p)$	

Source: Adapted from Hankerson & Menezes (2011) and Hoffstein et al. (2008).

Table 3.18 Double-and-add algorithm

Double-and-add algorithm to solve $Q = lP,\ P, Q \in E(\mathbb{F}_p),\ 1 \le l \le n-1$	
Step 1	- We write l as $l = l_0 + l_1 \cdot 2 + l_2 \cdot 2^2 + l_3 \cdot 2^3 + \cdots + l_r \cdot 2^r$, where $l_0, l_1, l_2, \ldots, l_{r-1} \in \{0, 1\}, l_r = 1$.
Step 2	- We let $Q_0 = P$. - We write $Q_1 = 2Q_0 = 2P$ $Q_2 = 2Q_1 = 2^2P$ $Q_3 = 2Q_2 = 2^3P$ ... $Q_r = 2Q_{r-1} = 2^rP$.
Step 3	- We write Q as $Q = lP = l_0P + l_12P + l_22^2P + l_32^3P + \cdots + l_r2^rP = l_0Q_0 + l_1Q_1 + l_2Q_2 + \cdots + l_rQ_r$.

Source: Adapted from Hoffstein et al. (2008) and Knuth (1981).

Chapter 1, the "double-and-add-algorithm" for the elliptic curve addition can be used with the steps provided in Table 3.18.

Example 3.6

Let $E(\mathbb{F}_{409}): y^2 = x^3 + 253x + 400$ be an elliptic curve over the finite field $\mathbb{F}_{409}$. Let also $P = (0, 20)$ be defined by a trusted third party. We assume that Alice chooses $a = 41$ and Bob chooses $b = 85$ as the private keys. Accordingly, Table 3.19 provides the basic steps of the elliptic curve Diffie-Hellman key exchange for this simple example.

Table 3.19 An example for the elliptic curve Diffie-Hellman key exchange

	Alice	*Bob*
Public: $P = (0, 20)$	- Chooses $a = 41$. - Computes $P_a = 41(0, 20) = (257, 393)$ in $E(\mathbb{F}_{409})$. - Sends $P_a = (257, 393)$ to Bob. - Computes $41(392, 100) = (380, 24)$ in $E(\mathbb{F}_{409})$.	- Chooses $b = 85$. - Computes $P_b = 85(0, 20) = (392, 100)$ in $E(\mathbb{F}_{409})$. - Sends $P_b = (392, 100)$ to Alice. - Computes $85(257, 393) = (380, 24)$ in $E(\mathbb{F}_{409})$.
Result: Common private (secret) key	$(380, 24)$ in $E(\mathbb{F}_{409})$	

Some details of the double-and-add-algorithm to find $P_a = 41P = 41(0, 20) = (257, 393)$ in $E(\mathbb{F}_{409})$ are given as follows:

- We write 41 as $41 = 1 + 2^3 + 2^5$.
- We let $Q_0 = P = (0, 20)$.
- We find $Q_1 = 2Q_0 = 2P = 2(0, 20) = (X_{Q_1}, Y_{Q_1}) = (142, 43) \in \mathbb{F}_{409}$, where we make the calculations modulo 409 as follows (recall the "elliptic curve addition algorithm" provided in Section 1.7.3 of Chapter 1):

$$\lambda = \frac{3(0)^2 + 253}{2(20)} = \frac{253}{40} \equiv 253 \cdot 317 \equiv 37 \pmod{409}$$

$$X_{Q_1} = 37 \cdot 37 - 0 - 0 \equiv 142 \pmod{409}$$

$$Y_{Q_1} = 37(0 - 142) - 20 \equiv 43 \pmod{409}$$

- We make all other calculations in this manner, and find the following results:

$$Q_2 = 2Q_1 = 2(142, 43) = (76, 149) \in \mathbb{F}_{409}$$

$$Q_3 = 2Q_2 = 2(76,149) = (378, 310) \in \mathbb{F}_{409}$$

$$Q_4 = 2Q_3 = 2(378, 310) = (190, 224) \in \mathbb{F}_{409}$$

$$Q_5 = 2Q_4 = 2(190,224) = (125, 56) \in \mathbb{F}_{409}$$

  Finally, we find $P_a = 41P = 41(0, 20) = Q_0 + Q_3 + Q_5 = (0, 20) + (378, 310) + (125, 56) = (257, 393) \in \mathbb{F}_{409}$.

Some details of the double-and-algorithm to find $P_b = 85P = 85(0, 20) = (392, 100)$ in $E(\mathbb{F}_{409})$ are as follows:

- We write 85 as $85 = 1 + 2^2 + 2^4 + 2^6$.
- The calculations for Q_1, Q_2, Q_3, Q_4, Q_5 were already made. We additionally need Q_6 which we can find as $Q_6 = 2Q_5 = 2(125, 56) = (204, 386) \in \mathbb{F}_{409}$.
- Finally, we find $P_b = 85P = Q_0 + Q_2 + Q_4 + Q_6 = (0, 20) + (76, 149) + (190, 224) + (204, 386) = (392, 100) \in \mathbb{F}_{409}$.

The calculations for $41P_b$ and $85P_a$ can be made analogously.

In the following, an extension to the "elliptic curve Diffie-Hellman key exchange", which is "tripartite Diffie-Hellman key exchange" that was developed based on the "modified Weil pairing" will be explained very briefly.

3.3.2.1 *Tripartite Diffie-Hellman key exchange developed based on the modified Weil pairing*

Recall that the basic and elliptic curve Diffie-Hellman key exchange algorithms have been defined for two parties to create a common private key. A

Table 3.20 Tripartite Diffie-Hellman key exchange

	Alice	Bob	Carl
Private: a, b, c	- Chooses a. - Computes	- Chooses b. - Computes	- Chooses c. - Computes
Public: p, $E(\mathbb{F}_p)$, $P \in E(\mathbb{F}_p)$, $P_a, P_b, P_c, \hat{e}_l$	$P_a = aP$ in $E(\mathbb{F}_p)$. - Sends P_a to Bob and Carl.	$P_b = bP$ in $E(\mathbb{F}_p)$. - Sends P_b to Alice and Carl.	$P_c = cP$ in $E(\mathbb{F}_p)$. Sends P_c to Alice and Bob.
	- Computes $\hat{e}_l(P_b, P_c)^a$ $= \hat{e}_l(bP, cP)^a$ $= \hat{e}_l(P, P)^{abc}$ in $E(\mathbb{F}_p)$.	- Computes $\hat{e}_l(P_a, P_c)^b$ $= \hat{e}_l(aP, cP)^b$ $= \hat{e}_l(P, P)^{bac}$ in $E(\mathbb{F}_p)$.	- Computes $\hat{e}_l(P_a, P_b)^c$ $= \hat{e}_l(aP, bP)^c$ $= \hat{e}_l(P, P)^{cab}$ in $E(\mathbb{F}_p)$.
Common private (secret) key		$\hat{e}_l(P, P)^{abc}$ in $(\mathbb{F}_p)$	

Source: Adapted from Hoffstein et al. (2008), Joux (2000), and Joux (2004).

tripartite Diffie-Hellman key exchange is a very special Diffie-Hellman key exchange since three parties (here Alice, Bob, and Carl due to the notations in Hoffstein et al., 2008) can create a common private key by considering the "modified Weil pairing". We provide the basic parameters in the following, and the basic steps in Table 3.20.

Basic parameters of the tripartite Diffie-Hellman key exchange (adapted from Hoffstein et al., 2008):

p: A large prime number (chosen by Alice, Bob, Carl, or a trusted party)
$E(\mathbb{F}_p)$: Elliptic curve over the finite field $\mathbb{F}_p$ (chosen by Alice, Bob, Carl, or a trusted party)
$P \in E(\mathbb{F}_p)$: ℓ-torsion point (chosen by Alice, Bob, Carl, or a trusted party)
ϕ: ℓ-distortion map for $P \in E(\mathbb{F}_p)$ (chosen by Alice, Bob, Carl, or a trusted party)
$\hat{e}_l$: Modified Weil pairing on $E[\ell]$ (chosen by Alice, Bob, Carl, or a trusted party)
a, b, c: Private (secret) integers of Alice, Bob, and Carl, respectively, satisfying $1 \le a \le l-1, 1 \le b \le l-1, 1 \le c \le l-1$

As in the basic and elliptic curve Diffie-Hellman key exchange, Eve should solve at least one of the ECDLPs in $E(\mathbb{F}_p)$, that is, $P_a = aP$, $P_b = bP$ or $P_c = cP$ so that she can recover either a or b or c to compute the common secret key.

3.3.3 Elliptic curve ElGamal public key cryptosystem

The basic ElGamal public key cryptosystem has been extended to the elliptic curve ElGamal public key cryptosystem. The basic parameters will be given and the basic steps of the elliptic curve ElGamal public key cryptosystem are provided in Table 3.21.

Table 3.21 Elliptic curve ElGamal public key cryptosystem

	Alice	*Bob*
Private: a	- Chooses $a \in \mathbb{Z}_+$.	
Public $p, E(\mathbb{F}_p), P, P_a$	- Computes $P_a = aP$ *in* $E(\mathbb{F}_p)$. - Sends P_a to Bob.	
Encryption Private: M, r Public: (C_1, C_2)		- Chooses $M \in E(\mathbb{F}_p)$. - Chooses (randomly) $r \in \mathbb{Z}_+$. - Computes $C_1 = rP$ in $E(\mathbb{F}_p)$. - Computes $C_2 = M + rP_a$ in $E(\mathbb{F}_p)$. - Sends (C_1, C_2) to Alice.
Decryption	- Computes $C_2 - aC_1 = M$ in $E(\mathbb{F}_p)$.	

Source: Adapted from Hoffstein et al. (2008) and Yan (2019).

Basic parameters for the elliptic curve ElGamal public key cryptosystem (adapted from Hoffstein et al., 2008; Koç, Özdemir, & Ödemiş Özger, 2021):

p: A large prime number (chosen by Alice or Bob or a trusted third party)
$E(\mathbb{F}_p)$: Elliptic curve over the finite field $\mathbb{F}_p$ (chosen by Alice or Bob or a trusted third party)
$P \in E(\mathbb{F}_p)$ of order n (chosen by Alice or Bob or a trusted third party)
a: Private (secret) integer of Alice satisfying $1 \le a \le n-1$
r: Integer ephemeral key satisfying $1 \le r \le n-1$ (chosen by Bob)
$M = (x_M, y_M) \in E(\mathbb{F}_p)$: Plaintext (chosen by Bob)
(C_1, C_2): Ciphertext

Notice the similarities between the elliptic curve ElGamal public key cryptosystem and the basic ElGamal public key cryptosystem. Note also that in the elliptic curve ElGamal public key cryptosystem, the exponentiation is replaced with the multiplication, and the multiplication is replaced with the addition, that is, $c_1 \equiv g^r \pmod{p}$ in the basic ElGamal public key cryptosystem is replaced with $C_1 = rP$ in $E(\mathbb{F}_p)$ in the elliptic curve ElGamal public key cryptosystem, and $c_2 \equiv m \cdot A^r \pmod{p}$ in the basic ElGamal public key cryptosystem is replaced with $C_2 = M + rP_a$ in $E(\mathbb{F}_p)$ in the elliptic curve ElGamal public key cryptosystem.

Example 3.7

We consider $p = 409$, $E(\mathbb{F}_{409})$: $y^2 = x^3 + 253x + 400$, and $P = (0, 20)$ as in Example 3.6. Then the steps of the elliptic curve ElGamal public key cryptosystem will be as given in Table 3.22.

Note that the calculations of $41(0, 20) = (257, 393)$, $85(0, 20) = (392, 100)$, and $85(257, 393) = (380, 24)$ in $E(\mathbb{F}_{409})$ have already been made in Example 3.6.

Table 3.22 Example for the elliptic curve ElGamal public key cryptosystem

	Alice	*Bob*
Public: $P=(0, 20)$	- Chooses $a=41$. - Computes $P_a=41(0, 20)$ $=(257, 393)$ in $E(\mathbb{F}_{409})$. - Sends $P_a=(257, 393)$ to Bob.	
Encryption		- Chooses $M=(23, 18)$ in $E(\mathbb{F}_{409})$. - Chooses (randomly) $r=85$. - Computes $C_1=85(0, 20)=(392, 100)$ in $E(\mathbb{F}_{409})$. - Computes $C_2=(23, 18)+85(257, 393)$ $=(23, 18)+(380, 24)$ $=(245, 102)$ in $E(\mathbb{F}_{409})$. - Sends (C_1, C_2) to Alice.
Decryption	- Computes $(245, 102)-41(392, 100)$ $=(245, 102)-(380, 24)$ $=(245, 102)+(380, -24)$ $=(23, 18)=M$ in $E(\mathbb{F}_{409})$.	

The calculations of $(23, 18)+(380, 24)=(245, 102)$ and $(245, 102)+(380, -24)=(23, 18)$ in $E(\mathbb{F}_{409})$ can also be made analogously by using the "elliptic curve addition algorithm" provided in Section 1.7.3 of Chapter 1.

3.3.4 Elliptic curve DSA (ECDSA)

The ECDSA is the elliptic curve counterpart of the DSA. ECDSA was developed by the American National Standard for Financial Services. Table 3.23 provides the basic steps for the ECDSA after the basic parameters for the ECDSA (see American National Standard for Financial Services (2020) for the latest version).

Basic parameters for the ECDSA (adapted from Hoffstein et al., 2008; Liao & Shen, 2006; Vanstone, 1992):

p, q: Large prime numbers (chosen by Samantha or Victor or a trusted third party)

$E(\mathbb{F}_p)$: Elliptic curve over the finite field $\mathbb{F}_p$ (chosen by Samantha or Victor or a trusted third party)

Table 3.23 ECDSA

	Samantha	*Victor*
Private: s	- Chooses s.	
Public: $p, E(\mathbb{F}_p), P, V$	- Computes $V = sP$ in $E(\mathbb{F}_p)$. - Sends V to Victor.	
Signing	- Chooses D.	
Private: r	- Chooses (randomly) r. - Computes $rP = (x_1, y_1)$ in $E(\mathbb{F}_p)$. - Computes $x_1 \equiv S_1 \pmod{q}$. - Computes $S_2 \equiv (D + s \cdot S_1) \cdot r^{-1} \pmod{q}$.	
Public: $D, D^{sig} = (S_1, S_2)$	- Sends D and $D^{sig} = (S_1, S_2)$ to Victor.	
Verification		- Computes $V_1 \equiv D \cdot S_2^{-1} \pmod{q}$ and $V_2 \equiv S_1 \cdot S_2^{-1} \pmod{q}$. - Computes $V_1P + V_2V = (x_2, y_2)$ in $E(\mathbb{F}_p)$. - Verifies $x_2 \equiv S_1 \pmod{q}$.

Source: Adapted from Hoffstein et al. (2008), Liao & Shen (2006), and Vanstone (1992).

$P \in E(\mathbb{F}_p)$: A point with large prime order q (chosen by Samantha or Victor or a trusted third party)
D: Digital document of Samantha satisfying $1 \le D \le q-1$
s: Private signing key of Samantha satisfying $1 < s \le q-1$
V: Public verification key to be used by Victor
r: Integer ephemeral key satisfying $1 \le r \le q-1$ (chosen by Samantha)
$D^{sig} = (S_1, S_2)$: Digital signature of the digital document D signed by Samantha

Note very high similarity between the DSA and the ECDSA.

Example 3.8

We consider $p = 1777$, $E(\mathbb{F}_{1777})$: $y^2 = x^3 + 253x + 400$, and $q = 223$. We assume $P = (179, 76)$ is chosen which has a prime order 223. Then the steps of the ECDSA will be as given in Table 3.24.

3.3.5 Cryptanalysis of the elliptic curve Diffie-Hellman key exchange, elliptic curve ElGamal public key cryptosystem, and ECDSA

According to Yan (2019), there is no "efficient classical attack" against the ECDLP and ECDLP-based cryptography. However, the ECDLP and ECDLP-based cryptography are vulnerable to quantum attacks (Yan, 2019).

Table 3.24 An example for the ECDSA

	Samantha	*Victor*
Public: $P=(179, 76)$	- Chooses $s=91$.	
	- Computes $V=91(179, 76)=(1652, 1235)$ in $E(\mathbb{F}_{1777})$.	
	- Sends V to Victor.	
Signing	- Chooses $D=129$.	
	- Chooses (randomly) $r=201$.	
	- Computes $201(179, 76)=(917, 1536)=(x_1, y_1)$ in $E(\mathbb{F}_{1777})$.	
	- Computes $x_1=917\equiv 25=S_1 \pmod{223}$.	
	- Computes $S_2\equiv(129+91\cdot 25)\cdot 201^{-1}\equiv 174\cdot 152\equiv 134 \pmod{223}$.	
	- Sends $D=129$ and $D^{sig}=(S_1, S_2)=(25, 134)$ to Victor.	
Verification		- Computes $V_1\equiv 129\cdot 134^{-1}\equiv 129\cdot 5\equiv 199 \pmod{223}$ and $V_2\equiv 25\cdot 134^{-1}\equiv 25\cdot 5\equiv 125 \pmod{223}$.
		- Computes $199(179, 76)+125(1652, 1235)=(161, 629)+(427, 1019)=(917, 1536)$ in $E(\mathbb{F}_{1777})$.
		- Verifies $917\equiv 25=S_1 \pmod{223}$.

3.3.5.1 *Cryptanalysis of the elliptic curve Diffie-Hellman key exchange and elliptic curve Elgamal public key cryptosystem*

There have been some attacks and cryptanalysis approaches against the elliptic curve Diffie-Hellman key exchange and elliptic curve ElGamal public key cryptosystem. In this section, we provide the basic contributions of some selected approaches.

Boneh and Shparlinski (2001) showed that predicting the least significant bit (LSB) (rightmost bit) of the elliptic curve Diffie-Hellman secret key is as hard as discovering the entire secret key. Jao, Jetchev, and Venkatesan (2007) studied the security of the elliptic curve Diffie-Hellman key exchange in the presence of oracles that provided partial information on the value of the common secret key abP. Yan (2013) provided the quantum attacks on the

ECDLP-based cryptosystems. The Eicher-Opoku's quantum attack on the ECDLP, Proos-Zalka's quantum attack on the ECDLP, and Eicher-Opoku's quantum attack on the elliptic curve Massey-Omura cryptosystem are some of these quantum attacks, which also hold for the elliptic curve ElGamal public key cryptosystem. Jacobson, Koblitz, and Silverman (2000) analyzed the so-called Xedni calculus attack proposed by Silverman (2000), which can also be applied against the elliptic curve ElGamal public key cryptosystem (see the respective references for more details).

3.3.5.2 *Cryptanalysis of the ECDSA*

There have also been some attacks and cryptanalysis approaches against the ECDSA. In this section, we provide the selected contributions of some selected references.

Johnson et al. (2001) classified the possible attacks on the ECDSA as attacks on the ECDLP, attacks on the hash function, and other attacks. Some selected attacks on the ECDLP are by using the Pohlig-Hellman algorithm, Pollard's rho algorithm, and Xedni calculus attacks. The attacks on the hash function differ according to whether the hash function has the preimage resistance/collision resistance or not. Some selected other attacks are related to the repeated use of some document-related secret parameters such as the ephemeral key, and implementation attacks. Nguyen and Shparlinski (2003) extended the approach of Nguyen and Shparlinski (2002) for the DSA to study the insecurity of the ECDSA with partially known nonces. For the details of the attack, see Nguyen and Shparlinski (2003).

Vaudenay (2003) proposed the signature manipulation in the ECDSA by replacing r with $-r$ and replacing S_2 with $-S_2$. Finally, the signature (S_1, S_2) will be replaced with $(S_1, -S_2)$, which will still be valid. As provided in Vaudenay (2003), it is possible to recover the private signing key s as $s = -\frac{D_1+D_2}{2S_1} \pmod{q}$ by assuming that a valid signature can be created for two different documents D_1, D_2 simultaneously, where the hashed documents can also be considered (Stern, Pointcheval, Malone-Lee, & Smart, 2002). According to Vaudenay (2003), the "Bleichenbacher attack against the pseudorandom generator" for the random ephemeral key r and "restart attack" applied for the DSA can also be applied analogously for the ECDSA (see details in Vaudenay (2003)).

3.4 BASIC ALGORITHMS FOR THE SOLUTION OF THE DLP AND ECDLP

Note that the security of the algorithms provided in this chapter is basically based on the hardness of the DLP or ECDLP. The solution of the DLP or ECDLP enables the attacker to recover the private decryption (signing) key in the DLP or ECDLP-related public key cryptosystems and digital signature algorithms. Some basic algorithms have been proposed for the solution of the DLP and ECDLP, which will be explained in this section.

3.4.1 Shanks' baby-step giant-step algorithm for the basic DLP and ECDLP

The Shanks' baby-step giant-step algorithm has been defined for any groups, not just for the finite fields (Hoffstein et al., 2008). We consider the basic DLP (Version 3) in Table 3.1 defined for the groups and assume the order of g, which is $N \geq 2$ to be known. The original baby-step giant-step algorithm is available in Shanks (1969). The steps of the Shanks' baby-step giant-step algorithm are provided in Table 3.25.

The multiplication by g in List 1 of Table 3.25 is a baby step, whereas the multiplication by g^{-n} in List 2 is a giant step.

Example 3.1 (revisited 1)

We reconsider the DLP $2^x \equiv 270 \pmod{347}$, $x = ?$ This time, we would like to find x by using the Shanks' baby-step giant-step algorithm. We should first find the order of 2 modulo 347, that is, the smallest integer N that satisfies $2^N \equiv 1 \pmod{347}$. We find $N = 346$ and consider the steps in Table 3.26 for the solution of the DLP. Note that this example is an application of the Shanks' baby-step giant-step algorithm in finite field.

Table 3.25 Shanks' baby-step giant-step algorithm for the DLP

Steps	*Shanks' baby-step giant-step algorithm*
Step 1: We compute	$n = 1 + \lfloor \sqrt{N} \rfloor$, where $\lfloor \sqrt{N} \rfloor$ is the greatest integer less than or equal to $\sqrt{N}$.
Step 2: We prepare two lists	List 1 $e, g, g^2, g^3, \ldots, g^i, \ldots, g^n$ List 2 $h, h \cdot g^{-n}, h \cdot g^{-2n}, h \cdot g^{-3n}, \ldots, h \cdot g^{-jn}, \ldots, h \cdot g^{-n^2}$
Step 3a	If for any j^*, we can find $h \cdot g^{-j^* n} = 1$ from List 2, then $x^* = j^* n$ is the solution.
Step 3b	If Step 3a does not hold, we find at most two collisions from List 1 and List 2, that is, we find $g^{i_1^*} = h \cdot g^{-j_1^* n}$ $g^{i_2^*} = h \cdot g^{-j_2^* n}$. We also determine $j^* = \min(j_1^*, j_2^*)$ $i^* = \begin{cases} i_1^* \text{ if } j_1^* = \min(j_1^*, j_2^*) \\ i_2^* \text{ if } j_2^* = \min(j_1^*, j_2^*) \end{cases}$ Finally, $x^* = i^* + j^* n$ is the solution.

Source: Adapted from Buchmann (2004), Coron, Lefranc, & Poupard (2005), and Hoffstein et al. (2008).

Table 3.26 An example for the Shanks' baby-step giant-step algorithm

Steps	*Shanks' baby-step giant-step algorithm*
Step 1	$n = 1 + \lfloor \sqrt{346} \rfloor = 1 + \lfloor 18.601 \rfloor = 1 + 18 = 19.$
Step 2	List 1
	$1, 2, 2^2, 2^3, \ldots, 2^{19} \pmod{347}$
	List 2
	$270, 270 \cdot 2^{-19}, 270 \cdot 2^{-2 \cdot 19}, 270 \cdot 2^{-3 \cdot 19}, \ldots, 270 \cdot 2^{-19^2} \pmod{347}$, where $2^{-19} \equiv 335 \pmod{347}$.
Step 3a	For any j^*, we cannot find $270 \cdot 2^{-j^* 19} \equiv 1 \pmod{347}$.
Step 3b	We find only one collision:
	$2^4 \equiv 16 \pmod{347}$ from List 1
	$270 \cdot 2^{-2 \cdot 19} \equiv 270 \cdot 335^2 \equiv 16 \pmod{347}$ from List 2.
	Finally, $2^4 = 270 \cdot 2^{-2 \cdot 19}$ and $x = 4 + 2 \cdot 19 = 42$ is the solution.

Coron et al. (2005) considered also the case of the unknown order of g for the Shanks' baby-step giant-step algorithm.

The Shanks' baby-step giant-step algorithm proposed for the solution of the DLP has also been adapted to the solution of the ECDLP.

3.4.1.1 Shanks' baby-step giant-step algorithm for the ECDLP

Recall the definition of the ECDLP from Section 3.3.1. The steps of the Shanks' baby-step giant-step algorithm for the ECDLP are given in Table 3.27.

Table 3.27 Shanks' baby-step giant-step algorithm for the ECDLP

	Shanks' baby-step giant-step algorithm for the ECDLP
Step 1: Compute	$m = \lfloor \sqrt{p} \rfloor$, where $\lfloor \sqrt{p} \rfloor$ is the greatest integer less than or equal to $\sqrt{p}$.
Step 2: Prepare two lists	List 1
	$iP\ 1 \le i \le m$ in $E(\mathbb{F}_p)$
	List 2
	$Q - jmP\ 1 \le j \le m - 1$ in $E(\mathbb{F}_p)$
Step 3a	If for any j^*, we can find $Q - j^* mP = 0$ from List 2, then the solution will be $l = j^* m$.
Step 3b	If Step 3a does not hold, we find at least one collision from List 1 and List 2, that is, we find
	$i^* P = Q - j^* mP$ in $E(\mathbb{F}_p)$.
	Finally, the solution will be $l = i^* + j^* m$.

Source: Adapted from Yan (2013).

Table 3.28 Pohlig-Hellman algorithm

Steps	*Pohlig-Hellman algorithm*	
Step 1: We factor N into prime numbers.	$N = p_1^{e_1} \cdot p_2^{e_2} \cdots p_i^{e_i} \cdots p_r^{e_r}$	
Step 2: We prepare two equation types for each $1 \le i \le r$.	Equation type 1 $g_i = g^{N/p_i^{e_i}}$	Equation type 2 $h_i = h^{N/p_i^{e_i}}$
Step 3: We find y_i for each $1 \le i \le r$.	$g_i^{y_i} = h_i$	
Step 4: We find simultaneous solution of the congruences to find the solution of the DLP.	$x \equiv y_i \left(\text{mod } p_i^{e_i}\right)$ for $1 \le i \le r$	

Source: Adapted from Buchmann (2004) and Hoffstein et al. (2008).

3.4.2 Pohlig-Hellman algorithm for the basic DLP

The Pohlig-Hellman algorithm is also defined for any groups, not only for the finite fields (Hoffstein et al., 2008). The original algorithm is available in Pohlig and Hellman (1978). We reconsider the basic DLP (Version 3) in Table 3.1 defined for the groups and assume again that the order of g, which is $N \ge 2$ to be known as in Section 3.4.1. Table 3.28 provides the basic steps of the Pohlig-Hellman algorithm.

Note that it is assumed that there is an efficient algorithm to solve the equations in Steps in Table 3.8. It is clear that the simultaneous solution of $x \equiv y_i \left(\text{mod } p_i^{e_i}\right)$ for $1 \le i \le r$ can be accomplished by using the CRT provided in Section 1.2.4 of Chapter 1. The Pohlig-Hellman algorithm tells us that if N is a product of powers of small prime numbers, then the DLP can be solved efficiently (Hoffstein et al., 2008).

Example 3.1 (revisited 2)

Recall the DLP $2^x \equiv 270 \left(\text{mod } 347\right)$ and $N = 346$ as the order of 2 modulo 347 from Example 3.1 (revisited 1). Then we consider the solution steps in Table 3.29 by using the Pohlig-Hellman algorithm.

Note that Example 3.1 (revisited 2) is an application of the Pohlig-Hellman algorithm in finite field. The simultaneous solution to the congruences in Step 4 of Table 3.29 is straightforward. However, it could also be found by considering the approach provided in Section 1.2.4 of Chapter 1 as follows: $M_1 = 173, M_2 = 2$, and $173N_1 \equiv 1 \left(\text{mod } 2\right)$, $2N_2 \equiv 1 \left(\text{mod } 173\right)$ hold, where $N_1 = 1, N_2 = 87$ can be found. Finally, we compute $x = 0 \cdot 1 \cdot 173 + 42 \cdot 87 \cdot 2 \equiv 42 \left(\text{mod } 346\right)$.

3.4.3 Index calculus method for the basic DLP

The index calculus method is defined for the finite field $\mathbb{F}_p$ (Hoffstein et al., 2008). We can consider either the basic DLP (Version 1) or the basic DLP (Version 2) provided in Table 3.1. In Table 3.30, the basic steps of the index calculus method are provided.

Table 3.29 An example for the Pohlig-Hellman algorithm

Steps	*Pohlig-Hellman algorithm*	
Step 1: We factor $N = 346$ into prime numbers.	$346 = 2 \cdot 173$	
Step 2: We prepare two equation types for each $1 \le i \le 2$.	Equation type 1	Equation type 2
	$g_1 = 2^{346/2} = 2^{173} \equiv 346 \pmod{347}$	$h_1 = 270^{346/2} = 270^{173} \equiv 1 \pmod{347}$
	$g_2 = 2^{346/173} = 2^2 \equiv 4 \pmod{347}$	$h_2 = 270^{346/173} = 270^2 \equiv 30 \pmod{347}$
Step 3: We find y_i for each $1 \le i \le 2$.	$346^{y_1} \equiv 1 \pmod{347}$, $y_1 = 0, 2$ $4^{y_2} \equiv 30 \pmod{347}$ $y_2 = 42$	
Step 4: We find simultaneous solution of the congruences to find x.	$x \equiv 0 \pmod 2$ $x \equiv 42 \pmod{173}$ Finally, $x = 42$ is the solution.	

Recall from Section 1.6.2 of Chapter 1 that B-smooth number is an integer number whose prime factors are less than or equal to B. Note also that "mod p" in Step 3 of Table 3.30 reduces to "mod $(p-1)$" in Step 4 due to the reason provided in Equation (3.1).

Example 3.1 (revisited 3)

This time, we would like to solve the DLP $2^x \equiv 270 \pmod{347}$ by using the index calculus method.

Step 1 and Step 2: We assume that we choose $B = 10$; thus, we should solve for all prime numbers $l \le 10$, $2^y \equiv l \pmod{347}$, which means that we solve the following DLPs:

$2^y \equiv 2 \pmod{347}$ from which $y = \log_2(2) \equiv 1 \pmod{347}$ is obtained.

$2^y \equiv 3 \pmod{347}$ from which $y = \log_2(3) \equiv 152 \pmod{347}$ is obtained.

Table 3.30 Index calculus method

Steps	*Index calculus method*
Step 1	We choose a positive integer B.
Step 2	We solve $g^y = l \pmod p$ for all prime numbers $l \le B$, that is, we find $\log_g(l) \pmod p$ for each prime $l \le B$.
Step 3	We calculate $h \cdot g^{-k} \pmod p$ for $k = 1, 2, \ldots$ until we find a B-smooth number $h \cdot g^{-k^*} \pmod p$, and factor it into prime numbers as $h \cdot g^{-k^*} \pmod p = \Pi_{l \le B} l^{e_l}$.
Step 4: We combine Step 2 and Step 3 to find the solution.	$\log_g(h) \equiv k^* + \Sigma_{l \le B} e_l \cdot \log_g(l) \bmod (p-1) \equiv x$

Source: Adapted from Hoffstein et al. (2008).

$2^y \equiv 5 \pmod{347}$ from which $y = \log_2(5) \equiv 277 \pmod{347}$ is obtained.

$2^y \equiv 7 \pmod{347}$ from which $y = \log_2(7) \equiv 289 \pmod{347}$ is obtained.

Step 3: $270 \cdot 2^{-1} \equiv 270 \cdot 174 \equiv 135 \pmod{347}$, where $135 = 3^3 \cdot 5$ is a 10-smooth number. Thus, we stop at $k^* = 1$.

Step 4 (Combination of Step 2 and Step 3): $\log_2(270) \equiv 1 + 3 \cdot \log_2(3) + 1 \cdot \log_2(5) \pmod{346} = 1 + 3 \cdot 152 + 1 \cdot 277 = 734 \equiv 42 \pmod{346}$.

3.5 CONCLUSIONS

This chapter was related to the DLP, ECDLP, and the related public key cryptosystems and digital signature algorithms. The Diffie-Hellman key exchange, ElGamal public key cryptosystem, ElGamal digital signature algorithm, and DSA were presented by considering the basic forms and elliptic curve analogs. The illustrative examples and some selected basic cryptanalysis approaches were also provided for these algorithms. Since the security of the DLP and ECDLP-related public key cryptosystems and digital signature algorithms depends basically on the hardness of the solution of the DLP and ECDLP, some selected basic algorithms to be used for the solution of the DLP and ECDLP were also given in the last section of the chapter. In this last section, a simple example that was solved by considering the trial-and-error method at the beginning of the chapter was revisited for the comparison of the algorithms. As mentioned in Chapters 1 and 2, it should be emphasized that the examples in this chapter are rather simple, and in real-life cryptographic applications, actually much larger values should be considered. The DLP- and ECDLP-related cryptographic algorithms have various real-life applications, including the application of the Diffie-Hellman key exchange for authentication in wireless mesh networks, wireless sensor networks, virtual private networks, openSSL, and the use of the DSA in virtual private networks, databases, and openSSL (see Chen, Blasco, & Kupwade Patil, 2019; Easttom, 2021, 2022; Roy & Khan, 2021; Xu, Thakur, Kamruzzaman, & Ali, 2021). Moreover, digital signature algorithms are used in blockchain technology, particularly ECDSA is the current digital signature algorithm used in Bitcoin transactions (Tanwar, 2022). More generally, elliptic curve cryptography is used in different applications such as wireless sensor networks, openSSL, and Financial Technology (Fin-Tech) including e-payment security (see Easttom, 2022; Khajuria & Tange, 2009; Othman, Trad, Alzaid, & Youssef, 2013; Thakur & Sharma, 2023; Vincent, Folorunso, & Akinde, 2010).

REFERENCES

American National Standard for Financial Services. (2020). *ANSI X9.142–2020. Public key cryptography for the financial services industry: The elliptic curve digital signature algorithm (ECDSA).* https://webstore.ansi.org/preview-pages/ASCX9/preview_ANSI+X9.142-2020.pdf

Bao, F., Deng, R. H., Han, Y., Jeng, A., Narasimhalu, A. D., & Ngair, T. (1997). Breaking public key cryptosystems on tamper resistant devices in the presence of transient faults. In B. Christianson, B. Crispo, M. Lomas, & M. Roe (Eds.), *Security protocols. Security protocols 1997.* Lecture Notes in Computer Science, 1361. Berlin, Heidelberg: Springer. https://doi.org/10.1007/BFb0028164

Bleichenbacher, D. (1996). Generating ElGamal signatures without knowing the secret key. In U. Maurer (Ed.), *Advances in cryptology – EUROCRYPT '96.* EUROCRYPT 1996. Lecture Notes in Computer Science, 1070. Berlin, Heidelberg: Springer. https://doi.org/10.1007/3-540-68339-9_2

Boneh, D., Joux, A., & Nguyen, P. Q. (2000). Why textbook ElGamal and RSA encryption are insecure. In T. Okamoto (Eds.), *Advances in cryptology – ASIACRYPT 2000.* ASIACRYPT 2000. Lecture Notes in Computer Science, 1976. Berlin, Heidelberg: Springer. https://doi.org/10.1007/3-540-44448-3_3

Boneh, D., & Shparlinski, I. E. (2001). On the unpredictability of bits of the elliptic curve Diffie-Hellman scheme. In J. Kilian (Ed.), *Advances in cryptology – CRYPTO 2001.* CRYPTO 2001. Lecture Notes in Computer Science, 2139. Berlin, Heidelberg: Springer. https://doi.org/10.1007/3-540-44647-8_12

Buchmann, J. A. (2004). *Introduction to cryptography.* Undergraduate Texts in Mathematics. New York, NY: Springer. https://doi.org/10.1007/978-1-4684-0496-8_11

Canetti, R., & Varia, M. (2011). Decisional Diffie–Hellman problem. In H. C. A. van Tilborg & S. Jajodia (Eds.), *Encyclopedia of cryptography and security.* Boston, MA: Springer. https://doi.org/10.1007/978-1-4419-5906-5_443

Chen, T. M., Blasco, J., & Kupwade Patil, H. (2019). Cryptography in WSNs. In H. Ammari (Ed.), *Mission-oriented sensor networks and systems: Art and science. Studies in systems, decision and control*, 163. Cham: Springer. https://doi.org/10.1007/978-3-319-91146-5_21

Coron, J. S., Lefranc, D., & Poupard, G. (2005). A new baby-step giant-step algorithm and some applications to cryptanalysis. In J. R. Rao & B. Sunar (Eds.), *Cryptographic hardware and embedded systems – CHES 2005.* Lecture Notes in Computer Science, 3659. Berlin, Heidelberg: Springer. https://doi.org/10.1007/11545262_4

Das, M., & Chakraborty, R. (2022). Statistical cryptanalysis of ElGamal cryptosystem for measuring security in disruptive technology. *Second international conference on computer science, engineering and applications (ICCSEA)*, Gunupur, India, 1–5. https://doi.org/10.1109/ICCSEA54677.2022.9936396

Diffie, W., & Hellman, M. (1976). New directions in cryptography. *IEEE Transactions on Information Theory*, 22(6), 644–654. https://doi.org/10.1109/TIT.1976.1055638

Easttom, W. (2022). SSL/TLS. In C. Easttom, *Modern cryptography.* Cham: Springer. https://doi.org/10.1007/978-3-031-12304-7_13

Easttom, W. (Ed.). (2021). Virtual private networks, authentication, and wireless security. In *Modern cryptography.* Cham: Springer. https://doi.org/10.1007/978-3-030-63115-4_14

ElGamal, T. (1985). A public key cryptosystem and a signature scheme based on discrete logarithms. In G. R. Blakley & D. Chaum (Eds.), *Advances in cryptology. CRYPTO 1984.* Lecture Notes in Computer Science, 196. Berlin, Heidelberg: Springer. https://doi.org/10.1007/3-540-39568-7_2

Giraud, C., & Knudsen, E. W. (2004). Fault attacks on signature schemes. In H. Wang, J. Pieprzyk, & V. Varadharajan (Eds.), *Information security and privacy. ACISP 2004.* Lecture Notes in Computer Science, 3108. Berlin, Heidelberg: Springer. https://doi.org/10.1007/978-3-540-27800-9_41

Gómez Pardo, J. L. (Ed.). (2013). Public-key encryption. In *Introduction to cryptography with maple.* Berlin, Heidelberg: Springer. https://doi.org/10.1007/978-3-642-32166-5_8

Gordon, D. (2011). Discrete logarithm problem. In H. C. A. van Tilborg & S. Jajodia (Eds.), *Encyclopedia of cryptography and security.* Boston, MA: Springer. https://doi.org/10.1007/978-1-4419-5906-5_445

Hankerson, D., & Menezes, A. (2011) Elliptic curve discrete logarithm problem. In H. C. A. van Tilborg, & S. Jajodia (Eds.), *Encyclopedia of cryptography and security.* Boston, MA: Springer. https://doi.org/10.1007/978-1-4419-5906-5_246

Hoffstein, J., Pipher, J., & Silverman, J. H. (2008). *An introduction to mathematical cryptography.* New York, NY: Springer Science + Business Media, LLC.

Inam, S., & Ali, R. (2018). A new ElGamal-like cryptosystem based on matrices over group ring. *Neural Computing Applications, 29*(11), 1279–1283.

Jacobson, M. J., Koblitz, N., & Silverman, J. H. et al. (2000). Analysis of the Xedni Calculus attack. *Designs, Codes and Cryptography, 20,* 41–64. https://doi.org/10.1023/A:1008312401197

Jao, D., Jetchev, D., & Venkatesan, R. (2007). On the bits of elliptic curve Diffie-Hellman keys. In K. Srinathan, C. P. Rangan, & M. Yung (Eds.), *Progress in cryptology – INDOCRYPT 2007.* INDOCRYPT 2007. Lecture Notes in Computer Science, 4859. Berlin, Heidelberg: Springer. https://doi.org/10.1007/978-3-540-77026-8_4

Jia, J., Wang, H., Zhang, H., Wang, S., & Liu, J. (2019). Cryptanalysis of an ElGamal-like cryptosystem based on matrices over group rings. In H. Zhang, B. Zhao, & F. Yan (Eds.), *Trusted computing and information security. CTCIS 2018. Communications in computer and information science,* 960. Singapore: Springer. https://doi.org/10.1007/978-981-13-5913-2_16

Johnson, D., Menezes, A., & Vanstone, S.. (2001). The elliptic curve digital signature algorithm (ECDSA). *International Journal of Information Security, 1,* 36–63. https://doi.org/10.1007/s102070100002

Joux, A. (2000). A one round protocol for tripartite Diffie–Hellman. In W. Bosma (Ed.), *Algorithmic number theory. ANTS 2000.* Lecture Notes in Computer Science, 1838. Berlin, Heidelberg: Springer. https://doi.org/10.1007/10722028_23

Joux, A. (2004). A one round protocol for tripartite Diffie-Hellman. *Journal of Cryptology, 17*(4), 263–276.

Khajuria, S., & Tange, H. (2009). Implementation of Diffie-Hellman key exchange on wireless sensor using elliptic curve cryptography. *2009 1st international conference on wireless communication, vehicular technology, information theory and aerospace & electronic systems technology,* Aalborg, Denmark. https://doi.org/10.1109/WIRELESSVITAE.2009.5172547

Knuth, D. E. (1981). *The art of computer programming. Volume 2: Seminumerical algorithms.* Reading, MA: Addison-Wesley.

Koç, Ç.K., Özdemir, F., & Ödemiş Özger, Z. (Eds.). (2021). ElGamal algorithm. In *Partially homomorphic encryption.* Cham: Springer. https://doi.org/10.1007/978-3-030-87629-6_5

Liao, H.-Z., & Shen, Y. Y. (2006). On the elliptic curve digital signature algorithm. *Tunghai Science, 8,* 109–126.

Naccache, D., Nguyên, P. Q., Tunstall, M., & Whelan, C. (2005). Experimenting with faults, lattices and the DSA. In S. Vaudenay (Ed.), *Public key cryptography – PKC 2005.* Lecture Notes in Computer Science, 3386. Berlin, Heidelberg: Springer. https://doi.org/10.1007/978-3-540-30580-4_3

National Institute of Standards and Technology. (2023a). *Digital signature standard (DSS).* https://csrc.nist.gov/pubs/fips/186-4/final

National Institute of Standards and Technology. (2023b). *FIPS 186-5. Digital signature standard (DSS).* Federal Information Processing Standards Publication. U.S. Department of Commerce. National Institute of Standards and Technology. https://nvlpubs.nist.gov/nistpubs/FIPS/NIST.FIPS.186-5.pdf

National Institute of Standards and Technology. (2013). *FIPS 186-4. Digital signature standard (DSS).* Federal Information Processing Standards Publication.

U.S. Department of Commerce. National Institute of Standards and Technology. https://nvlpubs.nist.gov/nistpubs/fips/nist.fips.186-4.pdf

Nguyen, P. Q., & Shparlinski, I. E. (2002). The insecurity of the digital signature algorithm with partially known nonces. *Journal of Cryptology*, *15*, 151–176.

Nguyen, P. Q., & Shparlinski, I. E. (2003). The insecurity of the elliptic curve digital signature algorithm with partially known nonces. *Designs, Codes and Cryptography*, *30*, 201–217. https://doi.org/10.1023/A:1025436905711

Othman, S. B., Trad, A., Alzaid, H., & Youssef, H. (2013). Performance evaluation of EC-ElGamal encryption algorithm for wireless sensor networks. In B. Godara & K. S. Nikita (Eds.), *Wireless mobile communication and healthcare. MobiHealth 2012*. Lecture Notes of the Institute for Computer Sciences, Social Informatics and Telecommunications Engineering, 61. Berlin, Heidelberg: Springer. https://doi.org/10.1007/978-3-642-37893-5_31

Paar, C., & Pelzl, J. (2010). *Understanding cryptography. A textbook for students and practitioners*. Berlin, Heidelberg: Springer-Verlag.

Phan, R. C. W., & Goi, B. M. (2006). Cryptanalysis of the n-party encrypted Diffie-Hellman key exchange using different passwords. In J. Zhou, M. Yung, & F. Bao (Eds.), *Applied cryptography and network security. ACNS 2006*. Lecture Notes in Computer Science, 3989. Berlin, Heidelberg: Springer. https://doi.org/10.1007/11767480_15

Pohlig, S., & Hellman, M. (1978). An improved algorithm for computing logarithms overGF(p)and its cryptographic significance. *IEEE Transactions on Information Theory*, *24*(1), 106–110. https://doi.org/10.1109/TIT.1978.1055817

Pointcheval, D., & Stern, J. (1996). Security proofs for signature schemes. In U. Maurer (Ed.), *Advances in cryptology – EUROCRYPT '96*. EUROCRYPT 1996. Lecture Notes in Computer Science, 1070. Berlin, Heidelberg: Springer. https://doi.org/10.1007/3-540-68339-9_33

Raymond, J.-F., & Stiglic, A. (2002). Security issues in the Diffie-Hellman key agreement protocol. *IEEE Transactions on Information Theory. 22*. https://www.researchgate.net/publication/2401745_Security_Issues_in_the_Diffie-Hellman_Key_Agreement_Protocol.

Roy, A. K., & Khan, A. K. (2021). Handoff authentication through Diffie-Hellman approach for wireless mesh networks. In A. K. Maji, G. Saha, S. Das, S. Basu, & J. M. R. S. Tavares (Eds.), *Proceedings of the international conference on computing and communication systems*. Lecture Notes in Networks and Systems, 170. Singapore: Springer. https://doi.org/10.1007/978-981-33-4084-8_59

Shanks, D. (1969). Class number, a theory of factorization and general. *Proceedings of symposium of pure mathematics*. Providence, RI: AMS.

Sharma, P., & Purushothama, B. R. (2023). Cryptanalysis of a secure and efficient Diffie–Hellman based key agreement scheme. *International Journal of Information Technology*, *15*, 981–989. https://doi.org/10.1007/s41870-023-01154-5

Shparlinski, I. (2011) Computational Diffie-Hellman problem. In H. C. A. van Tilborg & S. Jajodia (Eds.), *Encyclopedia of cryptography and security*. Boston, MA: Springer. https://doi.org/10.1007/978-1-4419-5906-5_882

Silverman, J. H. (2000). The Xedni Calculus and the elliptic curve discrete logarithm problem. *Designs, Codes and Cryptography*, *20*(1), 5–40.

Stern, J., Pointcheval, D., Malone-Lee, J., & Smart, N. P. (2002). Flaws in applying proof methodologies to signature schemes. In M. Yung (Ed.), *Advances in cryptology – CRYPTO 2002. CRYPTO 2002*. Lecture Notes in Computer Science, 2442. Berlin, Heidelberg: Springer. https://doi.org/10.1007/3-540-45708-9_7

Tanwar, S. (Ed.). (2022). Basics of cryptographic primitives for blockchain development. In *Blockchain technology. Studies in autonomic, data-driven and industrial computing*. Singapore: Springer. https://doi.org/10.1007/978-981-19-1488-1_4

Thakur, N., & Sharma, V. (2023). Enhancing Fintech security-A comparative analysis of advanced security algorithms. *2023 2nd international conference on edge computing and applications (ICECAA)*, Namakkal, India. https://doi.org/10.1109/ICECAA58104.2023.10212129

van Tilborg, H. C. A. (Ed.). (1988). The discrete logarithm problem. In *An introduction to cryptology*. The Kluwer International Series in Engineering and Computer Science, 52. Boston, MA: Springer. https://doi.org/10.1007/978-1-4613-1693-0_8

Vanstone, S. (1992). Responses to NIST's proposal. *Communications of the ACM*, *35*(7), 41–54.

Vaudenay, S. (2003). The security of DSA and ECDSA. In Y. G. Desmedt (Ed.), *Public key cryptography – PKC 2003*. Lecture Notes in Computer Science, 2567. Berlin, Heidelberg: Springer. https://doi.org/10.1007/3-540-36288-6_23

Vaudenay, S. (Ed.). (2006) Digital signature. In *A classical introduction to cryptography*. Boston, MA: Springer. https://doi.org/10.1007/0-387-25880-9_10

Vincent, O. R., Folorunso, O., & Akinde, A. D. (2010). Improving e-payment security using elliptic curve cryptosystem. *Electronic Commerce Research*, *10*, 27–41. https://doi.org/10.1007/s10660-010-9047-z

Xu, H., Thakur, K., Kamruzzaman, A. S., & Ali, M. L. (2021). Applications of cryptography in database: A review. *IEEE international IOT, electronics and mechatronics conference (IEMTRONICS)*, Toronto, ON, Canada. https://doi.org/10.1109/IEMTRONICS52119.2021.9422663

Yan, S. Y. (Ed.). (2013). Quantum attacks on ECDLP-based cryptosystems. In *Quantum attacks on public-key cryptosystems*. Boston, MA: Springer. https://doi.org/10.1007/978-1-4419-7722-9_4

Yan, S. Y. (Ed.). (2019). Elliptic curve cryptography. In *Cybercryptography: applicable cryptography for cyberspace security*. Cham: Springer. https://doi.org/10.1007/978-3-319-72536-9_7

Chapter 4

RSA public key cryptosystem, RSA digital signature algorithm, and integer factorization

4.1 INTRODUCTION

This chapter is devoted to the Rivest, Shamir, Adleman (RSA) public key cryptosystem, RSA digital signature algorithm, and integer factorization. The RSA public key cryptosystem is the first public key cryptosystem, and its security basically depends on the hardness of factoring a large integer number into two prime numbers. In Section 4.2, the RSA public key cryptosystem and RSA digital signature, which were introduced in the same paper, are provided. Regarding the RSA public key cryptosystem, RSA-Chinese Remainder Theorem (CRT), which is proposed to be used to speed up the decryption process, and multi-factor RSA including multi-prime RSA and multi-power RSA as the variations of the RSA public key cryptosystem are also presented in Section 4.2.1. The RSA digital signature algorithm given in Section 4.2.2 is directly analogous to the RSA public key cryptosystem. Regarding the RSA digital signature algorithm, the RSA-CRT digital signature algorithm and blind RSA digital signature are also provided as the variations of the RSA digital signature algorithm. If an attacker can factor the large modulus into two prime numbers, then (s)he can recover the private decryption key and plaintext. However, there are several other possible attacks against the RSA public key cryptosystem and RSA digital signature algorithm. Some of these attacks are explained briefly in Section 4.3, including the attacks due to the low public encryption key, Wiener's attack, Boneh-Durfee attack and May's attack, homomorphic attack, chosen ciphertext attack of Davida and chosen ciphertext attack of Bleichenbacher, and implementation attacks.

Since the basic security issue in RSA is related to factoring the large modulus into two prime numbers, Section 4.4 is devoted to the basic approaches and algorithms for factoring an integer number into two prime numbers. We first consider the basic classification of the approaches as (1) Trial division, (2) Factorization via difference of squares, and (3) Faster algorithms. We first provide the simplest approach "trial division" in Section 4.4.1 very briefly. Afterward, we provide "factorization via difference of squares" in Section 4.4.2, and "three-step factorization procedure" in Section 4.4.3 that is developed based on "factorization via difference of squares". As faster algorithms,

DOI: 10.1201/9781003514190-4

continued fraction factorization algorithm (CFRAC), quadratic sieve (QS), and the number field sieve (NFS) are explained briefly in Section 4.4.4. CFRAC is related to "three-step factorization procedure", while QS is also based on CFRAC. On the other hand, NFS is much faster algorithm which considers polynomials and ring homomorphism. In addition to the basic classification for factoring a large integer number into two prime numbers, there are additional approaches proposed in the literature. The basic steps of Pollard's $p-1$ factorization algorithm, Lenstra's elliptic curve factorization algorithm, and Pollard's ρ (rho) algorithm are explained in Sections 4.4.5, 4.4.6, and 4.4.7, respectively, while the basic idea of the Shor's algorithm is given in Section 4.4.8. The RSA public key cryptosystem, RSA digital signature algorithm, and almost all integer factorization methods presented in this chapter are illustrated with examples to show their practicality.

4.2 RSA PUBLIC KEY CRYPTOSYSTEM AND RSA DIGITAL SIGNATURE ALGORITHM

4.2.1 RSA public key cryptosystem

RSA is the first public key cryptosystem developed by Ron Rivest, Adi Shamir, and Leonard Adleman in 1978, and its security is based on the hardness of integer factoring. After the basic parameters of the RSA public key cryptosystem, Table 4.1 provides the basic steps of the RSA public key cryptosystem.

Basic parameters of the RSA public key cryptosystem (adapted from Hoffstein, Pipher, & Silverman, 2008; Rivest, Shamir, & Adleman, 1978):

p, q: Large prime numbers (chosen by Alice)
N: Large integer number with about 200 digits long satisfying $N = p \cdot q$ (computed by Alice and sent to Bob by Alice)
m: Plaintext satisfying $0 < m \leq N-1$ (chosen by Bob)

Table 4.1 RSA public key cryptosystem

	Alice	*Bob*
Private: p, q Public: N, e	- Chooses p, q. - Computes $N = p \cdot q$. - Chooses e satisfying $\gcd(e, (p-1)\cdot(q-1)) = 1$. - Sends N and e to Bob.	
Encryption Private: m Public: c		- Chooses m. - Computes $c \equiv m^e \pmod N$. - Sends c to Alice.
Decryption Private: d	- Computes d satisfying $d \cdot e \equiv 1 \pmod{(p-1)\cdot(q-1)}$. - Computes $c^d \equiv m \pmod N$.	

Source: Adapted from Hoffstein et al. (2008) and Rivest et al. (1978).

e: Public encryption key (exponent) of Bob
d: Private decryption key (exponent) of Alice
c: Ciphertext

The function $c \equiv m^e \pmod{N}$ is called the "RSA function", where two nominal values for the public encryption key (exponent) are $e = 3$ and $e = 65537$ (Boneh & Shacham, 2002; Rivest & Kaliski, 2011). Note that the "RSA function" has a multiplicative structure, which means that for the same modulus N and the same public encryption key e, it is possible to construct the ciphertext of $m_1 \cdot m_2$ from the ciphertexts of two plaintexts m_1 and m_2; that is, it is easy to generate $(m_1 \cdot m_2)^e \pmod{N} = m_1^e \cdot m_2^e \pmod{N} \equiv c_1 \cdot c_2$, where $c_1 \equiv m_1^e \pmod{N}$ and $c_2 \equiv m_2^e \pmod{N}$.

The RSA public key cryptosystem is based on the hardness of factoring a large integer number N into two prime numbers p and q. If Eve can factor N into the prime numbers p and q, then she can calculate the private decryption key (exponent) d of Alice, and recover the plaintext m.

Note from Table 4.1 that Alice considers the congruence $e \cdot d \equiv 1 \bmod ((p-1)\cdot(q-1))$ to determine the decryption key (exponent) d, where e is public, but d,p,q are private. Since $N = p \cdot q$ is known publicly and since $(p-1)\cdot(q-1) = pq - p - q + 1 = N - (p+q) + 1$ holds, it is actually sufficient for Eve to know only $p+q$ to recover d (Hoffstein et al., 2008).

In the following section, a version of the RSA public cryptosystem, which is RSA-CRT, will be explained.

4.2.1.1 RSA-CRT

Instead of the decryption step given in Table 4.1, we can use the so-called RSA-CRT to speed up the decryption process with the steps given in Equations (4.1)–(4.6) (adapted from Quisquater & Couvreur, 1982):

$$d \equiv d_p \pmod{(p-1)} \tag{4.1}$$

$$d \equiv d_q \pmod{(q-1)} \tag{4.2}$$

$$c^{d_p} \equiv m_p \pmod{p} \tag{4.3}$$

$$c^{d_q} \equiv m_q \pmod{q} \tag{4.4}$$

Finally, by using the CRT, m can be recovered from the solution of the congruences (4.5) and (4.6):

$$m \equiv m_p \pmod{p} \tag{4.5}$$

$$m \equiv m_q \pmod{q} \tag{4.6}$$

Example 4.1

We assume that Alice chooses $p = 347, q = 653$ as two private prime numbers, and Bob chooses $m = 200821$ as the plaintext. Table 4.2 illustrates the basic steps of the RSA public key cryptosystem for this simple example.

Table 4.2 An example for the RSA public key cryptosystem

	Alice	*Bob*
	- Chooses $p = 347, q = 653$. - Computes $N = p \cdot q = 347 \cdot 653 = 226591$. - Chooses e satisfying $\gcd(e, 346 \cdot 652) = \gcd(e, 225592) = 1$ as $e = 213743$. - Sends $N = 226591$ and $e = 213743$ to Bob.	
Encryption		- Chooses $m = 200821$. - Computes $c \equiv 200821^{213743} \equiv 189967 \pmod{226591}$. - Sends $c = 189967$ to Alice.
Decryption	- Computes d satisfying $d \cdot 213743 \equiv 1 \pmod{225592}$ as $d = 103743$. - Computes $189967^{103743} \equiv 200821 = m \pmod{226591}$.	

We can also consider the RSA-CRT for the decryption step in Example 4.1. First we adapt the Equations (4.1)–(4.4) as follows:

$$103743 \equiv 289 \pmod{346}$$
$$103743 \equiv 75 \pmod{652}$$
$$189967^{289} \equiv 255 \pmod{347}$$
$$189967^{75} \equiv 350 \pmod{653}$$

Finally, we obtain the following two linear congruences to find m by adapting Equations (4.5) and (4.6):

$$m \equiv 255 \pmod{347}$$
$$m \equiv 350 \pmod{653}$$

The solution for m can be found by considering the approach given in Section 1.2.4 of Chapter 1. Finally, we recover the plaintext as follows:

$$m = 255 \cdot 110 \cdot 653 + 350 \cdot 446 \cdot 347 \equiv 200821 \pmod{226591}$$

As mentioned previously, the RSA-CRT can be used to speed up the decryption process in RSA; however, it is not the unique approach for speeding up the decryption process in RSA. There are also three variants of the RSA to be used for speeding up the decryption process, which are "batch RSA", "multi-factor RSA", and "rebalanced RSA" (Boneh & Shacham, 2002). In this section, the "multi-factor RSA" will be explained very briefly.

4.2.1.2 Multi-factor RSA

A multi-factor RSA public key cryptosystem can be either "multi-prime RSA" or "multi-power RSA", which will be explained next (Boneh & Shacham, 2002).

4.2.1.2.1 Multi-prime RSA

The "multi-prime RSA" was proposed by Collins, Hopkins, Langford, and Sabin (1997) in a US patent (Boneh & Shacham, 2002). In this section, we will provide the details of the multi-prime RSA in Table 4.3 as presented by Boneh and Shacham (2002).

Basic parameters of the multi-prime RSA (adapted from Boneh & Shacham, 2002)

b: Number of the prime factors, $b > 2$ (chosen by Alice)
$p_1, p_2 \cdots p_b$: Large distinct prime numbers with $\lfloor n / b \rfloor$-bits long, where n is the security parameter (chosen by Alice)
N: Large integer number satisfying $N = p_1 \cdot p_2 \cdot \cdots \cdot p_b$ (computed by Alice and sent to Bob by Alice)

Table 4.3 Multi-prime RSA algorithm

	Alice	*Bob*
Private: $p_1, p_2 \cdots p_b$	- Chooses $p_1, p_2 \cdots p_b$. - Computes $N = p_1 \cdot p_2 \cdot \cdots \cdot p_b$.	
Public: N, e	- Chooses e that satisfies $\gcd\left(e, (p_1 - 1) \cdot (p_2 - 1) \cdot \cdots \cdot (p_b - 1)\right) = 1$. - Sends N and e to Bob.	
Encryption		- Chooses m. - Computes $c \equiv m^e \pmod N$. - Sends c to Alice.
Decryption	- Computes d satisfying $d \cdot e \equiv 1 \bmod \left((p_1 - 1) \cdot (p_2 - 1) \cdot \cdots \cdot (p_b - 1)\right)$. - Determines $d \equiv d_i \left(\bmod\ (p_i - 1)\right) 1 \le i \le b$. - Computes $c^{d_i} \equiv m_i \pmod{p_i}\ 1 \le i \le b$. - Computes $m \equiv m_i \pmod{p_i} 1 \le i \le b$ by using the CRT.	

Source: Adapted from Boneh and Shacham (2002).

m: Plaintext satisfying $0 < m \leq N - 1$ (chosen by Bob)
e: Public encryption key (exponent) of Bob
d: Private decryption key (exponent) of Alice
c: Ciphertext

As clear from Table 4.3, CRT is used during the decryption process in multi-prime RSA as in the RSA-CRT.

4.2.1.2.2 *Multi-power RSA*

In a multi-power RSA, N can be defined as $N = p^{b-1} \cdot q$, where $b \in \mathbb{Z}_{+}$, $b \geq 3$ hold, and p,q are the distinct prime numbers with $\lfloor n / b \rfloor$-bit long, where n is again the security parameter (Boneh & Shacham, 2002; Takagi & Naito, 1999). In a special case of the multi-power RSA, $N = p^2 \cdot q$ can be considered.

4.2.2 RSA digital signature algorithm

The RSA digital signature algorithm has been presented in the same paper in which the RSA public key cryptosystem was introduced. After the basic parameters for the RSA digital signature algorithm, Table 4.4 provides the basic steps of the RSA digital signature algorithm.

Basic parameters for the RSA digital signature algorithm (adapted from Buchmann, 2004; Hoffstein et al., 2008):

p,q: Large prime numbers (chosen by Samantha)
N: Integer number satisfying $N = p \cdot q$ (computed by Samantha and sent to Victor by Samantha)

Table 4.4 RSA digital signature algorithm

	Samantha	*Victor*
Private: p,q	- Chooses p, q.	
Public: N, v	- Computes $N = p \cdot q$.	
	- Chooses v satisfying $\gcd(v,(p-1)\cdot(q-1)) = 1$.	
	- Sends N and v to Victor.	
Signing	- Chooses D.	
Private: s	- Determines s satisfying	
Public: $D, D^{sig} = S$	$s \cdot v \equiv 1 \pmod{(p-1)\cdot(q-1)}$.	
	- Computes $S \equiv D^s \pmod{N}$.	
	- Sends D and $D^{sig} = S$ to Victor.	
Verification		- Computes and verifies $S^v \equiv D \pmod{N}$.

Source: Adapted from Buchmann (2004), Hoffstein et al. (2008), and Rivest et al. (1978).

Table 4.5 Comparison of the RSA public key cryptosystem and RSA digital signature algorithm

RSA public key cryptosystem	*RSA digital signature algorithm*
$\gcd(e, (p-1)\cdot(q-1)) = 1$ e: Public encryption key	$\gcd(v, (p-1)\cdot(q-1)) = 1$ v: Public verification key
$d \cdot e \equiv 1 \bmod ((p-1)\cdot(q-1))$ d: Private decryption key	$s \cdot v \equiv 1 \pmod{(p-1)\cdot(q-1)}$ s: Private signing key
$c \equiv m^e \pmod N$ m: Plaintext, c: Ciphertext	$S \equiv D^s \pmod N$ D: Digital document, S: Digital signature of D
$c^d \equiv m \pmod N$	$S^v \equiv D \pmod N$

D: Digital document of Samantha satisfying $1 < D \le N-1$ (according to Buchmann (2004), $0 \le D \le N-1$)
v: Public verification key (exponent) to be used by Victor satisfying $1 < v < (p-1)\cdot(q-1)$
s: Private signing key (exponent) of Samantha satisfying $1 < s < (p-1)\cdot(q-1)$
$D^{sig} = S$: Digital signature of the digital document D signed by Samantha

As in the other digital signature algorithms presented in Chapter 3, instead of D, the hash function $h(D)$ can also be considered during signing and verification. As in the RSA public key cryptosystem, Eve must find p,q (or simply $p+q$) to recover the private signing key s of Samantha. Very high similarity between the steps of the RSA public key cryptosystem and the RSA digital signature algorithm is evident as provided in Table 4.5.

Example 4.2:

We consider the values $p = 59$, $q = 29$, and $D = 9$ for the RSA digital signature algorithm. Then the steps in Table 4.6 will follow.

Table 4.6 An example for the RSA digital signature algorithm

	Samantha	*Victor*
	- Chooses $p = 59, q = 29$.	
	- Computes $N = 59 \cdot 29 = 1711$.	
	- Chooses $v = 729$ since 729 satisfies $\gcd(729, 58 \cdot 28) = \gcd(729, 1624) = 1$.	
	- Sends $N = 1711$ and $v = 729$ to Victor.	
Signing	- Chooses $D = 9$.	
	- Determines $s = 225$ since $225 \cdot 729 \equiv 1 \pmod{1624}$ is satisfied.	
	- Computes $S \equiv 9^{225} \equiv 1169 \pmod{1711}$.	
	- Sends $D = 9$ and $S = 1169$ to Victor.	
Verification		- Computes and verifies $1169^{729} \equiv 9 = D \pmod{1711}$.

As in the public key cryptosystems and digital signature algorithms provided in Chapter 3, small values are used also in the examples of this chapter for illustration purposes. Actually, the values should be much larger.

ISO 9796 signature standards are a series of standards that specify three digital signature algorithms based on the hardness of integer factoring (ISO, 2024; Tibouchi, 2011). In these standards, $\mu(D)$ is used as the "encoding function" instead of D which helps to avoid the so-called "homomorphic attacks" to be explained in Section 4.3 briefly (Tibouchi, 2011). ISO/IEC 9796-1 is the first international standard, which was initially published in 1991, while ISO/IEC 9796-2:1997 was published in 1997, which was updated by ISO/IEC 9796-2:2002 that was also updated by ISO/IEC 9796-2:2010 as the "last reviewed and confirmed" standard (ISO, 2024; Tibouchi, 2011).

Analogous to the RSA public key cryptosystem, speeding up the signing process can be a concern. Thus, instead of computing $S \equiv D^s \pmod{N}$ as given in Table 4.4, we can use the RSA-CRT digital signature algorithm for signing, which will be provided next.

4.2.2.1 RSA-CRT digital signature algorithm

Note that only the signing step differs in the RSA-CRT digital signature algorithm. Other steps are as provided in Table 4.4. First, we consider the congruences in (4.7) and (4.8) (adapted from Brier, Naccache, Nguyen, & Tibouchi, 2011):

$$S_p \equiv D^{s\ (mod(p-1))} \pmod{p} \tag{4.7}$$

$$S_q \equiv D^{s\ (mod(q-1))} \pmod{q} \tag{4.8}$$

Then, by using the CRT, the digital signature S can be computed from the congruences (4.9) and (4.10) (adapted from Brier et al., 2011):

$$S \equiv S_p \pmod{p} \tag{4.9}$$

$$S \equiv S_q \pmod{q} \tag{4.10}$$

In congruences (4.7) and (4.8), instead of D, the encoded digital document $\mu(D)$ can also be used to increase security.

Blind RSA digital signature algorithm is another variation of the RSA digital signature algorithm, which will be explained next.

4.2.2.2 Blind RSA digital signature algorithm

The blind signatures were generally introduced by David Chaum in 1982 (Chaum, 1983). The basic idea of the blind signatures is that the "sender" (Alice) sends a blinded version D' of the original digital document D to the "signer" (Samantha), the "signer" signs the document D' as S' without

Table 4.7 Blind RSA digital signature algorithm

	Alice (Sender)	*Samantha (Signer)*
Private: p, q, D, r	- Chooses v and sends v to Samantha.	- Chooses p, q.
Public: N, v	- Chooses D. - Chooses (randomly) r.	- Computes $N = p \cdot q$. - Sends N to Alice.
Blinding D as D'	- Computes $D' \equiv D \cdot r^v \pmod N$.	
Public: D'	- Sends D' to Samantha.	
Signing D' Private: s Public: S'		- Chooses s satisfying $s \cdot v \equiv 1 \left(\bmod\ (p-1)\cdot(q-1)\right)$. - Computes $S' \equiv (D')^s \equiv D^s \cdot r \pmod N$. - Sends S' to Alice.
Obtaining the digital signature for D Private: S	- Computes $S' \cdot r^{-1} \equiv D^s = S \pmod N$.	

Source: Adapted from Hoffstein et al. (2014).

knowing D, and finally the "sender" can obtain the digital signature of the original document D as S through S' although the "sender" does not possess the private signing key of the "signer" (Atallah, 1999; Carminati, 2018; Chaum, 1983). Two examples of blinded signatures are the RSA blind digital signature algorithm and blind DSA (Carminati, 2018). The basic parameters for the blind RSA digital signature algorithm will be given, and the basic steps of the algorithm will be provided in Table 4.7.

Basic parameters for the blind RSA digital signature algorithm (adapted from Carminati, 2018; Hoffstein, Pipher, & Silverman, 2014):

p,q: Large prime numbers (chosen by Samantha)
N: Integer number satisfying $N = p \cdot q$ (computed by Samantha and sent to Alice by Samantha)
r: Integer ephemeral key satisfying $1 \le r \le N-1$, $\gcd(N,r)=1$ (chosen by Alice)
s: Private signing key (exponent) of Samantha satisfying $1 < s < (p-1)(q-1)$
v: Public key for blinding the document and computing the private signing key (chosen by Alice and sent to Samantha by Alice)
D: Original digital document of Alice satisfying $1 < D \le N-1$
D': Blinded digital document (blinded by Alice)
S: Digital signature of the original digital document D (obtained by Alice)
S': Digital signature of the blinded digital document D' (signed by Samantha)

Note that the digital document D and the digital signature S of D are private for Alice, whereas the prime numbers p,q, and the signing key s are private for Samantha. Please note also that in Table 4.7, “obtaining the signature for D” is also called the “signature unblinding step” (Carminati, 2018).

4.3 CRYPTANALYSIS OF RSA PUBLIC KEY CRYPTOSYSTEM AND RSA DIGITAL SIGNATURE ALGORITHM

We first provide the definitions of the “RSA problem”, “RSA assumption”, and “strong RSA assumption”, which are the basic concepts regarding the security of the RSA public key cryptosystem.

Definition 4.1 (RSA problem)

Recall from Section 4.2.1 that the function $c \equiv m^e \pmod N$ is called the “RSA function”. The “RSA problem” is a problem in which the adversary recovers m from the “RSA function” (adapted from Rivest & Kaliski, 2011).

Definition 4.2 (RSA assumption)

According to the “RSA assumption”, the “RSA problem” provided in Definition 4.1 is hard to solve when N is a sufficiently large random number, and the plaintext m (and the ciphertext c) is a random integer between 0 and $N-1$ (adapted from Rivest & Kaliski, 2011).

Definition 4.3 (Strong RSA assumption)

It is infeasible to find any pair (m,e) that satisfies $c = m^e \pmod N$, if the factorization of the integer N into two prime numbers is not accomplished (adapted from Rivest & Kaliski, 2011).

There are several attacks and cryptanalysis approaches proposed for the RSA public key cryptosystem. In this section, some selected approaches will be provided very briefly.

4.3.1 Attacks related to factoring the modulus *N*

This is the basic attack against the RSA public key cryptosystem. In case of the efficient factoring algorithms, some of which will be provided very basically in Section 4.4, the modulus N can be factored into two prime numbers and the private decryption key can be recovered (Boneh, 1999; Dubey, Ratan, Verma, & Saxena, 2014; Jordan & Liu, 2018).

4.3.2 Attacks due to the low public encryption key

Recall from Section 4.2.1 that two nominal values for the public encryption key are $e = 3$ and $e = 65537$. If e is small (such as $e = 3$) and m is very short, then m can be recovered from the RSA function $c \equiv m^e \pmod N$ easily (Boneh, 1999; Coppersmith, Franklin, Patarin, & Reiter, 1996; Dubey et al., 2014; Rivest & Kaliski, 2011).

4.3.3 Wiener's attack, Boneh-Durfee attack, and May's attack

"Wiener's attack" is a very well-known attack against the RSA public key cryptosystem based on the "continued fractions method" to factor N when d is relatively small compared to N, where $d < \sqrt[4]{N}/3$ and $q < p < 2q$ hold (Boneh, 1999; Dubey et al., 2014; Wiener, 1990). The "continued fractions method" is used to find the numerator and denominator of a fraction if a close estimate of the fraction is assumed to be known (Wiener, 1990). One countermeasure proposed by Wiener (1990) is to use a public encryption key e that is much larger than the modulus N (Durfee, 2011). The "Boneh-Durfee attack" proposed for the RSA public key cryptosystem presented in Boneh and Durfee (2000) is a lattice-based attack to recover the private decryption key d from the modulus N and public encryption key e if $d < N^{0.292}$ holds. May (2002) proposed also lattice-based attacks for the RSA-CRT in case of small d_p, d_q values and unbalanced prime numbers p and q, where p is much larger than q. In their lattice-based attacks, both Boneh and Durfee (2000) and May (2002) used Coppersmith's technique presented in Coppersmith (1997) for the solution of modular polynomials with two variables. Coppersmith (1997) developed a technique to find "sufficiently small integer" solutions to a polynomial with a single variable modulo N, also to a polynomial with two variables modulo N that can be extended to multiple variables, and as an illustration applied his technique to the RSA public key cryptosystem to show that RSA is vulnerable in case of low public key exponent if there is partial information of the plaintext. For the details of the attacks, please see Boneh and Durfee (2000), Coppersmith (1997), May (2002), and Wiener (1990).

4.3.4 Homomorphic attack

Recall the "multiplicative structure" of the "RSA function" from Section 4.2.1. The homomorphic attack is based on the "multiplicative structure" of the RSA function. It is assumed that the adversary knows $c_1 \equiv m_1^e \pmod{N}$ and $c_2 \equiv m_2^e \pmod{N}$. Then the adversary can construct $c = c_1 \cdot c_2 \equiv m_1^e \cdot m_2^e \pmod{N} = (m_1 \cdot m_2)^e \pmod{N} = m^e \pmod{N}$ for the message $m = m_1 \cdot m_2$ very easily due to the "multiplicative structure" of the "RSA function" (Dubey et al., 2014).

4.3.5 Chosen ciphertext attack of Davida and chosen ciphertext attack of Bleichenbacher

Davida also exploited the "multiplicative structure" of the RSA and considered a "chosen ciphertext attack" with the steps as follows (adapted from Davida, 1982; Desmedt & Odlyzko, 1986; Rivest & Kaliski, 2011):

- The adversary considers $c \equiv m^e \pmod{N}$, where (s)he is assumed to know c, e, N. The basic objective of the adversary is to recover the plaintext m.
- (S)he chooses a random integer r.

- (S)he computes $c' \equiv c \cdot r^e \pmod{N}$
- (S)he considers $(c')^d \equiv c^d \cdot r \equiv m \cdot r \pmod{N}$
- (S)he requests a signer with the private signing key d to sign c', since it is assumed that there is a signer who has the same private signing key as the private decryption key d.
- (S)he recovers m from $(c')^d \equiv c^d \cdot r \equiv m \cdot r \pmod{N}$ since $(c')^d, r, N$ are already known by the adversary.

Bleichenbacher (1998) proposed also the "chosen ciphertext attack" against the RSA public key cryptosystem and believed that the basic RSA public key cryptosystem is susceptible to the "chosen ciphertext attack"; thus, he recommended to "pad" a message with random bits. For the details of Bleichenbacher's attack, please see Bleichenbacher (1998).

4.3.6 Implementation attacks

Recall the "implementation attacks" from Section 2.12.1 of Chapter 2. The "implementation attacks" are also applicable for the RSA public key cryptosystem. Specifically, the RSA public key cryptosystem can be vulnerable to the "timing attacks", "power analysis attacks", particularly "differential power analysis attacks", and "fault attacks" (Boneh, 1999; Dubey et al., 2014).

The attacks against the RSA public key cryptosystems are not limited to the abovementioned attacks. Some other attacks against the RSA public key cryptosystem are "Hastad's broadcasting attack", "Franklin-Reiter's related-message attack", "cyclic attack", "short pad attack", "common modulus attack", and "partial key exposure attack", whose details can be found in various references including Boneh, Durfee, and Frankel (1998), Boneh (1999), Coppersmith et al. (1996), Dubey et al. (2014), and Yan (2008). For more details about the cryptanalysis of the RSA and its variants, the interested reader is strongly recommended to read the book by Hinek (2009).

The recent literature regarding the cryptanalysis of the RSA public key cryptosystem is also very rich. We present here just three examples from the literature. Santosh Kumar, Prakash, and Krishna (2024) showed that even if the private decryption key is sufficiently large, the RSA public key cryptosystem can still be vulnerable to attacks if the private decryption key has a special structure. Alquié, Chassé, and Nitaj (2022) proposed the cryptanalysis of the multi-power RSA cryptosystem variant with the modulus $N = p^r \cdot q^s$ satisfying $\gcd(r,s) = 1$ by using the Coppersmith's method and lattice reduction techniques. Cherkaoui-Semmouni, Nitaj, Susilo, and Tonien (2021) considered four variants of the RSA public key cryptosystem with the modulus $N = p \cdot q$ and with the special form $e \cdot d - k \cdot (p^2 - 1) \cdot (q^2 - 1) = 1$ and showed that if e and d share the most significant bits, then the equation $e \cdot d - k \cdot (p^2 - 1) \cdot (q^2 - 1) = 1$ can be solved for larger values of d. Please see the respective references for details.

Note that since the RSA public key cryptosystem and RSA digital signature algorithm are very similar as provided in Table 4.5, some attacks proposed for the RSA public key cryptosystem including "attacks related to factoring the modulus N", "homomorphic attack", and "fault attacks" can also be applied against the RSA digital signature algorithm (Coron, Joux, Kizhvatov, Naccache, & Paillier, 2009; de Jonge & Chaum, 1986; Seifert, 2005). Additional attacks including "attacks on the right-padded redundancy" and "attacks on the left-padded redundancy" have also been proposed in the literature for forging the RSA digital signature of a digital document (de Jonge & Chaum, 1986). Krämer, Nedospasov, and Seifert (2012) also showed that the RSA blind digital signature algorithm in case of the RSA-CRT is vulnerable against the side-channel attacks, specifically "simple power analysis attacks".

4.4 BASIC APPROACHES AND ALGORITHMS FOR FACTORING AN INTEGER NUMBER INTO TWO PRIME NUMBERS

The security of the RSA public key cryptosystem and RSA digital signature algorithm is fundamentally based on the hardness of factoring the large modulus into two prime numbers. Some approaches and algorithms have been proposed in the literature for the factorization of an integer number into two prime numbers. These approaches can be classified into (1) Trial division, (2) Factorization via difference of squares, and (3) Faster algorithms. Faster algorithms include the CFRAC, QS, and NFS (Landquist, 2001).

4.4.1 Trial division

Let N be the integer number to be factored. The trial division is the process of checking all the prime numbers $p \le B$ whether they divide N or not, and finding the smallest prime number which divides N. The value B is recommended to be less than 10^6 (Lenstra, 2011).

4.4.2 Factorization via difference of squares

One of the oldest methods for factoring an integer number into two prime numbers is "factorization via difference of squares" method proposed by Fermat. Let N be the integer number to be factored. Then it can be written as $N + b^2 = a^2$ from which $N = a^2 - b^2 = (a+b)(a-b)$ holds for $a, b \in \mathbb{Z}$ satisfying $a \ne \pm b$ (Hoffstein et al., 2008).

Example 4.3

The factorization of $N = 319$ into two prime numbers can be "via difference of squares" by using the "trial-and-error method" with the steps given in Table 4.8.

Table 4.8 An example for the factorization via difference of squares

Factorization of $N = 319$	
$319 + 1^2 = 320$	$\sqrt{320}$: Not integer
$319 + 2^2 = 323$	$\sqrt{323}$: Not integer
$319 + 3^2 = 328$	$\sqrt{328}$: Not integer
$319 + 4^2 = 335$	$\sqrt{335}$: Not integer
$319 + 5^2 = 344$	$\sqrt{344}$: Not integer
$319 + 6^2 = 355$	$\sqrt{355}$: Not integer
$319 + 7^2 = 368$	$\sqrt{368}$: Not integer
$319 + 8^2 = 383$	$\sqrt{383}$: Not integer
$319 + 9^2 = 400$	$\sqrt{400} = 20$ Integer
$319 + 9^2 = 400$	
$319 + 9^2 = 20^2$	
$319 = 20^2 - 9^2 = (20+9)(20-9) = 29 \cdot 11$	

An alternative approach for the basic "factorization via difference of squares" is to write $kN + b^2 = a^2$ from which $kN = a^2 - b^2 = (a+b)(a-b)$ holds for $a,b \in \mathbb{Z}$ satisfying $a \neq \pm b$, and $k \in \mathbb{Z}_+$ (Hoffstein et al., 2008). Hopefully, $\gcd(N, a+b)$ and $\gcd(N, a-b)$ are two nontrivial prime factors of N. Please note that a nontrivial factor is a factor other than 1 or N.

Example 4.4

Let $N = 253$ be the integer number to be factored. We assume that $k = 3$ is chosen. Then after some trials, it can be found that $3 \cdot 253 + 5^2 = 28^2$ holds. Then we consider $3 \cdot 253 = 28^2 - 5^2 = (28+5)(28-5) = 33 \cdot 23$. Finally, $\gcd(253, 33) = 11$ and $\gcd(253, 23) = 23$ are two prime factors of 253.

4.4.3 Three-step factorization procedure

Note that $kN = a^2 - b^2$ is equivalent to $a^2 \equiv b^2 \pmod N$ for $a \not\equiv \pm b \pmod N$, where a and b should actually be found by using a systematic procedure instead of the "trial-and-error method" as applied in Example 4.4. The three-step factorization procedure with the steps given in Table 4.9 is a basic factorization procedure to find a and b efficiently (Hoffstein et al., 2008).

Example 4.4 (revisited 1)

We reconsider the factorization of $N = 253$ by using the "three-step factorization procedure".

Table 4.9 Three-step factorization procedure

	Three-step factorization procedure
Step 1	- We choose randomly many integers a_i, $i = 1, 2, \ldots, r$. - We compute $b_i \equiv a_i^2 \pmod{N}$, $i = 1, 2, \ldots, r$. - We choose b_i values that have small prime factors. Let B^* be the set of the selected b_i values that have small prime factors.
Step 2	- We choose $b_{i_1}, b_{i_2}, \ldots, b_{i_s}$ in B^* that satisfy $b_{i_1} \cdot b_{i_2} \cdot \cdots \cdot b_{i_s} \equiv b^2 \pmod{N}$. - We compute $a \equiv a_{i_1} \cdot a_{i_2} \cdot \ldots \cdot a_{i_s} \pmod{N}$. - We obtain $a^2 \equiv b^2 \pmod{N}$.
Step 3	$\gcd(N, a-b)$ and $\gcd(N, a+b)$ are two nontrivial prime factors of N with high probability.

Source: Adapted from Hoffstein et al. (2008).

Step 1: We choose randomly the integer numbers 8, 10, 12, 13, 25, 32, 44, 48, 84. Next, we calculate

$$b_1 \equiv 8^2 \equiv 64 = 2^6 \pmod{253}$$

$$b_2 \equiv 10^2 \equiv 100 = 2^2 \cdot 5^2 \pmod{253}$$

$$b_3 \equiv 12^2 \equiv 144 = 2^4 \cdot 3^2 \pmod{253}$$

$$b_4 \equiv 13^2 \pmod{253}$$

$$b_5 \equiv 25^2 \equiv 119 = 7 \cdot 17 \pmod{253}$$

$$b_6 \equiv 32^2 \equiv 12 = 2^2 \cdot 3 \pmod{253}$$

$$b_7 \equiv 44^2 \equiv 165 = 3 \cdot 5 \cdot 11 \pmod{253}$$

$$b_8 \equiv 48^2 \equiv 27 = 3^3 \pmod{253}$$

$$b_9 \equiv 84^2 \equiv 225 = 3^2 \cdot 5^2 \pmod{253}$$

We only consider b_1, b_2, b_3, b_6, b_8, b_9 since they have small prime factors, thus $B^* = \{b_1, b_2, b_3, b_6, b_8, b_9\}$ will be obtained.

Step 2: When we consider all the elements in B^*, we see that the multiplication gives a perfect square modulo 253, that is

$b_1 \cdot b_2 \cdot b_3 \cdot b_6 \cdot b_8 \cdot b_9 = 2^6 \cdot 2^2 \cdot 5^2 \cdot 2^4 \cdot 3^2 \cdot 2^2 \cdot 3 \cdot 3^3 \cdot 3^2 \cdot 5^2 \equiv \left(2^7 \cdot 3^4 \cdot 5^2\right)^2 \equiv 128^2 = b^2 \pmod{253}$

The multiplication of the corresponding a_i values modulo 253 will be $a = 8 \cdot 10 \cdot 12 \cdot 32 \cdot 48 \cdot 84 = 123863040 \equiv 59 \pmod{253}$.

Finally $59^2 \equiv 128^2 \pmod{253}$ holds.

Step 3: As a result, $\gcd(253, 59-128) = \gcd(253, -69) = 23$ and $\gcd(253, 59+128) = \gcd(253, 187) = 11$ are again two prime factors of 253.

4.4.4 Continued fraction factorization algorithm (CFRAC), quadratic sieve (QS), and the number field sieve (NFS)

According to Kaliski (2011), sieving refers to "a process for selecting candidates for further processing among a set of candidates, typically by employing arithmetic progressions to identify candidates to be filtered out". The QS and the NFS are two faster algorithms based on sieving used for factoring an integer number into two prime numbers. Since the QS has been developed based on the CFRAC, in this section, the CFRAC will be explained first very briefly.

4.4.4.1 *CFRAC*

Recall again that in the method of "factorization via difference of squares", $N = a^2 - b^2$ and $kN = a^2 - b^2$ are equivalent to $a^2 \equiv b^2 \pmod{N}$, where $a \not\equiv \pm b \pmod{N}$. Recall also the steps of the "three-step factorization procedure" given in Table 4.9. According to Table 4.9, we need to find a list of numbers b_i, compute $b_i \equiv a_i^2 \pmod{N}, i = 1, 2, \ldots, r$, and choose b_i values that have small prime factors more systematically, which can be accomplished by using the CFRAC. The basic steps of the CFRAC are provided as follows by considering the notations in Wagstaff and Smith (1987):

Basic step 1: Let $\{Q_n\}$ and $\{A_n\}$ be two sequences that can be found by using the recursion formulae given in Wagstaff and Smith (1987) that satisfy $A_{n-1}^2 \equiv (-1)^n Q_n \pmod{N}, 0 < Q_n < 2\sqrt{N}$, where N is the integer number to be factored.

Basic step 2: Let S be the set of the selected values of Q_n and A_n from the sequences $\{Q_n\}$ and $\{A_n\}$ such that $\Pi_{n \in S} A_n = a$ and $\Pi_{n \in S} (-1)^n Q_n = b^2$ hold, where the factoring of Q_n can be made by using the "trial division". (For details of the systematic trial division algorithm, please see Wagstaff and Smith (1987).)

Finally, as in the "three-step factorization procedure" given in Section 4.4.3, $a^2 \equiv b^2 \pmod{N}$ holds, and $\gcd(N, a-b)$ and $\gcd(N, a+b)$ are two nontrivial prime factors of N with high probability.

4.4.4.2 *Quadratic sieve (QS)*

The QS is based on the CFRAC, but the factoring of $\{Q_n\}$ is made by "sieving" not by the "trial division" as in the CFRAC. In this section, instead of Q_n given in the CFRAC, we will use $Q(X)$ to consider different polynomials that can be used for the QS. Two basic polynomials as given in (4.11) and (4.12) have been proposed (Wagstaff & Smith, 1987):

$$X^2 \equiv Q(X) \pmod{N} \tag{4.11}$$

$$(X \le \sqrt{N})^2 \equiv Q(X) \pmod{N}, \text{where} Q(X) < 2\sqrt{N}|X| + X^2 \tag{4.12}$$

Crandall and Pomerance (2001) defined also the general case for the polynomial $Q(X)$ as follows:

Table 4.10 Quadratic sieve

	Basic steps of quadratic sieve method for factorization
Step 1	- We select a positive number B.
	- We determine the factor base as $FB = \{p_i\text{: } i\text{th prime number} \mid p_i \le B\}$, where $p_1 = 2$.
Step 2: Sieving process	- We choose an appropriate positive value M for the sieve array over the interval $X \in [-M, M]$.
	- We choose the polynomial $Q(X)$.
	- We find the values of $Q(X) - N$ for all X.
	- We do the following steps for each $p_i \in FB$ one by one:
	- We solve $Q(X) \equiv N \pmod{p_i}$ for $p_i \in FB$.
	- We find (at most) two solutions of $Q(X) \equiv N \pmod{p_i}$ as $\alpha_{p_i}, \beta_{p_i}$, where $\beta_{p_i} = p_i - \alpha_{p_i}$. (If there is no solution, then we discard this p_i value.)
	- We divide the following array of values by $p_i \in FB$:
	$Q(\alpha_{p_i}) - N, Q(\alpha_{p_i} \pm p_i) - N, Q(\alpha_{p_i} \pm 2p_i) - N, \ldots$
	$Q(\beta_{p_i}) - N, Q(\beta_{p_i} \pm p_i) - N, Q(\beta_{p_i} \pm 2p_i) - N, \ldots$
Step 3	- We determine which $Q(X) - N$ values are sieved away to 1.
Step 4	- We consider those X values, for which $Q(X) - N$ values are sieved away to 1, which satisfy $\prod Q(X) = Y^2$ as a (perfect) square.
	- Finally, $\gcd(N, X - Y)$ is hopefully a nontrivial factor of N.

Source: Adapted from Buchmann (2004), Hoffstein et al. (2008), Kechlibar (2005), Silverman (1987), and Wagstaff and Smith (1987).

Let $Q(X) = aX^2 + 2bX + c$ be defined, where a, b, c are integers, a is square, $0 \le b < a$, and $b^2 \equiv N \pmod{a}$ holds with $b^2 - ac = N$.

Then $aQ(X) = (aX)^2 + 2abX + ac = (aX + b)^2 - N$ holds and consequently $(aX + b)^2 \equiv aQ(X) \pmod{N}$ is the general case for the polynomial.

Please note that for $a = 1, b = 0$, we obtain (4.11), and for $a = 1, b = \lfloor \sqrt{N} \rfloor$, we obtain (4.12).

The basic steps of the QS are provided in Table 4.10.

According to Hoffstein et al. (2008), $[0, M]$ or even $[M_1, M_2]$ for positive values M_1, M_2 can be considered in Step 2 so that $Q(X) - N$ will be non-negative. We can also consider the prime powers of $p_i \in FB$ in Step 2 (Hoffstein et al., 2008; Landquist, 2001). If the first trial does not work in Step 4, we should try for another set of X values that satisfy $\prod Q(X) = Y^2$ until $\gcd(N, X - Y)$ is hopefully a nontrivial factor of N.

Example 4.4 (revisited 2)

We reconsider the factorization of $N = 253$ by using the QS method.

Step 1: We consider $B = 10$, thus $FB = \{2, 3, 5, 7\}$ will be the factor base.

Table 4.11 The values of X and $X^2 - 253$ for Example 4.4 (revisited 2)

X	$X^2 - 253$
17	36
18	71
19	108
20	147
21	188
22	231
23	276
24	323
25	372
26	423
27	476
28	531
29	588
30	647
31	708
32	771
33	836
34	903
35	972

Step 2: We consider the sieve array over the interval $X \in [17, 35]$ and the polynomial in (4.11). Please note that the reason for starting with the value 17 is that we would like to start with a non-negative $X^2 - 253$ value. The values of X and $X^2 - 253$ by considering $X \in [17, 35]$ are given in Table 4.11.

We start with $p_1 = 2$ from FB and find $X^2 \equiv 253 \equiv 1 \pmod{2}$. There is only one solution for this congruence, which is $\alpha_{p_1} = 1$. Then we would divide $X^2 - 253$ values corresponding to $X = 1, 3, 5, 7, 9,\ldots,17, 19, 21,\ldots,35$ by 2. However, since we start with $X = 17$ as given in Table 4.11, we only divide $X^2 - 253$ values corresponding to $X = 17, 19, 21,\ldots,35$ as provided in Table 4.12.

Next we consider $p_2 = 3$ from FB and find also $X^2 = 253 \equiv 1 \pmod{3}$. There are two solutions for this congruence, which are $\alpha_{p_2} = 1, \beta_{p_2} = 2$. Then we would divide the updated $X^2 - 253$ values in Table 4.12 corresponding to $X = 1, 4, 7, \ldots,16, 19, 22,\ldots,34$ and also corresponding to $X = 2, 5, 8, \ldots,17, 20, 23,\ldots,35$ by 3. However, since we start with $X = 17$ as given in Tables 4.11 and 4.12, we only divide $X^2 - 253$ values corresponding to $X = 19, 22, 25, 28, 31, 34$ and $X = 17, 20, 23, 26, 29, 32, 35$ by 3 as provided in Table 4.13.

Table 4.12 Update of Table 4.11 by considering the division by $p_1 = 2$

X	$X^2 - 253$	*Results after the division by* $p_1 = 2$
17	36 →	18
18	71	71
19	108 →	54
20	147	147
21	188 →	94
22	231	231
23	276 →	138
24	323	323
25	372 →	186
26	423	423
27	476 →	238
28	531	531
29	588 →	294
30	647	647
31	708 →	354
32	771	771
33	836 →	418
34	903	903
35	972 →	486

Next we consider $p_3 = 5$ from *FB* and find $X^2 = 253 \equiv 3 \pmod{5}$. However, there is no solution for this congruence, thus we discard $p_3 = 5$.

As provided before, we can also consider the prime powers of $p_i \in FB$ in Step 2; thus, we consider $2^2 = 4$ and find $X^2 = 253 \equiv 1 \pmod{4}$. There are two solutions for this congruence, which are 1 and 3. Then we would divide the updated $X^2 - 253$ values in Table 4.13 corresponding to $X = 1, 5, 9, \ldots, 25, 29, 33$ and also corresponding to $X = 3, 7, 11, \ldots, 27, 31, 35$. However, since we start with $X = 17$ as given in Tables 4.11–4.13, we only divide $X^2 - 253$ values corresponding to $X = 17, 21, 25, 29, 33$ and $X = 19, 23, 27, 31, 35$ by 4 as provided in Table 4.14. Note that since the $X^2 - 253$ values corresponding to $X = 17, 21, 25, 29, 33$ and $X = 19, 23, 27, 31, 35$ were divided by 2 before (please see Table 4.12), the respective $X^2 - 253$ values in the fourth column of Table 4.14 (the entries with arrows) are only divided by 2.

Next, we consider $p_4 = 7$ from *FB* and find $X^2 = 253 \equiv 1 \pmod{7}$. There are two solutions for this congruence, which are $\alpha_{p4} = 1$, $\beta_{p4} = 6$. Then we would divide the updated $X^2 - 253$ values in Table 4.14 corresponding to $X = 1, 8, 15, 22, 29$ and also corresponding to $X = 6, 13, 20, 27, 34$ by 7. However, since we start with $X = 17$ as given in Tables 4.11–4.14, we only divide $X^2 - 253$ values corresponding to $X = 22, 29$ and $X = 20, 27, 34$ by 7 as provided in Table 4.15.

Table 4.13 Update of Table 4.12 by considering the division by $p_2 = 3$

X	$X^2 - 253$	*Results after the division by $p_1 = 2$*	*Results after the division by $p_2 = 3$*
17	36	18 →	6
18	71	71	71
19	108	54 →	18
20	147	147 →	49
21	188	94	94
22	231	231 →	77
23	276	138 →	46
24	323	323	323
25	372	186 →	62
26	423	423 →	141
27	476	238	238
28	531	531 →	177
29	588	294 →	98
30	647	647	647
31	708	354 →	118
32	771	771 →	257
33	836	418	418
34	903	903 →	301
35	972	486 →	162

We can also consider $3^2 = 9$ and find $X^2 = 253 \equiv 1 \pmod{9}$. There are two solutions for this congruence, which are 1 and 8. Then we would divide the updated $X^2 - 253$ values in Table 4.15 corresponding to $X = 1, 10, 19, 28, 37$ and also corresponding to $X = 8, 17, 26, 35$. However, since we start with $X = 17$ and end with $X = 35$ as given in Tables 4.11–4.15, we only divide $X^2 - 253$ values corresponding to $X = 19, 28$ and $X = 17, 26, 35$ by 9 as provided in Table 4.16.

In this example, given $FB = \{2, 3, 5, 7\}$ from Step 1, there is only one X value, which is 17, for which $X^2 - 253$ is sieved away to 1, as clear from Table 4.16. We can write $17^2 \equiv 2^2 \cdot 3^2 = (2 \cdot 3)^2 \pmod{253}$ and calculate $\gcd(253, 17 - 2 \cdot 3) = \gcd(253, 11) = 11$, which is a nontrivial factor of 253. As a result, 253 can be factored as $253 = 11 \cdot 23$ as in Example 4.4 and Example 4.4 (revisited 1).

4.4.4.3 Number field sieve (NFS)

NFS has been first proposed by Pollard. There are two forms of NFS: (1) General NFS, where N is a general integer to be factored. (2) Special NFS, where N has an especially simple form to be factored (Kruppa & Leyland,

Table 4.14 Update of Table 4.13 by considering the division by 4

X	$X^2 - 253$	*Results after the division by $p_1 = 2$*	*Results after the division by $p_2 = 3$*	*Results after the division by 4*
17	36	18	6→	3
18	71	71	71	71
19	108	54	18→	9
20	147	147	49	49
21	188	94	94→	47
22	231	231	77	77
23	276	138	46→	23
24	323	323	323	323
25	372	186	62→	31
26	423	423	141	141
27	476	238	238→	119
28	531	531	177	177
29	588	294	98→	49
30	647	647	647	647
31	708	354	118→	59
32	771	771	257	257
33	836	418	418→	209
34	903	903	301	301
35	972	486	162→	81

2011). As in the previous methods, the basic objective is to find a structure $X^2 \equiv Y^2 \pmod{N}$ such that $\gcd(N, X-Y)$ will be hopefully a nontrivial factor of N. The general NFS is based on the idea of the "ring homomorphism" from a ring of algebraic integers to a ring of integers modulo N. We consider the following parameters for the general NFS and provide the basic steps in Table 4.17 (adapted from Briggs, 1998; Buhler, Lenstra, & Pomerance, 1993; Pomerance, 1994):

$\mathbb{Z}[\alpha]$: Ring of algebraic integers, where an algebraic integer is a complex number that is a root of a monic polynomial with integer coefficients
$f(t)$: Monic irreducible polynomial over $\mathbb{Z}[\alpha]$
S: A set of polynomials of $g(t)$ over $\mathbb{Z}[\alpha]$

Note that $(\varphi(\beta))^2 \equiv \varphi(\beta^2)$ holds in Step 4 of Table 4.17 due to ring homomorphism. For the details of the NFS, see references regarding the NFS including Buhler et al. (1993) and Pomerance (1994).

In addition to the classification given at the beginning of Section 4.4 for factoring a large integer number into two prime numbers, there are additional approaches proposed in the literature which will be provided next.

Table 4.15 Update of Table 4.14 by considering the division by $p_4 = 7$

X	$X^2 - 253$	*Results after the division by* $p_1 = 2$	*Results after the division by* $p_2 = 3$	*Results after the division by* **4**	*Results after the division by* $p_4 = 7$
17	36	18	6	3	3
18	71	71	71	71	71
19	108	54	18	9	9
20	147	147	49	49 →	7
21	188	94	94	47	47
22	231	231	77	77 →	11
23	276	138	46	23	23
24	323	323	323	323	323
25	372	186	62	31	31
26	423	423	141	141	141
27	476	238	238	119 →	17
28	531	531	177	177	177
29	588	294	98	49 →	7
30	647	647	647	647	647
31	708	354	118	59	59
32	771	771	257	257	257
33	836	418	418	209	209
34	903	903	301	301 →	43
35	972	486	162	81	81

4.4.5 Pollard's $p-1$ factorization algorithm

Let N be the integer number to be factored as $N = p \cdot q$. The Pollard's $p-1$ factorization algorithm is a factorization algorithm which is based on three assumptions and an observation of Pollard (adapted from Hoffstein et al., 2008; Koblitz, 1994; Pollard, 1974; Yan, 2002).

Assumption 1

$(p-1)$ is assumed to have (many) small prime factors.

Assumption 2

It is assumed that there is a value $l \in \mathbb{Z}$ which is divided by $p-1$, but not divided by $q-1$, that is, for a value $k \in \mathbb{Z}$, $l = k(p-1)$ holds, but for all $k \in \mathbb{Z}, l \neq k(q-1)$ holds.

Assumption 3

Since $l = k(p-1)$ holds for a value $k \in \mathbb{Z}$, but $l \neq k(q-1)$ holds for all $k \in \mathbb{Z}$ from Assumption 2, $a^l \equiv 1 \pmod{p}$ and $a^l \not\equiv 1 \pmod{q}$ will hold for all $a \in \mathbb{Z}$ due to the "Fermat's little theorem", and it can be assumed that $p = \gcd(a^l - 1, N)$.

Table 4.16 Update of Table 4.15 by considering the division by 9

X	X^2-253	*Results after the division by* $p_1=2$	*Results after the division by* $p_2=3$	*Results after the division by 4*	*Results after the division by* $p_4=7$	*Results after the division by 9*
17	36	18	6	3	3→	1
18	71	71	71	71	71	71
19	108	54	18	9	9→	3
20	147	147	49	49	7	7
21	188	94	94	47	47	47
22	231	231	77	77	11	11
23	276	138	46	23	23	23
24	323	323	323	323	323	323
25	372	186	62	31	31	31
26	423	423	141	141	141→	47
27	476	238	238	119	17	17
28	531	531	177	177	177→	59
29	588	294	98	49	7	7
30	647	647	647	647	647	647
31	708	354	118	59	59	59
32	771	771	257	257	257	257
33	836	418	418	209	209	209
34	903	903	301	301	43	43
35	972	486	162	81	81→	27

Table 4.17 The basic steps of NFS

	Basic steps of NFS method for factorization
Step 1	If $f(\alpha)\equiv 0$ for $\alpha\in\mathbb{C}$ in $\mathbb{Z}[\alpha]$ and $f(m)\equiv 0\ (\text{mod } N)$ for $m\in\mathbb{Z}$ hold, then $\varphi:\mathbb{Z}[\alpha]\to\mathbb{Z}/N\mathbb{Z}$ is a ring homomorphism; that is, there is a mapping $\varphi(\alpha)\equiv m(\text{mod } N)$ or $\varphi(g(\alpha))\equiv g(m)(\text{mod } N)$ hold.
Step 2	We assume that the perfect squares $\beta^2=\Pi_{g\in S}g(\alpha)$ in $\mathbb{Z}[\alpha]$ and $Y^2=\Pi_{g\in S}\,g(m)\ (\text{mod } N)$ in $\mathbb{Z}/N\mathbb{Z}$ exist.
Step 3	We assume also that there exists X satisfying $\varphi(\beta)\equiv X\ (\text{mod } N)$.
Step 4	$X^2\equiv(\varphi(\beta))^2\equiv\varphi(\beta^2)\equiv\varphi(\Pi_{g\in S}\,g(\alpha))\equiv\Pi_{g\in S}\,g(m)\equiv Y^2(\text{mod } N)$ holds by connecting Step 2 and Step 3.
Step 5	Finally, $\gcd(N, X-Y)$ is hopefully a nontrivial factor of N.

Source: Adapted from Buhler et al. (1993) and Pomerance (1994).

Pollard's observation and the final result: Please recall that, according to Assumption 2, $p-1$ is assumed to divide l. Then $p-1$ can also divide $n!$, where n is an integer number that is not too large. As a result, we can replace $p = \gcd\left(a^l - 1, N\right)$ from Assumption 3 with $p = \gcd\left(a^{n!} - 1, N\right)$, $2 \le a \le N-1$.

Note that the first trial can be made with $a = 2$. If it does not work, it can be continued with $a = 3, 4, 5, \ldots$ We can also try for different n values until we find a nontrivial factor of N. Note also that in Assumption 1, p can be replaced with q; that is, it is sufficient that $(p-1)$ or $(q-1)$ has (many) small prime factors. For a practical Pollard's $p-1$ factorization algorithm, see Hoffstein et al. (2008) and Yan (2002).

Example 4.4 (revisited 3)

We reconsider the factorization of $N = 253$ by using the Pollard's $p-1$ factorization algorithm.

Trial 1: We choose $a = 2$ and start with $n = 2$. Then $p = \gcd\left(2^{2!} - 1, 253\right) = \gcd(3, 253) = 1$. Trial 1 did not work, so we can proceed with Trial 2.

Trial 2: Let $a = 2$, $n = 3$ be chosen. Then $p = \gcd\left(2^{3!} - 1, 253\right) = \gcd(63, 253) = 1$. Trial 2 did not work either, so we can proceed with Trial 3.

Trial 3: Let $a = 3$, $n = 2$ be chosen. Then $p = \gcd\left(3^{2!} - 1, 253\right) = \gcd(8, 253) = 1$. Trial 3 did not work either, so we can proceed with Trial 4.

Trial 4: Let $a = 4, n = 2$ be chosen. Then $p = \gcd\left(4^{2!} - 1, 253\right) = \gcd(15, 253) = 1$. Trial 4 did not work either.

After several trials, we find for $a = 10$ and $n = 2$, $p = \gcd\left(10^{2!} - 1, 253\right) = \gcd(99, 253) = 11$. Indeed, 253 can be factored as $253 = 11 \cdot 23$ as in the previous approaches. Note that the Pollard's $p-1$ factorization algorithm worked for the factorization of $N = 253$ since $p - 1 = 10$ can be factored as $10 = 2 \cdot 5$ with small prime numbers.

Example 4.5

We want to factor $N = 763$ by using the Pollard's $p-1$ factorization algorithm.

Trial 1: We choose $a = 2$ and start with $n = 2$. Then $p = \gcd\left(2^{2!} - 1, 763\right) = \gcd(3, 763) = 1$. Trial 1 did not work, so we can proceed with Trial 2.

Trial 2: Let $a = 2, n = 3$ be chosen. Then $p = \gcd\left(2^{3!} - 1, 763\right) = \gcd(63, 763) = 7$.

We found one of the factors of 763, which is $p = 7$. The other factor should be $763/7 = 109$. As a result, 763 can be factored as $763 = 7 \cdot 109$. Please note that the Pollard's $p-1$ factorization algorithm worked also for the factorization of $N = 763$, since $q - 1 = 108$ can be factored as $108 = 2^2 \cdot 3^3$ with small prime numbers.

4.4.6 Lenstra's elliptic curve factorization algorithm

The Lenstra's elliptic curve factorization algorithm has been inspired by the "Pollard's $p-1$ factorization algorithm" (Hoffstein et al., 2008; Lenstra, 1987). An elliptic curve modulo N, where the integer N is not a prime number, is considered in this algorithm so the ring $\mathbb{Z}/N\mathbb{Z}$ is not a field. Then, it is possible to factor the integer number N by using the Lenstra's elliptic curve factorization algorithm with the steps given in Table 4.18.

According to Koblitz (1994), any other method can also be applied to generate the elliptic curve deterministically or randomly in Steps 1 and 2 of Table 4.18. An alternative approach for Step 3 has also been proposed by Koblitz (1994) (see details in Koblitz (1994)).

Example 4.4 (revisited 4)

We reconsider the factorization of $N = 253$ by using the Lenstra's elliptic curve factorization algorithm.

Step 1: We choose the random values $a = 2, x_P = 3, y_P = 4$ modulo $N = 253$.
Step 2: We set $P = (3, 4)$. We compute $b \equiv 4^2 - 3^3 - 2 \cdot 3 = -17 \pmod{253}$ and check that $4 \cdot 2^3 + 27 \cdot (-17)^2 = 7835 \neq 0$, $\gcd(7835, 253) = 1$

Table 4.18 Lenstra's elliptic curve factorization algorithm

	Lenstra's elliptic curve factorization algorithm to factor N
Step 1	- We choose the random values a, x_P, y_P modulo N.
Step 2	- We set $P = (x_P, y_P)$. - We compute $b \equiv y_P^2 - x_P^3 - a \cdot x_P \pmod{N}$, where $4a^3 + 27b^2 \neq 0$ and $\gcd(4a^3 + 27b^2, N) = 1$ should be satisfied. Otherwise, we choose other random values for a, x_P, y_P. - We determine the elliptic curve $E: y^2 = x^3 + ax + b \pmod{N}$ by using a and b.
Step 3	We attempt to compute $Q_j \equiv jP \pmod{N}$, $j = 2, 3, 4, \ldots$ by using the elliptic curve addition algorithm, where we assume incremental additions as follows: Let $Q_1 = P$. Then $Q_2 = 2P = P + P = P + Q_1 \pmod{N}$ $Q_3 = 3P = P + 2P = P + Q_2 \pmod{N}$ ... $Q_j = jP = P + (j-1)P = P + Q_{j-1} \pmod{N}$
Step 4	If the computation in Step 3 fails for any $j = 2, 3, 4, \ldots$, that is, if the extended Euclidean algorithm fails to find the inverse during any addition, then there exists a nontrivial factor p of N if it is less than N. More specifically, let Q_{j^*} be the computation from Step 3 for which $Q_{j^*} = j^*P = P + Q_{j-1^*} \pmod{N}$ is not possible, where $P = (x_P, y_P)$, $Q_{j-1^*} = \left(x_{Q_{j-1^*}}, y_{Q_{j-1^*}}\right)$. Then, $p = \gcd\left(x_P - x_{Q_{j-1^*}}, N\right)$ is a nontrivial factor of N, if $p < N$.

Source: Adapted from Hoffstein et al. (2008), Koblitz (1994), and Lenstra (1987).

hold. Thus, we can determine the elliptic curve $E: y^2 = x^3 + 2x - 17 \pmod{253}$.

Step 3: We start with $Q_2 = 2P = P + P = (3, 4) + (3, 4) = (19, 191) \pmod{253}$ by applying the "elliptic curve addition algorithm" provided in Section 1.7.3 of Chapter 1. Other results are also given as follows:

$$Q_3 = 3P = P + 2P = (3, 4) + (19, 191) = (165, 95) \pmod{253}$$

$$Q_4 = 4P = P + 3P = (3, 4) + (165, 95) = (86, 79) \pmod{253}$$

$$Q_5 = 5P = P + 4P = (3, 4) + (86, 79) = (213, 44) \pmod{253}$$

$$Q_6 = 6P = P + 5P = (3, 4) + (213, 44) = (64, 141) \pmod{253}$$

$$Q_7 = 7P = P + 6P = (3, 4) + (64, 141) = (11, 202) \pmod{253}$$

$$Q_8 = 8P = P + 7P = (3, 4) + (11, 202) = (140, 84) \pmod{253}$$

$$Q_9 = 9P = P + 8P = (3, 4) + (140, 84) = (47, 227) \pmod{253}$$

Step 4: Although the calculations given in Step 3 could be made, the calculation $Q_{10} = 10P = P + 9P = (3, 4) + (47, 227)$ cannot be accomplished since in the calculation of $\lambda = \frac{227-4}{47-3} = \frac{223}{44} \pmod{253}$, there is no result for $44^{-1} \pmod{253}$, that is, 44 has no multiplicative inverse modulo 253. Thus $p = \gcd(47 - 3, 253) = \gcd(44, 253) = 11$ can be found, where 11 is a nontrivial factor of 253. As a result, 253 can be factored as $253 = 11 \cdot 23$ as in the previous approaches.

4.4.7 Pollard's ρ (rho) algorithm

There are two main approaches for the Pollard's ρ (rho) algorithm in the literature.

Approach 1 (Based on true random number generator)

We assume that we pick some distinct random numbers $x_1, x_2, \ldots, x_\ell$ uniformly distributed in $[0, N-1]$, where $\ell \approx \sqrt{p}$ is assumed. We also assume for $1 \le i < j \le \ell$ there exists $x_i \equiv x_j \pmod{p}$. Then $p \mid (x_i - x_j)$ holds and $p = \gcd(x_i - x_j, N)$ is a nontrivial factor of N (adapted from Goemans, 2015).

Approach 2 (Based on pseudo-random number generator)

The steps in Table 4.19 are considered for the Pollard's ρ (rho) algorithm based on pseudo random number generator.

An example for the function $f : S \to S$ to be used in Step 1 of Table 4.19 is $f(x_i) \equiv x_i^2 \pm a \pmod{N}$ for $a \ne -2, 0$. Note that the congruences in Step 1 of Table 4.19 will finally cycle since S is a finite set. Note also that $x_j \equiv x_k \pmod{p}$, $x_j \not\equiv x_k \pmod{N}$ will be satisfied in Step 3.

Table 4.19 Pollard's ρ (rho) algorithm

	Pollard's ρ (rho) algorithm
Step 1	We consider a sequence of congruences $x_{i+1} = f(x_i) \pmod N$ for $i = 0, 1, 2, \ldots$, where $f: S \rightarrow S$, S is a finite set of cardinality N, and $x_0 \in S$ is a starting random element.
Step 2	From Step 2, we find two values x_j and x_k such that $f(x_j) \equiv f(x_k) \pmod N$ holds.
Step 3	As a result, $p = \gcd(x_j - x_k, N)$ is hopefully a nontrivial factor of N.

Source: Adapted from Menezes, van Oorschot, and Vanstone (1996) and Yan (2009).

Example 4.4 (revisited 5)

We reconsider the factorization of $N = 253$ by using the Pollard's ρ (rho) algorithm. We consider the approach based on pseudo-random number generator and assume $x_{i+1} = f(x_i) \equiv x_i^2 + 1 \pmod{253}$. $x_0 = 97$ is assumed as a random starting value. Accordingly, we perform the following calculations:

$$x_1 \equiv x_0^2 + 1 = 97^2 + 1 = 9410 \equiv 49 \pmod{253}$$

$$x_2 \equiv x_1^2 + 1 = 49^2 + 1 = 2402 \equiv 125 \pmod{253}$$

$$x_3 \equiv x_2^2 + 1 = 125^2 + 1 = 15626 \equiv \mathbf{193} \pmod{253}$$

$$x_4 \equiv x_3^2 + 1 = 193^2 + 1 = 37250 \equiv 59 \pmod{253}$$

$$x_5 \equiv x_4^2 + 1 = 59^2 + 1 = 3482 \equiv \mathbf{193} \pmod{253}$$

Since $x_3 = f(x_2) = x_5 = f(x_4) \equiv 193 \pmod{253}$, we calculate $\gcd(x_2 - x_4, N) = \gcd(125 - 59, 253) = \gcd(66, 253) = 11$ as a nontrivial factor of 253. As a result, 253 can be factored as $253 = 11 \cdot 23$ as in the previous approaches.

4.4.8 Shor's algorithm

Shor's algorithm, which was proposed by a mathematician named Peter Shor in 1994, has been a breakthrough in the history of cryptography since it is a polynomial-time quantum algorithm for factoring the integer numbers (LaPierre, 2021). In the following, we provide merely the basic idea of the Shor's algorithm (adapted from Yan, 2015):

N : Integer to be factored
$G = \mathbb{Z}_N^*$ (Finite multiplicative group)
$x \in G$: Randomly chosen integer satisfying $\gcd(x, N) = 1$, $2 \le x \le N - 2$
Order-finding problem: The smallest integer r satisfying $x^r \equiv 1 \pmod N$, $r = ?$ (Please note that the order-finding problem is normally intractable, but it is tractable on quantum computers.)
Nontrivial factors of N: $p = \gcd(x^{r/2} + 1, N)$ and $q = \gcd(x^{r/2} - 1, N)$

The whole steps of Shor's algorithm are provided in various sources including Neuenschwander (2004), Pittenger (2001), and Yan (2015).

4.5 CONCLUSIONS

This chapter included the RSA public key cryptosystem, which is the first public key cryptosystem, RSA digital signature algorithm, basic cryptanalysis approaches, and the basic approaches and algorithms for factoring an integer number into two prime numbers. As in Chapter 3, simple examples were given for showing the practicality of the steps. Some selected variations of the RSA public key cryptosystem and RSA digital signature algorithm were also provided in this chapter. The security of both RSA public key cryptosystem and RSA digital signature algorithm depends basically on factoring the large modulus into two large prime numbers; thus, the last section was devoted to integer factoring and some examples were solved in this section some of which were revisited multiple times for the comparison of the methods. However, the security of RSA is not limited to integer factoring, several attacks have been proposed in the literature against RSA; thus, one section of the chapter was devoted to the selected attacks against RSA. Like the DLP- and ECDLP-based public key cryptosystems, the RSA public key cryptosystem and RSA digital signature algorithm are used in various real-life cryptographic applications including e-commerce security, wireless sensor networks, virtual private networks, secure sockets layer (SSL) and transport layer security (TLS), and databases (please see Chang, Lin, Sun, & Wu, 2012; Easttom, 2021; Li & Ying, 2012; Li, Wu, Zhou, & Chen, 2008; Martin, 2012; Singh, Kumar, & Kumar, 2015; Xu, Thakur, Kamruzzaman, & Ali, 2021).

REFERENCES

Alquié, D., Chassé, G., & Nitaj, A. (2022). Cryptanalysis of the multi-power RSA cryptosystem variant. In A. R. Beresford, A. Patra, & E. Bellini (Eds.), *Cryptology and network security. CANS 2022*. Lecture Notes in Computer Science, 13641. Cham: Springer. https://doi.org/10.1007/978-3-031-20974-1_12

Atallah, M. J. (1999). *Algorithms and theory of computation handbook*. New York: CRC Press.

Bleichenbacher, D. (1998). Chosen ciphertext attacks against protocols based on the RSA encryption standard PKCS #1. In H. Krawczyk (Ed.), *Advances in cryptology – CRYPTO '98*. Lecture Notes in Computer Science, 1462. Berlin, Heidelberg: Springer. https://doi.org/10.1007/BFb0055716

Boneh, D. (1999). Twenty years of attacks on the RSA cryptosystem. *Notices of the AMC*, *46*, 203–213.

Boneh, D., & Durfee, G. (2000). Cryptanalysis of RSA with private key less than. *IEEE Transactions on Information Theory*, *46*(4), 1339–1349.

Boneh, D., Durfee, G., & Frankel, Y. (1998). An attack on RSA given a small fraction of the private key bits. In K. Ohta, D. Pei (Eds.), *Advances in cryptology - ASIACRYPT'98*. Lecture Notes in Computer Science, 1514. Berlin, Heidelberg: Springer. https://doi.org/10.1007/3-540-49649-1_3

Boneh, D., & Shacham, H. (2002). *Fast variants of RSA*. https://hovav.net/ucsd/dist/survey.pdf

Brier, É, Naccache, D., Nguyen, P. Q., & Tibouchi, M. (2011). Modulus fault attacks against RSA-CRT signatures. In B. Preneel, T. Takagi (Eds.), *Cryptographic hardware and embedded systems – CHES 2011*. Lecture Notes in Computer Science, 6917. Berlin, Heidelberg: Springer. https://doi.org/10.1007/978-3-642-23951-9_13

Briggs, M. E. (1998). *An introduction to the general number field sieve*. Thesis submitted to the Faculty of the Virginia Polytechnic Institute and State University in partial fulfillment of the requirements for the degree of master of science in mathematics. https://personal.math.vt.edu/brown/doc/briggs_gnfs_thesis.pdf

Buchmann, J. A. (2004). *Introduction to cryptography*. New York, NY: Springer. https://doi.org/10.1007/978-1-4419-9003-7_9)

Buhler, J. P., Lenstra, H. W., & Pomerance, C. (1993). Factoring integers with the number field sieve. In A. K. Lenstra, H. W. Lenstra (Eds.), *The development of the number field sieve*. Lecture Notes in Mathematics, 1554. Berlin, Heidelberg: Springer. https://doi.org/10.1007/BFb0091539

Carminati, B. (2018). Blind signatures. In L. Liu, M. T. Özsu (Eds.), *Encyclopedia of database systems*. New York, NY: Springer. https://doi.org/10.1007/978-1-4614-8265-9_1488

Chang, S. Y., Lin, Y. H., Sun, H. M., & Wu, M. E. (2012). Practical RSA signature scheme based on periodical rekeying for wireless sensor networks. *ACM Transactions on Sensor Networks*, *8*(2), 1–13.

Chaum, D. (1983). Blind signatures for untraceable payments. In D. Chaum, R. L. Rivest, & A. T. Sherman (Eds.), *Advances in cryptology*. Boston, MA: Springer. https://doi.org/10.1007/978-1-4757-0602-4_18

Cherkaoui-Semmouni, M., Nitaj, A., Susilo, W., & Tonien, J. (2021). Cryptanalysis of RSA variants with primes sharing most significant bits. In J. K. Liu, S. Katsikas, W. Meng, W. Susilo, & R. Intan (Eds.), *Information security. ISC 2021*. Lecture Notes in Computer Science, 13118. Cham: Springer. https://doi.org/10.1007/978-3-030-91356-4_3

Collins, T., Hopkins, D., Langford, S., & Sabin, M. (1997). *Public key cryptographic apparatus and method*. US Patent US5848159A. https://patents.google.com/patent/US5848159A/en

Coppersmith, D. (1997). Small solutions to polynomial equations, and low exponent RSA vulnerabilities. *Journal of Cryptology*, *10*, 233–260. https://doi.org/10.1007/s001459900030

Coppersmith, D., Franklin, M., Patarin, J., & Reiter, M. (1996). Low-exponent RSA with related messages. In U. Maurer (Eds.), *Advances in cryptology – EUROCRYPT '96*. Lecture Notes in Computer Science, 1070. Berlin, Heidelberg: Springer. https://doi.org/10.1007/3-540-68339-9_1

Coron, J. S., Joux, A., Kizhvatov, I., Naccache, D., & Paillier, P. (2009). Fault attacks on RSA signatures with partially unknown messages. In C. Clavier, K. Gaj (Eds.), *Cryptographic hardware and embedded systems – CHES 2009*. Lecture Notes in Computer Science, 5747. Berlin, Heidelberg: Springer. https://doi.org/10.1007/978-3-642-04138-9_31

Crandall, R., & Pomerance, C. B. (Eds.). (2001). Subexponential factoring algorithms. In*Prime numbers: A computational perspective*. New York, NY: Springer. https://doi.org/10.1007/978-1-4684-9316-0_6

Davida, D. (1982). Chosen signature cryptanalysis of the RSA (MIT) public key cryptosystem. *Technical Report TR-CS-82-2*. Department of Electrical Engineering and Computer Science, University of Wisconsin, Milwaukee, Wisconsin.

de Jonge, W., & Chaum, D. (1986). Attacks on some RSA signatures. In H. C. Williams (Ed.), *Advances in cryptology – CRYPTO '85 proceedings*. Lecture Notes in Computer Science, 218. Berlin, Heidelberg: Springer. https://doi.org/10.1007/3-540-39799-X_3

Desmedt, Y., & Odlyzko, A. M. (1986). A chosen text attack on the RSA cryptosystem and some discrete logarithm schemes. In H. C. Williams (Ed.), *Advances in cryptology – CRYPTO '85 proceedings*. Lecture Notes in Computer Science, 218. Berlin, Heidelberg: Springer. https://doi.org/10.1007/3-540-39799-X_40

Dubey, M. K., Ratan, R., Verma, N., & Saxena, P. K. (2014) Cryptanalytic attacks and countermeasures on RSA. In M. Pant, K. Deep, A. Nagar, & J. Bansal (Eds.), *Proceedings of the third international conference on soft computing for problem solving. Advances in intelligent systems and computing*, 258. New Delhi: Springer. https://doi.org/10.1007/978-81-322-1771-8_70

Durfee, G. (2011). Wiener, Boneh–Durfee, and May attacks on the RSA public key cryptosystem. In H. C. A. van Tilborg, S. Jajodia (Eds.), *Encyclopedia of cryptography and security*. Boston, MA: Springer. https://doi.org/10.1007/978-1-4419-5906-5_260

Easttom, W. (Ed.). (2021). Virtual private networks, authentication, and wireless security. In *Modern cryptography*. Cham: Springer. https://doi.org/10.1007/978-3-030-63115-4_14

Goemans, M. (2015). *Factoring. 18.310 Lecture notes*. http://math.mit.edu/~goemans/18310S15/factoring-notes.pdf

Hinek, M. J. (2009). *Cryptanalysis of RSA and its variants*. Boca Raton, London, New York: Chapman & Hall/CRC Press.

Hoffstein, J., Pipher, J., & Silverman, J. H. (2008). *An introduction to mathematical cryptography*. New York, NY: Springer Science + Business Media, LLC.

Hoffstein, J., Pipher, J., & Silverman, J. H. (2014). *An introduction to mathematical cryptography*. New York, NY: Springer Science + Business Media, LLC.

ISO. (2024). *ISO/IEC 9796-2:2010. Information technology - Security techniques – Digital signature schemes giving message recovery. Part 2: Integer factorization based mechanisms*. https://www.iso.org/standard/54788.html

Jordan, S. P., & Liu, Y. (2018). Quantum cryptanalysis: Shor, grover, and beyond. *IEEE Security & Privacy*, *16*(5), 14–21. https://doi.org/10.1109/MSP.2018.3761719

Kaliski, B. (2011). Sieving. In H. C. A. van Tilborg, S. Jajodia (Eds.), *Encyclopedia of cryptography and security*. Boston, MA: Springer. https://doi.org/978-1-4419-5906-5_435

Kechlibar, M. (2005). *The quadratic sieve. Introduction to theory with regard to implementation issues*. Ph.D. Thesis. https://www.karlin.mff.cuni.cz/~krypto/Implementace_MPQS_SIQS_files/main_file.pdf.

Koblitz, N. (Eds.). (1994). Elliptic curves. In *A course in number theory and cryptography*. Graduate Texts in Mathematics, 114. New York, NY: Springer. https://doi.org/10.1007/978-1-4419-8592-7_6

Krämer, J., Nedospasov, D., & Seifert, J. P. (2012). Weaknesses in current RSA signature schemes. In H. Kim (Ed.), *Information security and cryptology – ICISC 2011*. Lecture Notes in Computer Science, 7259. Berlin, Heidelberg: Springer. https://doi.org/10.1007/978-3-642-31912-9_11

Kruppa, A., & Leyland, P. (2011). Number field sieve for factoring. In H. C. A. van Tilborg & S. Jajodia (Eds.), *Encyclopedia of cryptography and security*. Boston, MA: Springer. https://doi.org/10.1007/978-1-4419-5906-5_465

Landquist, E. (2001). *The quadratic sieve factoring algorithm. MATH 488: Cryptographic algorithms*. https://www.cs.virginia.edu/crab/QFS_Simple.pdf

LaPierre, R. (2021). Shor algorithm. *Introduction to quantum computing*. The Materials Research Society Series. Cham: Springer. https://doi.org/10.1007/978-3-030-69318-3_13

Lenstra, A. K. (2011). Integer factoring. In H. C. A. van Tilborg & S. Jajodia (Eds.), *Encyclopedia of cryptography and security*. Boston, MA: Springer. https://doi.org/10.1007/978-1-4419-5906-5_455

Lenstra, H. W. Jr (1987). Factoring integers with elliptic curves. *Annals of Mathematics*, *126*, 649–673.

Li, S., Wu, Y.-D., Zhou, J. Y., & Chen, K.-F. (2008). A practical SSL server performance improvement algorithm based on batch RSA decryption. *Journal of Shanghai Jiaotong University (Science)*, *13*(1), 67–70. https://doi.org/10.1007/s12204-008-0067-y

Li, Z., & Ying, S. (2012). The application of information encrypted in e-commerce security. In D. Jin & S. Lin (Eds.), *Advances in electronic engineering, communication and management*, 1. Lecture Notes in Electrical Engineering, 139. Berlin, Heidelberg: Springer. https://doi.org/10.1007/978-3-642-27287-5_79

Martin, K. M. (2012). *Everyday cryptography: Fundamental principles and applications*. New York, NY: Oxford Academic.

May, A. (2002). Cryptanalysis of unbalanced RSA with small CRT-exponent. In M. Yung (Ed.), *Advances in cryptology – CRYPTO 2002*. Lecture Notes in Computer Science, 2442. Berlin, Heidelberg: Springer. https://doi.org/10.1007/3-540-45708-9_16

Menezes, A., van Oorschot, P., & Vanstone, S. (1996). *Handbook of applied cryptography*. Boca Raton, London, New York: CRC Press.

Neuenschwander, D. (Ed.). (2004). Factorization with quantum computers: Shor's algorithm. In *Probabilistic and statistical methods in cryptology*. Lecture Notes in Computer Science, 3028. Berlin, Heidelberg: Springer. https://doi.org/10.1007/978-3-540-25942-8_4

Pittenger, A. O. (Ed.). (2001). Quantum algorithms. In *An introduction to quantum computing algorithms. Progress in computer science and applied logic*, 19. Boston, MA: Birkhäuser. https://doi.org/10.1007/978-1-4612-1390-1_3

Pollard, J. M. (1974). Theorems on factorization and primality testing. *Mathematical Proceedings of the Cambridge Philosophical Society*, 76, 521–528.

Pomerance, C. (1994). The number field sieve. *Proceedings of symposia in applied mathematics*, 48

Quisquater, J. J., & Couvreur, C. (1982). Fast decipherment algorithm for RSA public-key cryptosystem. *Electronics Letters*, *18*(21), 905–907.

Rivest, R. L., & Kaliski, B. (2011). RSA problem. In H. C. A. van Tilborg & S. Jajodia (Eds.), *Encyclopedia of cryptography and security*. Boston, MA: Springer. https://doi.org/10.1007/978-1-4419-5906-5_475

Rivest, R. L., Shamir, A., & Adleman, L. M. (1978). A method for obtaining digital signature and public-key cryptosystems. *Communications of the ACM*, *21*(2), 120–126.

Santosh Kumar, R., Prakash, K. L. N. C., & Krishna, S. R. M. (2024). Cryptanalysis of RSA with composed decryption exponent with few most significant bits of one of the primes. *Journal of Computer Virology and Hacking Techniques*, *20*, 195–202. https://doi.org/10.1007/s11416-023-00508-8

Seifert, J.-P. (2005). On authenticated computing and RSA-based authentication. *Proceedings of the 12th ACM conference on computer and communications security*, 122–127. https://doi.org/10.1145/1102120.1102138

Silverman, R. D. (1987). The multiple polynomial quadratic sieve. *Mathematics of Computation*, *48*(177), 329–339.

Singh, J., Kumar, V., & Kumar, R. (2015). An RSA based certificateless signature scheme for wireless sensor networks. 2015 International conference on green computing and internet of things (ICGCIoT), Greater Noida, India. https://doi.org/10.1109/ICGCIoT.2015.7380504

Takagi, T., & Naito, S. (1999). *Scheme for fast realization of encryption, decryption and authentication*. US Patent US6396926B1. https://patents.google.com/patent/US6396926

Tibouchi, M. (2011). ISO-9796 signature standards. In H. C. A. van Tilborg & S. Jajodia (Eds.), *Encyclopedia of cryptography and security*. Boston, MA: Springer. https://doi.org/10.1007/978-1-4419-5906-5_512

Wagstaff, S. S., & Smith, J. W. (1987). Methods of factoring large integers. In D. V. Chudnovsky, G. V. Chudnovsky, H. Cohn, & M. B. Nathanson (Eds.), *Number theory*. Lecture Notes in Mathematics, 1240. Berlin, Heidelberg: Springer. https://doi.org/10.1007/BFb0072986

Wiener, M. (1990). Cryptanalysis of short RSA secret exponents. *IEEE Transactions on Information Theory*, *36*, 553–558.

Xu, H., Thakur, K., Kamruzzaman, A. S., & Ali, M. L. (2021). Applications of cryptography in database: A review. IEEE international IOT, electronics and mechatronics conference (IEMTRONICS), Toronto, ON, Canada. https://doi.org/10.1109/IEMTRONICS52119.2021.9422663

Yan, S. Y. (Ed.). (2002). Computational/algorithmic number theory. In *Number theory for computing*. Berlin, Heidelberg: Springer. https://doi.org/10.1007/978-3-662-04773-6_2

Yan, S. Y. (Ed.). (2008). Public exponent attacks. In Cryptanalytic attacks on RSA. Boston, MA: Springer. https://doi.org/10.1007/978-0-387-48742-7_7

Yan, S. Y. (Ed.). (2009). Integer factorization and discrete logarithms. In *Primality testing and integer factorization in public-key cryptography*. Advances in Information Security, 11. Boston, MA: Springer. https://doi.org/10.1007/978-0-387-77268-4_3

Yan, S. Y. (Ed.). (2015). Quantum algorithms for integer factorization. In *Quantum computational number theory*. Cham: Springer. https://doi.org/10.1007/978-3-319-25823-2_3

Chapter 5

Goldreich, Goldwasser, Halevi (GGH) public key cryptosystem, GGH digital signature algorithm, NTRU public key cryptosystem, and NTRU signature scheme

5.1 INTRODUCTION

This chapter is related to the Goldreich, Goldwasser, Halevi (GGH) public key cryptosystem, GGH digital signature algorithm, NTRUEncrypt, and NSS. The GGH public key cryptosystem given in Section 5.2.1 is an example of a lattice-based cryptography in which the "good basis" corresponds to the private decryption key, whereas the "bad basis" corresponds to the public encryption key. In a "good basis" the basis vectors are reasonably orthogonal to one another, while in a "bad basis" the basis vectors are not sufficiently orthogonal to one another. Like in the ElGamal public key cryptosystem provided in Chapter 3, the ephemeral key is used in the GGH public key cryptosystem; thus, GGH is also an example of probabilistic encryption. The decryption process of the GGH public key cryptosystem is based on the solution of apprCVP by using the Babai's closest vertex (round-off) algorithm provided in Chapter 1, Section 1.8.2.2.

The basic idea of the GGH public key cryptosystem has been adapted to the GGH digital signature algorithm, which is provided in Section 5.2.2. In the GGH digital signature algorithm, the "good basis" is used during signing as the private signing key, while the "bad basis" is considered during verification as the public verification key. Both the GGH public key cryptosystem and GGH digital signature algorithm are illustrated with examples. The basic cryptanalysis approaches for the GGH public key cryptosystem and GGH digital signature algorithm are provided in Section 5.2.3. Some basic flaws regarding the GGH public key cryptosystem are presented in this section, while the literature regarding some improvement suggestions and discussions of the improvement suggestions are also mentioned. The basic findings of a paper regarding the vulnerability of the GGH public key cryptosystem in case of the partial information of the plaintext and one approach for estimating the good basis used as the private signing key in the GGH digital signature algorithm are also explained briefly in this section.

The NTRU public key cryptosystem is based on either convolution polynomial rings or lattice problems, and we present the NTRU public key cryptosystem based on convolution polynomial rings in Section 5.3.1. An example is also given to show the steps of the NTRU public key cryptosystem clearly.

DOI: 10.1201/9781003514190-5

There are three types of the NTRU digital signature scheme, which are NTRU signature scheme (NSS), R-NSS, and NTRUSign, and we provide the NSS in Section 5.3.2. We also illustrate the applicability of the NSS with an example in this section. Section 5.3.3 is about the cryptanalysis of the NTRU public key cryptosystem and NTRU digital signature algorithm. In this section, the "NTRU key recovery problem" is defined, which is a basic mathematical problem to break the NTRU public key cryptosystem. Some selected approaches for the cryptanalysis of the NTRU public key cryptosystem and NSS are also discussed in this section.

5.2 GGH PUBLIC KEY CRYPTOSYSTEM, GGH DIGITAL SIGNATURE ALGORITHM, AND CRYPTANALYSIS

5.2.1 GGH public key cryptosystem

The GGH public key cryptosystem is a lattice analog of the so-called McEliece cryptosystem, which is a code-based public key cryptosystem introduced in 1978 in which the public key is a random binary Goppa code, and the ciphertext is a codeword randomized with random errors (Micciancio & Regev, 2009; Overbeck & Sendrier, 2009). The GGH public key cryptosystem is based on the idea of using a "good basis" as the private decryption key and using a "bad basis" of a lattice as the public encryption key. A "good basis" of a lattice means that the vectors in the basis are reasonably orthogonal to one another, while in a "bad basis" of the same lattice the basis vectors are not reasonably orthogonal to one another (Goldreich, Goldwasser, & Halevi, 1997). We give the basic parameters of the GGH public key cryptosystem in the following and provide the basic steps of the GGH public key cryptosystem in Table 5.1.

Basic parameters of the GGH public key cryptosystem (adapted from Hoffstein, Pipher, & Silverman, 2008):

$\mathbf{v}_1, \mathbf{v}_2, \ldots, \mathbf{v}_n \in \mathbb{Z}^n$: Linearly independent vectors that are reasonably orthogonal to one another (chosen by Alice)
V: An $n \times n$ matrix with the columns $\mathbf{v}_1, \mathbf{v}_2, \ldots, \mathbf{v}_n \in \mathbb{Z}^n$ (good basis to be used as the private decryption key by Alice)
L: Lattice generated by the basis vectors $\mathbf{v}_1, \mathbf{v}_2, \ldots, \mathbf{v}_n \in \mathbb{Z}^n$
U: An $n \times n$ unimodular matrix (a square integer matrix with determinant +1 or −1) (chosen by Alice)
$\mathbf{w}_1, \mathbf{w}_2, \ldots, \mathbf{w}_n \in \mathbb{Z}^n$: Linearly independent vectors of L that are not reasonably orthogonal to one another
W: An $n \times n$ matrix with the columns $\mathbf{w}_1, \mathbf{w}_2, \ldots, \mathbf{w}_n \in \mathbb{Z}^n$ (generated by Alice, bad basis to be used as the public encryption key by Bob)
$\mathbf{m}$: Plaintext as an n-dimensional vector (Binary vector is also possible.) (chosen by Bob)
$\mathbf{r}$: Ephemeral key as an n-dimensional vector (chosen by Bob)
$\mathbf{c}$: Ciphertext as an n-dimensional vector

Table 5.1 GGH public key cryptosystem

	Alice	*Bob*
Private: V, U	- Chooses $\mathbf{v}_1, \mathbf{v}_2, \ldots, \mathbf{v}_n$.	
Public: W	- Determines V.	
	- Generates the lattice L.	
	- Chooses U.	
	- Computes $W = VU$.	
	- Sends W to Bob.	
Encryption		- Chooses $\mathbf{m}$.
Private: $\mathbf{m}, \mathbf{r}$		- Chooses $\mathbf{r}$.
Public: $\mathbf{c}$		- Computes $\mathbf{c} = W\mathbf{m} + \mathbf{r}$.
		- Sends $\mathbf{c}$ to Alice.
Decryption	- Finds $W\mathbf{m}$ in L that is close to $\mathbf{c}$ (by using the good basis V and considering the Babai's algorithm).	
	- Computes $W^{-1} \cdot (W\mathbf{m}) = \mathbf{m}$.	

Source: Adapted from Hoffstein et al. (2008).

Note that W is a "Hermite Normal Form (HNF)" of V if it is obtained by the multiplication of V by an unimodular matrix U, and if W is an upper triangular matrix, all its elements on the diagonal are strictly positive and any other element w_{ij} satisfies $0 \le w_{ij} < w_{ii}$ (Micciancio, 2001; Micciancio & Regev, 2009). Micciancio (2001) and Micciancio and Regev (2009) proposed to use HNF of a good basis as a bad basis.

Some examples for the selection of the basic parameters are as follows (adapted from Lee & Hahn, 2010; Nguyen, 1999):

$\mathrm{m} \in [-128, 127]^n$, where $n = 300$ can be a typical value.
$\mathrm{r} \in \{-\sigma, \sigma\}^n$ is uniformly distributed, where $\sigma = 3$ can be a typical value.
$V = kI_n + V'$, where $k = \ell\lceil \sqrt{n} + 1 \rceil$ holds with typical values of $\ell = 4$, $n = 300$, I_n is an $n \times n$ identity matrix, and $V' = (-\ell, \ell)^{n \times n}$ is a uniformly distributed $n \times n$ matrix. (Goldreich et al. (1997) proposed $V = \sqrt{n} I_n + V'$ as another example of the good basis to be used as the private decryption key.)

Example 5.1

We assume the following steps as an example:

Alice chooses $\mathbf{v}_1 = \begin{bmatrix} -3 \\ 2 \\ 1 \end{bmatrix}$, $\mathbf{v}_2 = \begin{bmatrix} -10 \\ -8 \\ 12 \end{bmatrix}$, $\mathbf{v}_3 = \begin{bmatrix} -5 \\ 4 \\ 7 \end{bmatrix}$ as the basis vectors

and determines $V = \begin{bmatrix} -3 & -10 & -5 \\ 2 & -8 & 4 \\ 1 & 12 & 7 \end{bmatrix}$ as the good basis which satisfies

$\mathcal{H}(\mathcal{B}) = \left(\frac{|252|}{(3.74)\cdot(17.55)\cdot(9.49)}\right)^{1/3} = 0.74$ in which $\det(V) = 252$, $\|\mathbf{v}_1\| = 3.74$, $\|\mathbf{v}_2\| = 17.55$, and $\|\mathbf{v}_3\| = 9.49$ hold.

Alice also chooses $U = \begin{bmatrix} 0 & 1 & 0 \\ 1 & 1 & 0 \\ 0 & 0 & 1 \end{bmatrix}$, where $\det(U) = -1$.

Alice computes $W = VU = \begin{bmatrix} -3 & -10 & -5 \\ 2 & -8 & 4 \\ 1 & 12 & 7 \end{bmatrix} \cdot \begin{bmatrix} 0 & 1 & 0 \\ 1 & 1 & 0 \\ 0 & 0 & 1 \end{bmatrix} = \begin{bmatrix} -10 & -13 & -5 \\ -8 & -6 & 4 \\ 12 & 13 & 7 \end{bmatrix}$

where $\mathbf{w}_1 = \begin{bmatrix} -10 \\ -8 \\ 12 \end{bmatrix}$, $\mathbf{w}_2 = \begin{bmatrix} -13 \\ -6 \\ 13 \end{bmatrix}$, $\mathbf{w}_3 = \begin{bmatrix} -5 \\ 4 \\ 7 \end{bmatrix}$ are the vectors of the "bad basis", and Alice sends W to Bob.

Encryption

We suppose that Bob chooses $\mathbf{m} = \begin{bmatrix} 3 \\ -5 \\ 7 \end{bmatrix}$ as the plaintext and chooses $\mathbf{r} = \begin{bmatrix} -2 \\ 1 \\ 3 \end{bmatrix}$ as the ephemeral key.

Bob computes $\mathbf{c} = W\mathbf{m} + \mathbf{r} = \begin{bmatrix} -10 & -13 & -5 \\ -8 & -6 & 4 \\ 12 & 13 & 7 \end{bmatrix} \cdot \begin{bmatrix} 3 \\ -5 \\ 7 \end{bmatrix} + \begin{bmatrix} -2 \\ 1 \\ 3 \end{bmatrix} = \begin{bmatrix} 0 \\ 34 \\ 20 \end{bmatrix} + \begin{bmatrix} -2 \\ 1 \\ 3 \end{bmatrix} = \begin{bmatrix} -2 \\ 35 \\ 23 \end{bmatrix}$, and sends the result $\mathbf{c} = \begin{bmatrix} -2 \\ 35 \\ 23 \end{bmatrix}$ to Alice as the ciphertext.

Decryption

Alice applies the Babai's algorithm with the following steps:

She writes $\mathbf{c} = t_1\mathbf{v}_1 + t_2\mathbf{v}_2 + t_3\mathbf{v}_3$ with $t_1, t_2, t_3 \in \mathbb{R}$, i.e. $\begin{bmatrix} -2 \\ 35 \\ 23 \end{bmatrix} = t_1 \begin{bmatrix} -3 \\ 2 \\ 1 \end{bmatrix} + t_2 \begin{bmatrix} -10 \\ -8 \\ 12 \end{bmatrix} + t_3 \begin{bmatrix} -5 \\ 4 \\ 7 \end{bmatrix}$ from which the following equations will follow:

$$-3t_1 - 10t_2 - 5t_3 = -2$$
$$2t_1 - 8t_2 + 4t_3 = 35$$
$$t_1 + 12t_2 + 7t_3 = 23$$

In matrix notation, these equations will be equivalent to

$$\begin{bmatrix} -3 & -10 & -5 \\ 2 & -8 & 4 \\ 1 & 12 & 7 \end{bmatrix} \cdot \begin{bmatrix} t_1 \\ t_2 \\ t_3 \end{bmatrix} = \begin{bmatrix} -2 \\ 35 \\ 23 \end{bmatrix}.$$

Accordingly

$$\begin{bmatrix} t_1 \\ t_2 \\ t_3 \end{bmatrix} = \begin{bmatrix} -3 & -10 & -5 \\ 2 & -8 & 4 \\ 1 & 12 & 7 \end{bmatrix}^{-1} \cdot \begin{bmatrix} -2 \\ 35 \\ 23 \end{bmatrix} = \begin{bmatrix} -26/63 & 5/126 & -20/63 \\ -5/126 & -4/63 & 1/126 \\ 8/63 & 13/126 & 11/63 \end{bmatrix} \cdot \begin{bmatrix} -2 \\ 35 \\ 23 \end{bmatrix} =$$

$$\begin{bmatrix} -641/126 \\ -247/126 \\ 929/126 \end{bmatrix}$$

will hold.

Alice sets a_i = rounding of t_i for $i = 1, 2, 3$ such that $\begin{bmatrix} a_1 \\ a_2 \\ a_3 \end{bmatrix} = \begin{bmatrix} -5 \\ -2 \\ 7 \end{bmatrix}$ will be obtained.

She computes $W\mathbf{m} = -5\mathbf{v}_1 - 2\mathbf{v}_2 + 7\mathbf{v}_3 = -5\begin{bmatrix} -3 \\ 2 \\ 1 \end{bmatrix} - 2\begin{bmatrix} -10 \\ -8 \\ 12 \end{bmatrix} + 7\begin{bmatrix} -5 \\ 4 \\ 7 \end{bmatrix} = \begin{bmatrix} 0 \\ 34 \\ 20 \end{bmatrix}$

Finally, Alice computes $W^{-1}(W\mathbf{m}) = \begin{bmatrix} -10 & -13 & -5 \\ -8 & -6 & 4 \\ 12 & 13 & 7 \end{bmatrix}^{-1} \cdot \begin{bmatrix} 0 \\ 34 \\ 20 \end{bmatrix} =$

$$\begin{bmatrix} 47/126 & -13/126 & 41/126 \\ -26/63 & 5/126 & -20/63 \\ 8/63 & 13/126 & 11/63 \end{bmatrix} \cdot \begin{bmatrix} 0 \\ 34 \\ 20 \end{bmatrix} = \begin{bmatrix} 3 \\ -5 \\ 7 \end{bmatrix} = \mathbf{m}.$$

Note that in Example 5.1, the bad basis W is not an HNF of the good basis V, since it does not satisfy the properties of being a HNF. However, $\mathbf{m}$ could be recovered as part of decryption. Note also that if V is defined as an $n \times n$ matrix with the rows (instead of columns) $\mathbf{v}_1, \mathbf{v}_2, \ldots, \mathbf{v}_n \in \mathbb{Z}^n$, and if W is defined as an $n \times n$ matrix with the rows (instead of columns) $\mathbf{w}_1, \mathbf{w}_2, \ldots, \mathbf{w}_n \in \mathbb{Z}^n$, then some changes should be made in Table 5.1 as follows: $W = UV$, $\mathbf{c} = \mathbf{m}W + \mathbf{r}$, and $(\mathbf{m}W) \cdot W^{-1} = \mathbf{m}$.

5.2.2 GGH digital signature algorithm

The basic idea of the GGH public key cryptosystem has been adapted to the GGH digital signature algorithm. The basic parameters for the GGH digital

Table 5.2 GGH digital signature algorithm

	Samantha	*Victor*
Private: V	- Chooses $V = (\mathbf{v}_1, \mathbf{v}_2, \ldots, \mathbf{v}_n)$.	
Public: W	- Chooses $W = (\mathbf{w}_1, \mathbf{w}_2, \ldots, \mathbf{w}_n)$.	
	- Sends W to Victor.	
Signing	- Chooses $\mathbf{d} \in \mathbb{Z}^n$.	
	- Computes $\mathbf{s} \in L$ that is close to $\mathbf{d} \in \mathbb{Z}^n$ (by using the good basis V and considering the Babai's algorithm).	
Public: $\mathbf{d}$,	- Writes $\mathbf{s} = x_1\mathbf{w}_1 + x_2\mathbf{w}_2 + \cdots + x_n\mathbf{w}_n$.	
$(x_1, x_2, \ldots, x_n)$	- Sends $\mathbf{d} \in \mathbb{Z}^n$ and $(x_1, x_2, \ldots, x_n)$ to Victor.	
Verification		- Computes
Public: ϵ		$\mathbf{s} = x_1\mathbf{w}_1 + x_2\mathbf{w}_2 + \cdots + x_n\mathbf{w}_n$.
		- Verifies $\lVert \mathbf{s} - \mathbf{d} \rVert \le \epsilon$.

Source: Adapted from Hoffstein et al. (2008) and Nguyen & Regev (2009).

signature algorithm are given, and the basic steps of the algorithm are provided in Table 5.2.

Basic parameters for the GGH digital signature algorithm (*adapted from* Hoffstein et al., 2008):

$\mathbf{v}_1, \mathbf{v}_2, \ldots, \mathbf{v}_n \in \mathbb{Z}^n$: Linearly independent vectors that are reasonably orthogonal to one another (chosen by Samantha)
V: An $n \times n$ matrix matrix with the columns $\mathbf{v}_1, \mathbf{v}_2, \ldots, \mathbf{v}_n \in \mathbb{Z}^n$ (good basis to be used as the private signing key by Samantha)
$\mathbf{w}_1, \mathbf{w}_2, \ldots, \mathbf{w}_n \in \mathbb{Z}^n$: Linearly independent vectors that are not reasonably orthogonal to one another (chosen by Samantha)
W: An $n \times n$ matrix with the columns $\mathbf{w}_1, \mathbf{w}_2, \ldots, \mathbf{w}_n \in \mathbb{Z}^n$ (bad basis to be used as the public verification key by Victor)
$\mathbf{d} \in \mathbb{Z}^n$: Digital document of Samantha
$\mathbf{s} \in \mathbb{Z}^n$: Digital signature of the digital document $\mathbf{d} \in \mathbb{Z}^n$ signed by Samantha
ϵ: A predetermined small threshold value (chosen by Samantha, Victor or a trusted third-party)

Nguyen and Regev (2009) provided an example for the selection of the good basis as $V = kI_n + V'$, where $k = 4\lceil \sqrt{n} + 1 \rfloor + 1$, I_n is an $n \times n$ identity matrix, V' is an $n \times n$ matrix with entries uniformly distributed in $[-4, +3]$. As in the digital signature algorithms provided in Chapters 3 and 4, instead of considering the original document $\mathbf{d} \in \mathbb{Z}^n$ for signing, the "hash value" of $\mathbf{d} \in \mathbb{Z}^n$ can be considered for signing. As in the GGH public key cryptosystem, $W = VU$ can be considered as the public verification key, where U is an $n \times n$ unimodular matrix (Hoffstein et al., 2008). The public verification key W can also be chosen by multiplying V by sufficiently many small U matrices or by using the HNF of L as in the GGH public key cryptosystem (Goldreich et al., 1997; Micciancio, 2001; Nguyen & Regev, 2009). According to Hoffstein et al. (2008), at each document signature, Samantha reveals some information about the good basis V of the lattice, thus changing the private signing key V after some number of digital signatures can be recommended.

Example 5.2

We will consider the same good basis and bad basis in Example 5.1.

Samantha chooses

$$V = \begin{bmatrix} -3 & -10 & -5 \\ 2 & -8 & 4 \\ 1 & 12 & 7 \end{bmatrix}, \text{ where } \mathbf{v}_1 = \begin{bmatrix} -3 \\ 2 \\ 1 \end{bmatrix}, \mathbf{v}_2 = \begin{bmatrix} -10 \\ -8 \\ 12 \end{bmatrix}, \mathbf{v}_3 = \begin{bmatrix} -5 \\ 4 \\ 7 \end{bmatrix} \text{ as the}$$

private signing key,

$$W = \begin{bmatrix} -10 & -13 & -5 \\ -8 & -6 & 4 \\ 12 & 13 & 7 \end{bmatrix}, \text{ where } \mathbf{w}_1 = \begin{bmatrix} -10 \\ -8 \\ 12 \end{bmatrix}, \mathbf{w}_2 = \begin{bmatrix} -13 \\ -6 \\ 13 \end{bmatrix}, \mathbf{w}_3 = \begin{bmatrix} -5 \\ 4 \\ 7 \end{bmatrix}$$

as the public verification key and sends W to Victor.

Signing

We assume that Samantha chooses $\mathbf{d} = \begin{bmatrix} 5 \\ 2 \\ 7 \end{bmatrix} \in \mathbb{Z}^3$. By using the Babai's algorithm with the following steps, Samantha finds $\mathbf{s}$:

She writes $\mathbf{d} = t_1\mathbf{v}_1 + t_2\mathbf{v}_2 + t_3\mathbf{v}_3$ with $t_1, t_2, t_3 \in \mathbb{R}$, i.e. $\begin{bmatrix} 5 \\ 2 \\ 7 \end{bmatrix} = t_1 \begin{bmatrix} -3 \\ 2 \\ 1 \end{bmatrix} +$ $t_2 \begin{bmatrix} -10 \\ -8 \\ 12 \end{bmatrix} + t_3 \begin{bmatrix} -5 \\ 4 \\ 7 \end{bmatrix}$ from which the following equations will follow:

$$-3t_1 - 10t_2 - 5t_3 = 5$$

$$2t_1 - 8t_2 + 4t_3 = 2$$

$$t_1 + 12t_2 + 7t_3 = 7$$

In matrix notation, these equations will be equivalent to

$$\begin{bmatrix} -3 & -10 & -5 \\ 2 & -8 & 4 \\ 1 & 12 & 7 \end{bmatrix} \cdot \begin{bmatrix} t_1 \\ t_2 \\ t_3 \end{bmatrix} = \begin{bmatrix} 5 \\ 2 \\ 7 \end{bmatrix}.$$

Accordingly

$$\begin{bmatrix} t_1 \\ t_2 \\ t_3 \end{bmatrix} = \begin{bmatrix} -3 & -10 & -5 \\ 2 & -8 & 4 \\ 1 & 12 & 7 \end{bmatrix}^{-1} \cdot \begin{bmatrix} 5 \\ 2 \\ 7 \end{bmatrix} = \begin{bmatrix} -26/63 & 5/126 & -20/63 \\ -5/126 & -4/63 & 1/126 \\ 8/63 & 13/126 & 11/63 \end{bmatrix} \cdot \begin{bmatrix} 5 \\ 2 \\ 7 \end{bmatrix} =$$

$$\begin{bmatrix} -265/63 \\ -17/63 \\ 130/63 \end{bmatrix}$$ will hold.

Samantha sets a_i = rounding of t_i for $i = 1, 2, 3$ such that she obtains $\begin{bmatrix} a_1 \\ a_2 \\ a_3 \end{bmatrix} = \begin{bmatrix} -4 \\ 0 \\ 2 \end{bmatrix}$.

She computes $\mathbf{s} = -4\mathbf{v}_1 + 0\mathbf{v}_2 + 2\mathbf{v}_3 = -4\begin{bmatrix} -3 \\ 2 \\ 1 \end{bmatrix} + 0\begin{bmatrix} -10 \\ -8 \\ 12 \end{bmatrix} + 2\begin{bmatrix} -5 \\ 4 \\ 7 \end{bmatrix} = \begin{bmatrix} 2 \\ 0 \\ 10 \end{bmatrix} \in L$ as the digital signature that is supposed to be close to $\mathbf{d} \in \mathbb{Z}^3$.

She writes $\mathbf{s} = x_1\mathbf{w}_1 + x_2\mathbf{w}_2 + x_3\mathbf{w}_3$, i.e. $\begin{bmatrix} 2 \\ 0 \\ 10 \end{bmatrix} = x_1\begin{bmatrix} -10 \\ -8 \\ 12 \end{bmatrix} + x_2\begin{bmatrix} -13 \\ -6 \\ 13 \end{bmatrix} + x_3\begin{bmatrix} -5 \\ 4 \\ 7 \end{bmatrix}$, finds

$$\begin{bmatrix} x_1 \\ x_2 \\ x_3 \end{bmatrix} = \begin{bmatrix} -10 & -13 & -5 \\ -8 & -6 & 4 \\ 12 & 13 & 7 \end{bmatrix}^{-1} \begin{bmatrix} 2 \\ 0 \\ 10 \end{bmatrix} = \begin{bmatrix} 47/126 & -13/126 & 41/126 \\ -26/63 & 5/126 & -20/63 \\ 8/63 & 13/126 & 11/63 \end{bmatrix} \cdot \begin{bmatrix} 2 \\ 0 \\ 10 \end{bmatrix} = \begin{bmatrix} 4 \\ -4 \\ 2 \end{bmatrix},$$

and sends $\begin{bmatrix} x_1 \\ x_2 \\ x_3 \end{bmatrix} = \begin{bmatrix} 4 \\ -4 \\ 2 \end{bmatrix}$ to Victor.

Verification

Victor computes $\mathbf{s} = x_1\mathbf{w}_1 + x_2\mathbf{w}_2 + x_3\mathbf{w}_3 = \begin{bmatrix} -10 & -13 & -5 \\ -8 & -6 & 4 \\ 12 & 13 & 7 \end{bmatrix} \cdot \begin{bmatrix} 4 \\ -4 \\ 2 \end{bmatrix} = \begin{bmatrix} 2 \\ 0 \\ 10 \end{bmatrix}$.

Victor is assumed to determine $\epsilon = 5$ as the predetermined threshold value. He computes and verifies that $\|\mathbf{s} - \mathbf{d}\| = 4.69 < \epsilon = 5$ holds, i.e. the digital signature $\mathbf{s}$ corresponds to the digital document $\mathbf{d}$ regarding the private signing key V of Samantha.

5.2.3 Cryptanalysis of the GGH public key cryptosystem and GGH digital signature algorithm

The security of the GGH public key cryptosystem and GGH digital signature algorithm is basically based on the hardness of the solution of apprCVP. However, two efficient cryptanalysis approaches were proposed by Nguyen (1999) and Lee and Hahn (2010) for the GGH public key cryptosystem, which will be presented in this section.

Nguyen (1999) made a cryptanalysis of the GGH public key cryptosystem, found that GGH public key cryptosystem has a basic flaw, and discussed that "GGH cannot provide sufficient security even for dimensions of ciphertext as high as 400." Please recall from Table 5.1 that $\mathbf{c} = W\mathbf{m} + \mathbf{r}$ holds, where $\mathbf{m} \in \mathbb{Z}^n$, $\mathbf{r} \in \mathbb{Z}^n$, and $\mathbf{c} \in \mathbb{Z}^n$. Nguyen (1999) considered $\mathbf{r} \in \{-\sigma, \sigma\}^n$ to be selected uniformly, and (n, σ) as the security parameters with the typical values $(300, 3)$. Nguyen (1999) showed that $\mathbf{r}$ disappeared by an appropriate choice of the modulus, as a result $\mathbf{m}$ could be recovered easily. Two cases that were considered in his cryptanalysis are given in Table 5.3.

Nguyen (1999) also discussed how to solve $\mathbf{m}$ by considering Cases 1 and 2 given in Table 5.3, and found that with high probability there were a few solutions which were easy to compute. He also found that with a non-negligible probability, there was a single solution. All details of the cryptanalysis are available in Nguyen (1999). After the cryptanalysis of Nguyen (1999) for the GGH public key cryptosystem, Yoshino and Kunihiro (2012) proposed a modified version of the GGH public key cryptosystem, which was analyzed by de Barros and Schechter (2014). Please see Yoshino and Kunihiro (2012) and de Barros and Schechter (2014) for the details.

The basic finding of the cryptanalysis of Lee and Hahn (2010) for the GGH public key cryptosystem is that the partial information of the plaintext can simplify the decryption in the GGH public key cryptosystem. They assumed that the first k of n bits of the plaintext $\mathbf{m}$ were known such that $\mathbf{m} = \begin{bmatrix} \mathbf{m}^1 \\ \mathbf{m}^2 \end{bmatrix}$ could be written, where $\mathbf{m}^1$ is the known k-bit part of the

Table 5.3 Two cases in the cryptanalysis of Nguyen (1999) for the GGH public key cryptosystem

Case 1: mod σ	*Case 2: mod 2σ*
Since each entry of the vector $\mathbf{r}$ is either σ or $-\sigma$, the following congruence is obtained:	Another n-dimensional vector with entries $\{\sigma\}$ is considered, and it is called $\mathbf{s}$. It is clear that the following congruences hold:
$\mathbf{c} \equiv W\mathbf{m} + \mathbf{r} \equiv W\mathbf{m} \pmod{\sigma}$	$\mathbf{r} + \mathbf{s} \equiv 0 \pmod{2\sigma}$ and accordingly
$\mathbf{m}$ can be recovered since $\mathbf{c}, W, \sigma$ are public.	$\mathbf{c} + \mathbf{s} \equiv W\mathbf{m} + \mathbf{r} + \mathbf{s} \equiv W\mathbf{m} \pmod{2\sigma}$
	$\mathbf{m}$ can be recovered since $\mathbf{c}, \mathbf{s}, W, \sigma$ are public.

Source: Adapted from Nguyen (1999).

plaintext, and $\mathbf{m}^2$ is the unknown $(n-k)$-bit part of the plaintext. Lee and Hahn (2010) also wrote $W = \left[W^1\ W^2\right]$, where W^1 corresponds to $\mathbf{m}^1$ and W^2 corresponds to $\mathbf{m}^2$. Then the ciphertext can be written as $\mathbf{c} = \left[W^1\ W^2\right] \begin{bmatrix} \mathbf{m}^1 \\ \mathbf{m}^2 \end{bmatrix} + \mathbf{r} = W^1\mathbf{m}^1 + W^2\mathbf{m}^2 + \mathbf{r}$, which is equivalent to $\mathbf{c} - W^1\mathbf{m}^1 = W^2\mathbf{m}^2 + \mathbf{r}$, where $\mathbf{c} - W_1\mathbf{m}^1$ is publicly known. Thus, only CVP related to the right-hand side for recovering $\mathbf{m}^2$ should be solved, which is expected to be simpler due to the smaller rank $n-k$ (Lee & Hahn, 2010). Note that the cryptanalysis of Lee and Hahn (2010) is effective only if there is partial information about the plaintext. For the details, please see Lee and Hahn (2010).

Nguyen and Regev (2006) and Nguyen and Regev (2009) provided the cryptanalysis of the GGH digital signature algorithm and proposed an attack against the GGH digital signature algorithm based on the so-called "Hidden Parallelepiped Problem (HPP)" to find a good approximation of the rows of $\pm V$. HPP is applicable if there is a list of document-signature pairs and the basic objective of the cryptanalysis is to recover the parallelepiped or an approximation of the parallelepiped, which can be transformed into a multivariate optimization model. Finally, a good approximation of the matrix $\pm V$ can be recovered (Nguyen & Regev, 2006; Nguyen & Regev, 2009). The details of this cryptanalysis are available in Nguyen and Regev (2006) and Nguyen and Regev (2009).

5.3 NTRU PUBLIC KEY CRYPTOSYSTEM (NTRUEncrypt), NTRU SIGNATURE SCHEME (NSS), AND CRYPTANALYSIS

5.3.1 NTRU public key cryptosystem

The NTRU public key cryptosystem can be based on the convolution polynomial rings or lattice problems like SVP and CVP (Hoffstein et al., 2008). In this section, the NTRU public key cryptosystem based on the convolution polynomial rings will be provided. Please see the basic parameters next and Table 5.4 for the steps of the NTRU public key cryptosystem.

Basic parameters of the NTRU public key cryptosystem (NTRUEncrypt) (adapted from Hoffstein et al., 2008; Jaulmes & Joux, 2000; Whyte & Hoffstein, 2011*):*

d_f, d_g, d: Positive integer numbers (chosen by Alice or Bob or a trusted third-party)

N: A prime number (chosen by Alice or Bob or a trusted third-party)

p: A small prime number (typically $p = 2$ or $p = 3$, chosen by Alice or Bob or a trusted third-party)

q: A large prime number satisfying $\gcd(N, q) = 1$, $q > (6d+1)p$ (chosen by Alice or Bob or a trusted third-party)

Table 5.4 NTRU public key cryptosystem based on convolution polynomial rings

	Alice	*Bob*
Private:	- Chooses (randomly)	
$\mathbf{f}(x), \mathbf{g}(x)$	$\mathbf{f}(x) \in \mathcal{T}(d_f+1, d_f)$	
$\mathbf{f}_p(x), \mathbf{f}_q(x)$	$\mathbf{g}(x) \in \mathcal{T}(d_g, d_g)$.	
	- Computes	
	$\mathbf{f}_q(x) = \mathbf{f}(x)^{-1}$ in R_q,	
	$\mathbf{f}_p(x) = \mathbf{f}(x)^{-1}$ in R_p, and	
Public:	$\mathbf{h}(x) = \mathbf{f}_q(x) \star \mathbf{g}(x)$ in R_q.	
$d_f, d_g, p, q, \mathbf{h}(x)$	- Sends $\mathbf{h}(x)$ to Bob.	
Encryption		- Chooses $\mathbf{m}(x) \in R$.
Private: $\mathbf{m}(x), \mathbf{r}(x)$		- Chooses $\mathbf{r}(x) \in \mathcal{T}(d, d)$ randomly.
Public: $d, \mathbf{c}(x)$		- Computes
		$\mathbf{c}(x) \equiv p\mathbf{r}(x) \star \mathbf{h}(x) + \mathbf{m}(x)$ in R_q.
		- Sends $\mathbf{c}(x)$ to Alice.
Decryption	- Computes	
	$\mathbf{a}(x) \equiv \mathbf{f}(x) \star \mathbf{c}(x)$ in R_q.	
	- Centerlifts $\mathbf{a}(x)$ in R_q to $\mathbf{a}'(x)$ in R.	
	- Computes	
	$\mathbf{f}_p(x) \star \mathbf{a}'(x) \equiv \mathbf{m}'(x)$ in R_p.	
	- Centerlifts $\mathbf{m}'(x)$ in R_p to $\mathbf{m}(x)$ in R.	

Source: Adapted from Hoffstein et al. (2008) and Hoffstein, Pipher, & Silverman (1998).

$R = \frac{\mathbb{Z}[x]}{(x^N-1)}$, $R_q = \frac{(\mathbb{Z}/q\mathbb{Z})[x]}{(x^N-1)}$, $R_p = \frac{(\mathbb{Z}/p\mathbb{Z})[x]}{(x^N-1)}$: Convolution polynomial rings

$\mathrm{f}(x) \in \mathcal{T}(d_f+1, d_f)$ (or $\mathrm{f}(x) \in \mathcal{T}(d_f, d_f-1)$): Randomly chosen ternary (trinary) polynomial from the distribution $\mathcal{D}_f$ (chosen by Alice)

$\mathrm{g}(x) \in \mathcal{T}(d_g, d_g)$: Randomly chosen ternary (trinary) polynomial from the distribution $\mathcal{D}_g$ (chosen by Alice)

$\mathrm{m}(x) \in R$: Plaintext as a randomly chosen polynomial from the distribution $\mathcal{D}_m$ with coefficients between $-\frac{1}{2}p$ and $\frac{1}{2}p$ (chosen by Bob)

$\mathrm{r}(x) \in \mathcal{T}(d, d)$: Ephemeral key as a randomly chosen ternary (trinary) polynomial from the distribution $\mathcal{D}_r$ (chosen by Bob)

According to Whyte and Hoffstein (2011), the public key $\mathrm{h}(x)$, ciphertext $\mathrm{c}(x)$, $\mathrm{a}(x)$, and the plaintext $\mathrm{m}(x)$ can also be computed as in Equations (5.1)–(5.4):

$$\mathrm{h}(x) = p\mathrm{g}(x) \star \mathrm{f}_q(x) \text{ in } R_q \tag{5.1}$$

$$c(x) \equiv r(x) \star h(x) + m(x) \text{ in } R_q \tag{5.2}$$

$$a(x) \equiv f(x) \star c(x) \text{ in } R_q \tag{5.3}$$

$$f_p(x) \star a(x) \equiv m(x) \text{ in } R_p \tag{5.4}$$

Example 5.3

We assume that that $N = 13$ and $d_f = d_g = d = 3$ are chosen by Alice or Bob or a trusted third-party. Accordingly, $f(x) \in \mathcal{T}(4,3)$, $g(x) \in \mathcal{T}(3,3)$ are assumed to be chosen as $f(x) = x^{12} + x^9 - x^8 - x^7 + x^6 + x^5 - x^3$ and $g(x) = x^{11} - x^7 + x^6 + x^5 - x^2 - 1$, respectively by Alice. We also assume that $p = 7$ and $q = 359 > (6d+1)p = 133$ are chosen as two prime numbers.

Alice

Alice computes $f_{359}(x) = f(x)^{-1} = 135x^{12} + 277x^{11} + 73x^{10} + 347x^9 + 241x^8 + 319x^7 + 186x^6 + 328x^5 + 185x^4 + 89x^3 + 225x^2 + 202x + 266$ in R_{359} and $f_7(x) = f(x)^{-1} = x^{12} + 6x^{11} + 2x^{10} + x^9 + 3x^8 + 2x^7 + 3x^6 + 3x^5 + x^4 + 4x^2 + 3x$ in R_7.

Alice also computes $h(x) = f_{359}(x) \star g(x) = 171x^{12} + 330x^{11} + 245x^{10} + 19x^9 + 117x^8 + 220x^7 + 203x^6 + 26x^5 + 115x^4 + 40x^3 + 232x^2 + 21x + 56$ in R_{359} as the public key, and sends $h(x)$ to Bob.

Bob

Bob chooses $m(x) = x^{10} - 3x^8 + 2x^7 + x^4 - x^3 - 1$ in R and $r(x) \in \mathcal{T}(3,3) = x^{10} - x^7 + x^6 + x^5 - x^3 - x$ randomly.

Bob computes $c(x) \equiv pr(x) \star h(x) + m(x) = 165x^{12} + 206x^{11} + 145x^{10} + 213x^9 + 188x^8 + 152x^7 + 90x^6 + 182x^5 + 34x^4 + 65x^3 + 226x^2 + 28x + 100$ in R_{359} and sends $c(x)$ to Alice.

Alice

Alice computes $a(x) \equiv f(x) \star c(x) = 337x^{12} + 17x^{11} + 7x^{10} + 349x^7 + 348x^6 + 350x^5 + 355x^4 + 36x^3 + 8x^2 + 2x + 344$ in R_{359}.

Alice centerlifts $a(x)$ in R_{359} to $a'(x)$ in R such that the entries of $a'(x)$ will be in $\left(-\frac{359}{2}, \frac{359}{2}\right]$, and determines $a'(x) = -22x^{12} + 17x^{11} + 7x^{10} - 10x^7 - 11x^6 - 9x^5 - 4x^4 + 36x^3 + 8x^2 + 2x - 15$.

Alice also computes $f_7(x) \star a'(x) \equiv m'(x) = x^{10} + 4x^8 + 2x^7 + x^4 + 6x^3 + 6$ in R_7 which she centerlifts to $m(x)$ in R such that the entries of $m(x)$ will be in $\left(-\frac{7}{2}, \frac{7}{2}\right]$. Accordingly, she recovers $m(x) = x^{10} - 3x^8 + 2x^7 + x^4 - x^3 - 1$.

Please note that we use the "extended Euclidean algorithm" (which was explained in Section 1.5.2 of Chapter 1) for the calculation of $f_{359}(x) = f(x)^{-1}$ in R_{359} and $f_7(x) = f(x)^{-1}$ in R_7. We also use the addition and multiplication (product) of two polynomials in the ring of convolution polynomials and center-lifting (which were explained in Sections 1.3.3.3 and 1.3.3.4 of Chapter 1) in various steps of the NTRU public key cryptosystem.

5.3.2 NTRU digital signature algorithm

There are three types of the NTRU digital signature schemes: The NTRU signature scheme (NSS), R-NSS, and the NTRUSign (Hoffstein, Howgrave-Graham,

Table 5.5 NSS

	Samantha	*Victor*
Private:	- Chooses $\mathbf{f}_1(x)$, $\mathbf{g}_1(x)$.	
$\mathbf{f}_1(x)$, $\mathbf{g}_1(x)$	- Computes	
$\mathbf{f}(x), \mathbf{g}(x)$	$\mathbf{f}(x) = \mathbf{f}_0(x) + p\mathbf{f}_1(x)$ and	
	$\mathbf{g}(x) = \mathbf{g}_0(x) + p\mathbf{g}_1(x)$ in R.	
Public: $p, q, \mathbf{f}_0(x)$, $\mathbf{g}_0(x), \mathbf{h}(x)$	- Finds $\mathbf{h}(x)$ satisfying $\mathbf{f}(x) \star \mathbf{h}(x) = \mathbf{g}(x)$ in R_q.	
	- Sends $\mathbf{h}(x)$ to Victor.	
Signing	- Chooses $\mathbf{d}(x)$.	
Private: $\mathbf{w}(x)$,	- Chooses randomly $\mathbf{w}_1(x), \mathbf{w}_2(x)$.	
$\mathbf{w}_1(x), \mathbf{w}_2(x)$ Public:	- Computes $\mathbf{w}(x) = \mathbf{d}(x) + \mathbf{w}_1(x) + p\mathbf{w}_2(x)$ in R.	
$\mathbf{d}(x), \mathbf{s}(x)$	- Computes $\mathbf{s}(x) \equiv \mathbf{f}(x) * \mathbf{w}(x)$ in R_q.	
	- Sends $\mathbf{d}(x)$ and $\mathbf{s}(x)$ to Victor.	
Verification		- Checks that $\mathbf{s}(x) \neq 0$ holds.
		- Computes $\mathbf{t}(x) \equiv \mathbf{s}(x) \star \mathbf{h}(x)$ in R_q.
Public: D_{min},		- Checks and verifies
D_{max}		$D_{min} \leq \mathrm{Dev}(\mathbf{s}(x), \mathbf{f}_0(x) \star \mathbf{d}(x)) \leq D_{max}$ and
		$D_{min} \leq \mathrm{Dev}(\mathbf{t}(x), \mathbf{g}_0(x) \star \mathbf{d}(x)) \leq D_{max}$.

Source: Adapted from Gentry et al. (2001) and Hoffstein et al. (2001)

Pipher, Silverman, & Whyte, 2003; Hoffstein, Pipher, & Silverman, 2001). The NSS was the first attempt of a digital signature algorithm based on the principle of the NTRU public key cryptosystem. Due to some weaknesses of NSS, a revised version of NSS, which is R-NSS, and NTRUSign that is based on the NTRU lattice, have been proposed (Hoffstein, Howgrave-Graham, Pipher, & Whyte, 2009). In this section, we merely provide the unmodified version of NSS with the steps given in Table 5.5. We provide the details of the NSS in Table 5.5, and give a definition that is used during the signature verification step.

Definition 5.1

Given two polynomials $\mathrm{f}(x), \mathrm{g}(x)$ of degree $N-1$, $Dev(\mathrm{f}(x), \mathrm{g}(x))$ gives the number of different coefficients in $\mathrm{f}(x) \equiv \bar{\mathrm{f}}(x) \pmod q \pmod p$ and $\mathrm{g}(x) \equiv \bar{\mathrm{g}}(x) \pmod q \pmod p$. More specifically, let $\bar{\mathrm{f}}(x) = \bar{a}_0 + \cdots + \bar{a}_{N-1}x^{N-1}$ and $\bar{g}(x) = \bar{b}_0 + \cdots + \bar{b}_{N-1}x^{N-1}$ be considered. Then, we can define $Dev(\mathrm{f}(x), \mathrm{g}(x)) = \#\{i \mid \bar{a}_i \neq \bar{b}_i\}$ (adapted from Gentry, Jonsson, Stern, & Szydlo, 2001; Hoffstein et al., 2001).

Basic parameters for the NSS (adapted from Gentry et al., 2001; Hoffstein et al., 2001*)*:

d_f, d_g, d_d: Positive integer numbers (chosen by Samantha or Victor or a trusted third-party)
N: Prime number (chosen by Samantha or Victor or a trusted third-party)
p, q: Integer numbers (chosen by Samantha or Victor or a trusted third-party)
$R = \frac{\mathbb{Z}[x]}{(x^N - 1)}$, $R_q = \frac{(\mathbb{Z}/q\mathbb{Z})[x]}{(x^N - 1)}$: Convolution polynomial rings
$\mathrm{f}_0(x), \mathrm{g}_0(x)$: Fixed small polynomials (chosen by Samantha or Victor or a trusted third-party)
$\mathrm{f}_1(x) \in \mathcal{T}(d_f, d_f), \mathrm{g}_1(x) \in \mathcal{T}(d_g, d_g)$: Randomly chosen ternary (trinary) polynomials (chosen by Samantha)
$\mathrm{f}(x), \mathrm{g}(x)$: Private polynomials (computed by Samantha)
$\mathrm{h}(x)$: Public verification key with a polynomial of degree $N-1$ (computed by Samantha and sent to Victor by Samantha)
$\mathrm{w}_1(x), \mathrm{w}_2(x)$: Two private polynomials with small coefficients generated randomly (chosen by Samantha)
$\mathrm{d}(x) \in \mathcal{T}(d_d, d_d)$: Digital document of Samantha as a randomly chosen ternary (trinary) polynomial
D_{min}, D_{max}: Parameters for the verification (chosen by Alice or Bob or a trusted third-party)

The typical values of the parameters are $p = 3$, $q = 128$, $d_f = 70, d_g = 40$, $N = 251$, $d_d = 32$, $D_{min} = 55$, $D_{max} = 87$, and $\mathrm{f}_0(x) = 1$, $\mathrm{g}_0(x) = 1 - 2x$ are typically chosen polynomials (Gentry et al., 2001; Hoffstein et al., 2001). For the selection of $\mathrm{w}_1(x), \mathrm{w}_2(x)$, please see Hoffstein et al. (2001).

As previously mentioned for all digital signature algorithms, instead of $\mathrm{d}(x)$, the hash value of $\mathrm{d}(x)$ can be considered for signing and verification.

Example 5.4

We assume that small values $d_f = 4$, $d_g = 3$, $d_d = 4$, $N = 11, p = 3, q = 7$, $D_{min} = 3$, $D_{max} = 15$, and also $\mathrm{f}_0(x) = 1$, $\mathrm{g}_0(x) = 1 - 2x$ are chosen. Then following steps will follow for the NSS.

Samantha
She chooses $\mathrm{f}_1(x) \in \mathcal{T}(4,4) = x^8 + x^7 - x^6 - x^5 + x^4 - x^3 + x^2 - 1$.
She chooses $\mathrm{g}_1(x) \in \mathcal{T}(3,3) = x^7 - x^5 - x^4 + x^3 + x^2 - x$.
She computes $\mathrm{f}(x) = \mathrm{f}_0(x) + p\mathrm{f}_1(x) = 1 + 3(x^8 + x^7 - x^6 - x^5 + x^4 - x^3 + x^2 - 1) = 3x^8 + 3x^7 - 3x^6 - 3x^5 + 3x^4 - 3x^3 + 3x^2 - 2$ in R.
She computes $\mathrm{g}(x) = \mathrm{g}_0(x) + p\mathrm{g}_1(x) = (1 - 2x) + 3(x^7 - x^5 - x^4 + x^3 + x^2 - x) = 3x^7 - 3x^5 - 3x^4 + 3x^3 + 3x^2 - 5x + 1$ in R.
For finding $\mathrm{h}(x)$ satisfying $\mathrm{f}(x) \star \mathrm{h}(x) = \mathrm{g}(x) \pmod 7$, first she finds $\mathrm{f}^{-1}(x) \pmod 7 = 4x^{10} + 4x^8 + 3x^7 + 3x^6 + 2x^5 + 5x^4 + 4x^3 + 4x^2 + 3x + 4$.

Then she computes $\mathbf{h}(x) = \mathbf{f}^{-1}(x) \star \mathbf{g}(x) \pmod 7 \equiv x^{10} + 3x^9 + 4x^7 + 4x^6 + x^5 + x^4 + 2x^3 + 3x^2 + x$ and sends $\mathbf{h}(x)$ to Victor.

Signing (Samantha)

Samantha chooses $\mathbf{d}(x) \in \mathcal{T}(4,4) = x^8 + x^7 + x^6 - x^5 - x^3 + x^2 - x - 1$.

She also chooses $\mathbf{w}_1(x) = 2x + 1$ and $\mathbf{w}_2(x) = x - 1$.

She computes $\mathbf{w}(x) = \mathbf{d}(x) + \mathbf{w}_1(x) + p\mathbf{w}_2(x) = (x^8 + x^7 + x^6 - x^5 - x^3 + x^2 - x - 1) + 2x + 1 + 3(x-1) = x^8 + x^7 + x^6 - x^5 - x^3 + x^2 + 4x - 3$ in R.

She also computes the digital signature $\mathbf{s}(x) \equiv \mathbf{f}(x) * \mathbf{w}(x) \pmod 7 \equiv 6x^{10} + x^9 + 3x^7 + x^6 + 6x^5 + 2x^4 + 5x^3 + 4x^2 + 3$ and sends $\mathbf{d}(x)$, $\mathbf{s}(x)$ to Victor.

Verification (Victor)

Victor checks $\mathbf{s}(x) \neq 0$.

He computes $\mathbf{s}(x) \pmod 3 \equiv x^9 + x^6 + 2x^4 + 2x^3 + x^2$.

He computes $\mathbf{f}_0(x) \star \mathbf{d}(x) = \mathbf{d}(x) = x^8 + x^7 + x^6 - x^5 - x^3 + x^2 - x - 1$, where $\mathbf{f}_0(x) = 1$. Then he computes $\mathbf{d}(x) \pmod 7 \equiv x^8 + x^7 + x^6 + 6x^5 + 6x^3 + x^2 + 6x + 6$ and finds $\mathbf{d}(x) \pmod 7 \pmod 3 \equiv x^8 + x^7 + x^6 + x^2$.

Finally, he determines $\mathrm{Dev}(\mathbf{s}(x), \mathbf{f}_0(x) \star \mathbf{d}(x)) = 3$ that satisfies $3 \leq 3 < 15$.

Victor computes $\mathbf{t}(x) \equiv \mathbf{s}(x) \star \mathbf{h}(x) \pmod 7 \equiv 3x^{10} + 4x^8 + 5x^7 + 2x^6 + 3x^5 + 4x^4 + 3x + 1$ and then he finds $\mathbf{t}(x) \pmod 3 \equiv x^8 + 2x^7 + 2x^6 + x^4 + 1$.

He computes $\mathbf{g}_0(x) \star \mathbf{d}(x) \pmod 7 = 5x^9 + 6x^8 + 6x^7 + 3x^6 + 6x^5 + 2x^4 + 4x^3 + 3x^2 + x + 4$ and finds $\mathbf{g}_0(x) \star \mathbf{d}(x) \pmod 7 \pmod 3 = 2x^9 + 2x^4 + x^3 + x + 1$.

Finally, he determines $\mathrm{Dev}(\mathbf{t}(x), \mathbf{g}_0(x) \star \mathbf{d}(x)) = 7$ that satisfies $3 < 7 < 15$.

As in the NTRU public key cryptosystem, we again use the "extended Euclidean algorithm" to find the multiplicative inverse $\mathbf{f}^{-1}(x) \pmod 7$. We also use the addition and multiplication (product) of two polynomials in the ring of convolution polynomials for various steps of the NSS.

5.3.3 Cryptanalysis of the NTRU public key cryptosystem and NTRU digital signature algorithm

5.3.3.1 Cryptanalysis of the NTRU public key cryptosystem

There is a basic mathematical problem to break the NTRU public key cryptosystem, which is called the "NTRU key recovery problem" (Hoffstein et al., 1998). Note that Equation (5.5) holds from Table 5.4, which is equivalent to Equation (5.6).

$$\mathbf{h}(x) = \mathbf{f}_q(x) \star \mathbf{g}(x) \text{ in } R_q \tag{5.5}$$

$$\mathbf{f}(x) \star \mathbf{h}(x) = \mathbf{g}(x) \text{ in } R_q \tag{5.6}$$

Please recall also that $\mathbf{f}(x), \mathbf{g}(x)$ are private, and $\mathbf{h}(x)$ is public. The "NTRU key recovery problem" is to recover $\mathbf{f}(x)$ and $\mathbf{g}(x)$ from Equation (5.6) given that $\mathbf{h}(x)$ is known publicly (Hoffstein et al., 1998). If the adversary can solve the "NTRU key recovery problem", then (s)he can recover the private keys $\mathbf{f}(x)$ and $\mathbf{g}(x)$, and also the plaintext $\mathbf{m}(x)$. Hoffstein et al. (1998) found that solving the "NTRU key recovery problem" is equivalent to solving SVP for a certain classes of lattices.

As provided in Easttom (2022), the basic security problem regarding the NTRU public key cryptosystem can be regarding the "implementation issues" rather than the fundamental mathematical structure of NTRU, which is found to be strong. However, there have been some attempts for the cryptanalysis of NTRUEncrypt in the literature. In the following, we will provide some basic contributions of the selected approaches.

Coppersmith and Shamir (1997) proposed a lattice-based attack on the NTRUEncrypt to find either the original private key $\mathbf{f}(x)$ or an alternative private key $\mathbf{f}'(x)$ which can be used as the original private key. Please recall the decryption steps of the NTRU public key cryptosystem from Table 5.4. Coppersmith and Shamir (1997) showed that if we assume the coefficients of $\mathbf{a}(x)$ as normally distributed with mean near 0 and standard deviation σ, then the decryption of the most plaintexts will be possible for $\sigma = q/10$, thus the parameters should be arranged to ensure $\sigma < q/10$ for higher reliability. As some other selected approaches from the literature, Jaulmes and Joux (2000) proposed a "chosen-ciphertext attack" against the NTRUEncrypt to recover the private decryption key. Gama and Nguyen (2007) proposed various chosen-ciphertext attacks on the NTRUEncrypt, which worked in case of the so-called "decryption failures". Hoffstein et al. (2009) also found that the decryption failures can occur under certain parameter choices of the NTRUEncrypt, which can be exploited by the adversary to recover the private decryption key. Shparlinski (2003) studied the bit security of the NTRUEncrypt and showed that each coefficient of the encrypted plaintext $\mathbf{m}(x)$ is as secure as the whole plaintext $\mathbf{m}(x)$. Please see the respective references for the details of the attacks against the NTRU public key cryptosystem.

5.3.3.2 Cryptanalysis of the NSS

Hoffstein et al. (2001) have already made a cryptanalysis of the NSS in the paper in which they introduced the NSS. As an example, one attack would be to try to recover the private key $\mathbf{f}(x)$ or an imitation of $\mathbf{f}(x)$ from the public key $\mathbf{h}(x)$. Some of the possible attacks on the NSS mentioned in Hoffstein et al. (2001) are "random search for a valid signature on a given message", "NTRU lattices and lattice attacks on the public key", and "lattice attack on transcripts", which can be avoided if the parameters are chosen properly according to Hoffstein et al. (2001). Please see details in Hoffstein et al. (2001).

As an example regarding the cryptanalysis of the NSS from the literature, Gentry et al. (2001) provided a cryptanalysis of the NSS and proposed the so-called "basic forgery attack", "forgery attack with lattice reduction", and "transcription attacks". As an example, in the "basic forgery attack", the attacker's objective is to find a pair of polynomials $(\mathbf{s}(x), \mathbf{t}(x))$ that satisfy the conditions in (5.7)–(5.9), which are the steps of the signature verification in

Table 5.5, where $D_{min} = 55$ and $D_{max} = 87$ are assumed (adapted from Gentry et al., 2001).

$$t(x) \equiv s(x) \star h(x) \pmod{q} \tag{5.7}$$

$$55 \leq \text{Dev}\left(s(x), f_0(x) \star d(x)\right) \leq 87 \tag{5.8}$$

$$55 \leq \text{Dev}\left(t(x), g_0(x) \star d(x)\right) \leq 87 \tag{5.9}$$

Accordingly, the attacker sets (5.10) for $\lfloor N/2 \rfloor$ coefficients of $s(x)$ and (5.11) for $\lceil N/2 \rceil$ coefficients of $t(x)$ (adapted from Gentry et al., 2001).

$$s_i(x) \equiv \left(f_0(x) \star d(x)\right)_i \pmod{p} \tag{5.10}$$

$$t_j(x) \equiv \left(g_0(x) \star d(x)\right)_j \pmod{p} \tag{5.11}$$

Note that the remaining coefficients of $s(x)$ and $t(x)$ are allowed to be random (Gentry et al., 2001). According to Gentry et al. (2001), if $p = 3$ and $D_{\max} \geq \frac{1}{3}N$, the "basic forgery attack" can generate signatures for any size of N. Please see Gentry et al. (2001) for the details of "basic forgery attack", "forgery attack with lattice reduction", and "transcription attacks".

5.4 CONCLUSIONS

This chapter provided the GGH public key cryptosystem, GGH digital signature algorithm, NTRU public key cryptosystem, NSS, and some selected cryptanalysis approaches to these algorithms. The GGH public key cryptosystem and GGH digital signature algorithm are two examples of lattice-based cryptography in which a good basis of the lattice is considered as the private key, whereas a bad basis of the lattice corresponds to the public key. Some major weaknesses of the GGH public key cryptosystem were identified as given in the literature; however, some papers were also published regarding the improvement potentials of the GGH public key cryptosystem. The NTRU public key cryptosystem based on the convolution polynomial rings and the NSS as an NTRU digital signature algorithm were also presented in this chapter. The NTRU public key cryptosystem is considered to be an example of post-quantum cryptography. However, there have been also attacks against the NTRU public key cryptosystem and NSS, some of which were explained very briefly in this chapter. As in Chapters 3 and 4, simple examples were provided to clarify the steps of the algorithms.

REFERENCES

Coppersmith, D., & Shamir, A. (1997). Lattice attacks on NTRU. In W. Fumy (Ed.), *Advances in cryptology - EUROCRYPT '97*. Lecture Notes in Computer Science, 1233. Berlin, Heidelberg: Springer. https://doi.org/10.1007/3-540-69053-0_5

de Barros, C. F., & Schechter, L. M. (2014). GGH may not be dead after all. *Proceeding series of the Brazilian society of computational and applied mathematics, CNMAC (2014)*, v3, n1. https://doi.org/10.5540/03.2015.003.01.0095.

Easttom, C. (2022). Lattice-based cryptography. In *Modern cryptography*. Cham: Springer. https://doi.org/10.1007/978-3-031-12304-7_20

Gama, N., & Nguyen, P. Q. (2007). New chosen-ciphertext attacks on NTRU. In T. Okamoto & X. Wang (Eds.), *Public key cryptography - PKC 2007*. Lecture Notes in Computer Science, 4450. Berlin, Heidelberg: Springer. https://doi.org/10.1007/978-3-540-71677-8_7

Gentry, C., Jonsson, J., Stern, J., & Szydlo, M. (2001). Cryptanalysis of the NTRU signature scheme (NSS) from eurocrypt 2001. In C. Boyd (Ed.), *Advances in cryptology - ASIACRYPT 2001*. Lecture Notes in Computer Science, 2248. Berlin, Heidelberg: Springer. https://doi.org/10.1007/3-540-45682-1_1

Goldreich, O., Goldwasser, S., & Halevi, S. (1997). Public-key cryptosystems from lattice reduction problems. In B. S. Kaliski (Ed.), *Advances in cryptology - CRYPTO '97*. Lecture Notes in Computer Science, 1294. Berlin, Heidelberg: Springer. https://doi.org/10.1007/BFb0052231

Hoffstein, J., Howgrave-Graham, N., Pipher, J., Silverman, J. H., & Whyte, W. (2003). NTRUSign: Digital signatures using the NTRU lattice. In M. Joye (Ed.), *Topics in cryptology CT-RSA 2003*. Lecture Notes in Computer Science, 2612. Berlin, Heidelberg: Springer. https://doi.org/10.1007/3-540-36563-X_9

Hoffstein, J., Howgrave-Graham, N., Pipher, J., & Whyte, W. (2009). Practical lattice-based cryptography: NTRUEncrypt and NTRUSign. In P. Nguyen & B. Vallée (Eds.), *The LLL algorithm. Information security and cryptography*. Berlin, Heidelberg: Springer. https://doi.org/10.1007/978-3-642-02295-1_11

Hoffstein, J., Pipher, J., & Silverman, J. H. (1998). NTRU: A ring-based public key cryptosystem. In J. P. Buhler (Ed.), *Algorithmic number theory. ANTS 1998*. Lecture Notes in Computer Science, 1423. Berlin, Heidelberg: Springer. https://doi.org/10.1007/BFb0054868

Hoffstein, J., Pipher, J., & Silverman, J. H. (2001). NSS: An NTRU lattice-based signature scheme. In B. Pfitzmann (Ed.), *Advances in cryptology - EUROCRYPT 2001*. Lecture Notes in Computer Science, 2045. Berlin, Heidelberg: Springer. https://doi.org/10.1007/3-540-44987-6_14

Hoffstein, J., Pipher, J., & Silverman, J. H. (2008). *An introduction to mathematical cryptography*. Springer Science + Business Media, LLC

Jaulmes, É, & Joux, A. (2000). A chosen-ciphertext attack against NTRU. In M. Bellare (Ed.), *Advances in cryptology - CRYPTO 2000*. Lecture Notes in Computer Science, 1880. Berlin, Heidelberg: Springer. https://doi.org/10.1007/3-540-44598-6_2

Lee, M. S., & Hahn, S. G. (2010). Cryptanalysis of the GGH cryptosystem. *Mathematics in Computer Science*, *3*, 201–208. https://doi.org/10.1007/s11786-009-0018-5

Micciancio, D. (2001). Improving lattice based cryptosystems using the hermite normal form. In J. H. Silverman (Ed.), *Cryptography and lattices. CaLC 2001*. Lecture Notes in Computer Science, 2146. Berlin, Heidelberg: Springer. https://doi.org/10.1007/3-540-44670-2_11

Micciancio, D., & Regev, O. (2009). Lattice-based cryptography. In D. J. Bernstein, J. Buchmann, & E. Dahmen (Eds.), *Post-quantum cryptography*. Berlin, Heidelberg: Springer. https://doi.org/10.1007/978-3-540-88702-7_5

Nguyen, P. (1999). Cryptanalysis of the goldreich-goldwasser-halevi cryptosystem from Crypto'97. In M. Wiener (Ed.), *Advances in cryptology - CRYPTO' 99*. Lecture Notes in Computer Science, 1666. Berlin, Heidelberg: Springer. https://doi.org/10.1007/3-540-48405-1_18

Nguyen, P. Q., & Regev, O. (2006). Learning a parallelepiped: Cryptanalysis of GGH and NTRU signatures. In S. Vaudenay (Ed.), *Advances in cryptology - EUROCRYPT 2006*. Lecture Notes in Computer Science, 4004. Berlin, Heidelberg: Springer. https://doi.org/10.1007/11761679_17

Nguyen, P. Q., & Regev, O. (2009). Learning a parallelepiped: Cryptanalysis of GGH and NTRU signatures. *Journal of Cryptology*, *22*, 139–160. https://doi.org/10.1007/s00145-008-9031-0

Overbeck, R., & Sendrier, N. (2009). Code-based cryptography. In D. J. Bernstein, J. Buchmann, & E. Dahmen (Eds.), *Post-quantum cryptography*. Berlin, Heidelberg: Springer. https://0-doi-org.divit.library.itu.edu.tr/10.1007/978-3-540-88702-7_4

Shparlinski, I. (Ed.). (2003). Bit security of NTRU. In *Cryptographic applications of analytic number theory. Progress in computer science and applied logic*, 22. Basel: Birkhäuser. https://doi.org/10.1007/978-3-0348-8037-4_21

Whyte, W., & Hoffstein, J. (2011). NTRU. In H. C. A. van Tilborg, S. Jajodia (Eds.), *Encyclopedia of cryptography and security*. Boston, MA: Springer. https://doi.org/10.1007/978-1-4419-5906-5_464

Yoshino, M., & Kunihiro, N. (2012). Improving GGH cryptosystem for large error vector. *International symposium on information theory and its applications*, Honolulu, HI, USA.

Chapter 6

Other selected public key cryptosystems and digital signature algorithms

6.1 INTRODUCTION

This chapter is related to other selected public key cryptosystems and digital signature algorithms. Section 6.2 covers the knapsack cryptosystems. Since the security of the first knapsack cryptosystem, which is the "single-iterated Merkle-Hellman knapsack cryptosystem" as a type of "additive knapsack cryptosystems", was based on the hardness of the "subset-sum problem" in case of the "superincreasing sequence of integers", we first define the "subset-sum problem" and "superincreasing sequence of integers" in Sections 6.2.1 and 6.2.2, respectively. Afterwards, we introduce the basic structure of the "additive knapsack cryptosystems", and the "single-iterated Merkle-Hellman knapsack cryptosystem" in Sections 6.2.3 and 6.2.4, respectively. An example is provided for the "single-iterated Merkle-Hellman knapsack cryptosystem" in Section 6.2.4. The single-iterated Merkle–Hellman public key cryptosystem was totally broken by Shamir and the basic approach of Shamir's attack is also included in Section 6.2.4. As another type of knapsack cryptosystem, Section 6.2.5 covers the "multiplicative knapsack cryptosystem" whose security is based on the factorization problem, not the "subset-sum problem". An example is intended to show the steps of the "multiplicative knapsack cryptosystem" clearly.

Section 6.3 is related to the identity-based (ID-based) public key cryptosystems, ID-based digital signature algorithms, and their cryptanalysis. In Section 6.3.1, the basic structure of the ID-based public key cryptosystems is provided. In Section 6.3.2, the basic structure of the ID-based digital signature algorithm and the ID-based digital signature algorithm proposed by Shamir are also given. Basic cryptanalysis approaches for the ID-based public key cryptosystems and ID-based digital signature algorithms proposed in the literature are the topics in Section 6.3.3. Section 6.4 covers the Goldwasser–Micali public key cryptosystem, which is the first probabilistic public key cryptosystem. In this section, an example and a basic cryptanalysis are also included.

DOI: 10.1201/9781003514190-6

6.2 KNAPSACK CRYPTOSYSTEMS (SUBSET-SUM CRYPTOSYSTEMS)

6.2.1 Subset-sum problem (SSP)

Let $\mathbf{a} = [a_1\ a_2 \ldots a_n]$ be a vector of positive integer numbers. Let b be another positive integer number. The subset-sum problem is related to finding the subset of **a** whose elements' sum is b such that $b = \Sigma_{i=1}^{n} a_i \cdot x_i$ holds, where $x_i = \{0, 1\}$ for $i = 1, 2, \ldots, n$, and $\mathbf{x} = [x_1\ x_2 \ldots x_n]$ is the solution to the subset-sum problem (adapted from van Tilborg, 1988).

Example 6.1

Let $\mathbf{a} = [3\,7\,6\,8\,5\,11]$ be a vector of positive integer numbers and let $b = 19$ be another positive integer number. The sum of the elements $\{6, 8, 5\}$ gives the sum $b = 19$. Thus, the solution to this subset-sum problem will be $\mathbf{x} = [0\,0\,1\,1\,1\,0]$.

6.2.2 Superincreasing sequence of integers

The subset-sum problem is easy to solve in the case of the superincreasing sequence of integers (Hoffstein, Pipher, & Silverman, 2008; van Tilborg, 1988). In this section, we provide two definitions of the superincreasing sequence of integers, and two solution approaches for the subset-sum problem by considering the superincreasing sequence of integers.

Definition 6.1

A superincreasing sequence of integers is a vector of positive integer numbers $\mathbf{a} = [a_1\ a_2 \ldots a_n]$ that satisfies $a_i \geq 2a_{i-1}, 2 \leq i \leq n$ (adapted from Hoffstein et al., 2008).

Definition 6.2

A superincreasing sequence of integers is a vector of positive integer numbers $\mathbf{a} = [a_1\ a_2 \ldots a_n]$ that satisfies $a_i > \Sigma_{j=1}^{i-1} a_j, 2 \leq i \leq n$ (adapted from van Tilborg, 1988).

Solution 6.1

Let $I = \{a_i : 1 \leq i \leq \frac{1}{2}n\}$, $J = \{a_j : \frac{1}{2}n < j \leq n\}$, and let $I_0 \subset I$ and $J_0 \subset J$ be defined. Then, (I_0, J_0) is the solution satisfying $\Sigma_{a_i \in I_0} a_i + \Sigma_{a_j \in J_0} a_j = b$ (adapted from Hoffstein et al., 2008).

Solution 6.2

We consider first x_n, then x_{n-1}, and so on in this solution. $x_n = 1$ holds if and only if $a_n \leq b$, otherwise $x_n = 0$. For $i = n-1, n-2, \ldots, 1$, $x_i = 1$ holds if and only if $a_i \leq b - \Sigma_{j=i+1}^{n} a_j \cdot x_j$ otherwise $x_i = 0$ (adapted from van Tilborg, 1988).

Example 6.2

According to both Definitions 6.1 and 6.2, the sequence of integers $\mathbf{a} = [a_1\ a_2\ a_3\ a_4\ a_5\ a_6] = [3\ 7\ 14\ 30\ 65\ 137]$ is a superincreasing sequence of integers. Let $b = 147$. We find the solution for this subset-sum problem by using Solution 6.2 with the following steps:

$$x_6 = 1(\text{Since}\,137 < 147)$$

$$x_5 = 0\,(\text{Since}\,65 > (147 - 137) = 10)$$

$$x_4 = 0\,(\text{Since}\,30 > 10)$$

$$x_3 = 0\,(\text{Since}\,14 > 10)$$

$$x_2 = 1\,(\text{Since}\,7 < 10)$$

$$x_1 = 1\,(\text{Since}\,3 = (10 - 7) = 3)$$

Thus, the solution to this subset-sum problem will be $\mathbf{x} = [1\ 1\ 0\ 0\ 0\ 1]$.

If we consider Solution 6.1, then it is clear that $I = \{a_1,\ a_2,\ a_3\}, J = \{a_4,\ a_5,\ a_6\}$, and $I_0 = \{a_1,\ a_2\} \subset I$, $J_0 = \{a_6\} \subset J$ hold.

6.2.3 Additive knapsack cryptosystems

The basic structure of the encryption and decryption in the additive knapsack cryptosystems is given below (adapted from Desmedt, 2011):

Encryption

Alice's public encryption key is $\mathbf{a} = [a_1\ a_2\ \dots\ a_n]$.

Bob's binary message is $\mathbf{x} = [x_1\ x_2\ \dots\ x_n]$.

Bob computes the ciphertext $c = \mathbf{a}^T \cdot \mathbf{x} = \Sigma_{i=1}^{n} a_i \cdot x_i$ and sends c to Alice. (Please note that the encryption function has to be a one-to-one function for a unique decryption.)

Decryption

It must be difficult to recover $\mathbf{x}$ from $(\mathbf{a}, c)$. The secret information used as the "trapdoor" is the private decryption key.

6.2.4 Single-iterated Merkle–Hellman knapsack cryptosystem

The single-iterated Merkle–Hellman knapsack cryptosystem with the basic parameters below and the basic steps in Table 6.1 is an additive knapsack cryptosystem proposed by Merkle and Hellman (1978). It was the first public key cryptosystem developed based on the subset-sum problem and superincreasing sequence of integers.

Basic parameters of the single-iterated Merkle–Hellman knapsack cryptosystem (adapted from Hoffstein et al., 2008*)*

$\mathbf{r} = [r_1\ r_2\ \dots\ r_n]$: A superincreasing sequence of integers (chosen by Alice)

Table 6.1 Single-iterated Merkle–Hellman knapsack cryptosystem

	Alice	Bob
Private: $\mathbf{r}, y, z$ Public: $\mathbf{a}$	- Chooses $\mathbf{r} = [r_1\ r_2\ \ldots\ r_n]$. - Chooses y, z. - Computes $a_i \equiv y \cdot r_i \pmod{z}$ for $1 \le i \le n$. - Sets $\mathbf{a} = [a_1\ a_2\ \ldots\ a_n]$ and sends $\mathbf{a}$ to Bob.	
Encryption Private: $\mathbf{x}$ Public: c		- Chooses $\mathbf{x} = [x_1\ x_2\ \ldots\ x_n]$. - Computes $c = \Sigma_{i=1}^{n} a_i \cdot x_i$. - Sends c to Alice.
Decryption	- Computes $c' \equiv y^{-1} \cdot c \pmod{z} = \Sigma_{i=1}^{n} r_i \cdot x_i$. - Recovers $\mathbf{x} = [x_1\ x_2\ \ldots\ x_n]$ by finding the solution to the subset-sum problem $c' = \Sigma_{i=1}^{n} r_i \cdot x_i$.	

Source: Adapted from Hoffstein et al. (2008).

y, z: Two private integers satisfying $z > 2r_n$, $\gcd(y, z) = 1$ (chosen by Alice)
$\mathbf{x} = [x_1\ x_2\ \ldots\ x_n]$: Plaintext as an n-dimensional binary vector (chosen by Bob)
c: Ciphertext

Example 6.3

We assume that $y = 23$, $z = 82$, and $\mathbf{r} = [1\ 3\ 9\ 20\ 40]$ are chosen by Alice. We also assume that Bob chooses the plaintext as $\mathbf{x} = [1\ 1\ 0\ 1\ 0]$. Table 6.2 provides the basic steps of the single-iterated Merkle–Hellman knapsack cryptosystem for this simple example.

In addition to the "single-iterated Merkle-Hellman knapsack cryptosystem", the "multiply-iterated Merkle-Hellman knapsack cryptosystem" has been proposed to increase security, where y_j, z_j, $j = 1, 2, \ldots, k$ are considered for multiple iterations (Brickell, Lagarias, & Odlyzko, 1984; Odlyzko, 1990).

Cryptanalysis of the single-iterated Merkle–Hellman knapsack cryptosystem

Merkle & Hellman provided some conditions for the parameters y, z and n, r_i, $i = 1, 2, \ldots, n$ to increase security (Shamir & Zippel, 1980). However, the single-iterated Merkle-Hellman public key cryptosystem was totally broken by Shamir (1984). Shamir's attack is based on finding a trapdoor pair of (y, z) such that $y \cdot a_i \pmod{z}$ for $\forall i$ build a superincreasing sequence of integers and the sum of this superincreasing sequence of integers is smaller than z (Shamir, 1984). Please note that the trapdoor pair (y, z) found in Shamir's attack need not be the same as the real (y, z) values. Shamir (1984) finally showed that if the public key elements $\mathbf{a} = [a_1\ a_2\ \ldots\ a_n]$ are modular multiples

Table 6.2 An example for the single-iterated Merkle–Hellman knapsack cryptosystem

	Alice	*Bob*
	- Chooses $\mathbf{r} = [1\ 3\ 9\ 20\ 40]$. - Chooses $y = 23$, $z = 82$. - Computes $a_1 = 23 \cdot 1 = 23 \equiv 23 \pmod{82}$, $a_2 = 23 \cdot 3 = 69 \equiv 69 \pmod{82}$, $a_3 = 23 \cdot 9 = 207 \equiv 43 \pmod{82}$, $a_4 = 23 \cdot 20 = 460 \equiv 50 \pmod{82}$, and $a_5 = 23 \cdot 40 = 920 \equiv 18 \pmod{82}$. - Sets $\mathbf{a} = [a_1\ a_2\ a_3\ a_4\ a_5] =$ $= [23\ 69\ 43\ 50\ 18]$ and sends **a** to Bob.	
Encryption		- Chooses $\mathbf{x} = [1\ 1\ 0\ 1\ 0]$. - Computes $c = [23\ 69\ 43\ 50\ 18]^T \cdot$ $[1\ 1\ 0\ 1\ 0] = 142$. - Sends $c = 142$ to Alice.
Decryption	- Computes $c' = 23^{-1} \cdot 142 = 25 \cdot 142 = 3550$ $\equiv 24 \pmod{82}$. - Recovers $\mathbf{x} = [x_1\ x_2\ x_3\ x_4\ x_5]$ as $\mathbf{x} = [1\ 1\ 0\ 1\ 0]$ by considering $[1\ 3\ 9\ 20\ 40]^T \cdot [x_1\ x_2\ x_3\ x_4\ x_5] = 24$.	

of a superincreasing sequence, i.e. if $a_i \equiv y \cdot r_i \pmod{z}$ holds for $i = 1, 2, \ldots, n$ as presented in Table 6.2, then the plaintext can be easily recovered. Please see Shamir (1984) for the details. Shamir's attack has been analyzed later by Lagarias (1984). The reader is also strongly recommended to read Desmedt (1988) for the general evaluation of the knapsack cryptosystems.

6.2.5 Multiplicative knapsack cryptosystem

The multiplicative knapsack cryptosystem proposed by Naccache and Stern (1997) is a special knapsack cryptosystem in which the encryption and decryption are multiplicative.

Basic parameters of the multiplicative knapsack cryptosystem (adapted from Naccache, 2011)

p_i: ith prime number

p: A large public prime number satisfying $p > \Pi_{i=1}^{n} p_i$ (chosen by Alice)

Table 6.3 Multiplicative knapsack cryptosystem

	Alice	Bob
Private: s	- Chooses a large prime number p satisfying $p > \Pi_{i=1}^{n} p_i$. - Chooses randomly $1 < s < p-1$.	
Public: $p_1, p_2, \ldots, p_n, p$ $[v_1\ v_2\ \ldots\ v_n]$	- Computes v_i satisfying $v_i^s \equiv p_i \pmod{p}$, $i = 1, 2, .., n$. - Sets $[v_1\ v_2\ \ldots\ v_n]$. - Sends p and $[v_1\ v_2\ \ldots\ v_n]$ to Bob.	
Encryption		- Chooses $\mathbf{x} = [x_1\ x_2\ \ldots\ x_n]$.
Private: $\mathbf{x}$		- Computes $c = \Pi_{i=1}^{n} v_i^{x_i} \pmod{p}$.
Public: c		
Decryption	- Computes $u \equiv c^s \pmod{p} \equiv \left(\Pi_{i=1}^{n} v_i^{x_i}\right)^s \pmod{p} \equiv \Pi_{i=1}^{n} p_i^{x_i}$. - Factors u and recovers $\mathbf{x} = [x_1\ x_2\ \ldots\ x_n]$.	

Source: Adapted from Naccache (2011) and Naccache and Stern (1997)

s: A random private decryption key satisfying $1 < s < p-1$ and $\gcd(s, p-1) = 1$ (chosen by Alice)

$[v_1 \quad v_2 \quad \ldots \quad v_n]$: Public encryption key

$\mathbf{x} = [x_1 \quad x_2 \quad \ldots \quad x_n]$: Plaintext

The basic steps given in Table 6.3 can be considered for the multiplicative knapsack cryptosystem.

As apparent from Table 6.3, the security of the multiplicative knapsack cryptosystem does not depend on the hardness of the subset-sum problem, but on the hardness of the integer factoring problem.

Example 6.4

We assume that $n = 9$. Then, the steps of the multiplicative knapsack cryptosystem will be as follows:

Alice

- Alice considers $p_1 = 2$, $p_2 = 3$, $p_3 = 5$, $p_4 = 7$, $p_5 = 11$, $p_6 = 13$, $p_7 = 17$, $p_8 = 19$, $p_9 = 23$, and calculates $p_1 \cdot p_2 \cdot p_3 \cdot p_4 \cdot p_5 \cdot p_6 \cdot p_7 \cdot p_8 \cdot p_9 = 2 \cdot 3 \cdot 5 \cdot 7 \cdot 11 \cdot 13 \cdot 17 \cdot 19 \cdot 23 = 223092870$.
- Alice chooses a large prime number $p = 275992897 > 223092870$.
- Alice chooses randomly $s = 236251 < 275992896$ as her private key satisfying $\gcd(236251, 275992896) = 1$.

- Alice considers the following congruences to find v_i, $i = 1, 2, \ldots, 9$:

$$v_1^{236251} \equiv 2 \pmod{275992897}$$
$$v_2^{236251} \equiv 3 \pmod{275992897}$$
$$v_3^{236251} \equiv 5 \pmod{275992897}$$
$$v_4^{236251} \equiv 7 \pmod{275992897}$$
$$v_5^{236251} \equiv 11 \pmod{275992897}$$
$$v_6^{236251} \equiv 13 \pmod{275992897}$$
$$v_7^{236251} \equiv 17 \pmod{275992897}$$
$$v_8^{236251} \equiv 19 \pmod{275992897}$$
$$v_9^{236251} \equiv 23 \pmod{275992897}$$

- Alice finds $v_1 = 225715704$, $v_2 = 142094955$, $v_3 = 131657371$, $v_4 = 127092272$, $v_5 = 229307670$, $v_6 = 242809248$, $v_7 = 232080003$, $v_8 = 114868269$, and $v_9 = 61537118$.
  (Note that Alice considers the following steps to compute v_1:
  She computes the multiplicative inverse of 236251 modulo 275992896 as 247837651. Then she calculates $v_1 = 2^{247837651} \equiv 225715704 \pmod{275992897}$. Other v_i, $i = 2, 3, \ldots, 9$ values can also be computed analogously.)
- Alice sends v_i, $i = 1, 2, \ldots, 9$ values to Bob.

Bob

- Bob chooses $\mathbf{x} = [1\ 0\ 0\ 1\ 0\ 1\ 1\ 0\ 1]$.
- Bob computes $c = v_1^{x1} \cdot v_2^{x2} \cdot v_3^{x3} \cdot v_4^{x4} \cdot v_5^{x5} \cdot v_6^{x6} \cdot v_7^{x7} \cdot v_8^{x8} \cdot v_9^{x9} = v_1 \cdot v_4 \cdot v_6 \cdot v_7 \cdot v_9 = 225715704 \cdot 127092272 \cdot 242809248 \cdot 232080003 \cdot 61537118 \equiv 181254061 \pmod{275992897}$ and sends $c = 181254061$ to Alice.

Alice

- Alice computes $u \equiv 181254061^{236251} \equiv 71162 \pmod{275992897}$.
- Alice factors 71162 as $2 \cdot 7 \cdot 13 \cdot 17 \cdot 23$, finds $x_1 = 1$, $x_4 = 1$, $x_6 = 1$, $x_7 = 1$, $x_9 = 1$, and finally she recovers $\mathbf{x} = [1\ \ 0\ \ 0\ \ 1\ \ 0\ \ 1\ \ 1\ \ 0\ \ 1]$.

There are some additional knapsack cryptosystems proposed in the literature. As an example, Chor and Rivest (1985) proposed a distinctive knapsack cryptosystem to encrypt the binary plaintexts. This knapsack cryptosystem is based on the arithmetic in finite field $GF(p^h)$, where p is a prime number that denotes the number of the bits of the plaintext, and h is the sum of 1 value in the plaintext. Scrambling of a sequence and a random value is used to create the public encryption key. A random irreducible monic polynomial of degree

h is also used during the decryption step. The security of the Chor–Rivest knapsack cryptosystem does not depend on the hardness of any well-known computational problem (Chor & Rivest, 1985; Lenstra, 1991).

6.3 IDENTITY-BASED (ID-based) PUBLIC KEY CRYPTOSYSTEMS, ID-based DIGITAL SIGNATURE ALGORITHMS, AND CRYPTANALYSIS

The basic idea of the ID-based public key cryptosystems and ID-based digital signature algorithms was proposed by Shamir (1985).

6.3.1 Basic idea of the ID-based public key cryptosystems

As it became clear from the other public key cryptosystems provided so far, in a typical public key cryptosystem, Alice creates her own private decryption key, generates the public encryption key from her private decryption key, and sends the public encryption key to Bob. However, the basic idea of an ID-based public key cryptosystem is different. In an ID-based public key cryptosystem, there is a "private key generator" (PKG) who generates the public encryption key to be used by any sender, and creates the private decryption key for the recipient (decryptor) corresponding to his/her unique public identity. The basic structure of an ID-based public key cryptosystem is based on four algorithms, which are provided in Table 6.4 according to Shamir's approach.

Although Shamir (1985) proposed the basic idea of an ID-based public key cryptosystem, he did not provide any specific algorithm, and the ID-based public key cryptosystem remained an open challenge for a long time. The "Boneh-Franklin public key cryptosystem" is the first practical and secure ID-based public key cryptosystem, which is based on the "Weil pairing"

Table 6.4 Four algorithms of an ID-based public key cryptosystem

Setup algorithm	*KeyGen*	*Encrypt*	*Decrypt*
- Run by the PKG.	- Run by the PKG.	- Run by any sender.	- Run by the recipient with identity i who owns the private decryption key d_i.
- Input: Security parameter.	- Input: PKG's msk, the user's unique public identity i.	- Input: Plaintext m, the recipient's identity i, PKG's mpk.	- Input: Ciphertext c, private decryption d_i.
- Output: Master public key (mpk), master secret key (msk) of the PKG.	- Output: Private decryption key d_i of the user with identity i.	- Output: Ciphertext c. (to be sent to the recipient with identity i.)	- Output: Plaintext m.

Source: Adapted from Libert and Quisquater (2011).

(Boneh & Franklin, 2001; Boneh & Franklin, 2003). The Boneh–Boyen (BB1) "hierarchical identity-based encryption" (HIBE) has also been proposed, which is based on the so-called "bilinear Diffie-Hellman (BDH)" assumption (Boneh & Boyen, 2004). Hoffstein et al. (2008) provided an ID-based public key cryptosystem based on the "modified Weil pairings" on elliptic curves. Cocks (2001) had a different approach and proposed an ID-based public key cryptosystem based on "quadratic residues".

Boneh and Franklin (2001) provided two algorithms related to the ID-based public key cryptosystems, which are "BasicIdent" and "identity-based encryption with chosen ciphertext security". The "BasicIdent" algorithm works on a bilinear map with the same two groups of prime order q as the inputs during the encryption and decryption steps. There are two hash functions in this algorithm. One hash function is used to hash the identity of the recipient, whereas the second hash function is used to hash the output of the bilinear map. The private decryption key of the recipient is created by multiplying the hash value of the identity by a secret random value in $\mathbb{F}_q^*$. An ephemeral key is also used during the encryption of the binary vector representing the plaintext. For more details, please see Boneh and Franklin (2001) and Boneh and Franklin (2003).

6.3.2 Basic idea of the ID-based digital signature algorithm

Like the ID-based public key cryptosystems, the basic structure of an ID-based digital signature algorithm is based on four algorithms, which are provided in Table 6.5.

As clear from Tables 6.4 and 6.5, an ID-based public key cryptosystem and an ID-based digital signature algorithm have almost the same structure. One basic difference between two is that the PKG's mpk is used during the encryption step in an ID-based public key cryptosystem, whereas it is used during the verification step in an ID-based digital signature algorithm.

Table 6.5 Four algorithms of an ID-based digital signature algorithm

Setup algorithm	*KeyGen*	*Sign*	*Verify*
- Run by the PKG.	- Run by the PKG.	- Run by the signer with identity i who owns the private signing key s_i.	- Run by any verifier.
- Input: Security parameter.	- Input: PKG's msk, the user's unique public identity i.	- Input: D, s_i.	- Input: D, D^{sig}, i, PKG's mpk.
- Output: mpk, msk of the PKG.	- Output: Private signing key s_i of the signer with identity i.	- Output: D^{sig}	- Output: 0 or 1.

Source: Adapted from Libert and Quisquater (2011).

Table 6.6 ID-based digital signature algorithm

	PKG	*Victor*
Private: p, q, s_i	- Chooses two large prime numbers p and q.	
	- Computes $N = p \cdot q$.	
Public: N, i, e, $f(\cdot)$	- Sends N to Samantha and Victor.	
	- Chooses e and $f(\cdot)$.	
	- Sends e and $f(\cdot)$ to Samantha and Victor.	
	- Computes the private signing key s_i for Samantha with identity i from the congruence $s_i^e \equiv i \pmod{N}$.	
	- Sends s_i to Samantha.	
Signing	**Samantha**	
Private: r	- Chooses D.	
Public: D,	- Chooses r.	
$D^{sig} = (S_1, S_2)$	- Computes $S_2 \equiv r^e \pmod{N}$ and $S_1 \equiv s_i \cdot r^{f(S_2,D)} \pmod{N}$.	
	- Sends D and $D^{sig} = (S_1, S_2)$ to Victor.	
Verification		- Verifies $S_1^e \equiv i \cdot S_2^{f(S_2,D)} \pmod{N}$.

Source: Adapted from Shamir (1985).

Although Shamir (1985) did not propose any basic algorithm for an ID-based public key cryptosystem, he proposed a basic idea for an ID-based digital signature algorithm, which is provided in Table 6.6.

Basic parameters for the ID-based digital signature algorithm (adapted from Shamir, 1985):

p,q: Two large prime numbers (chosen by the PKG)
$N = p \cdot q$ (computed by the PKG)
e: A large prime number satisfying $\gcd(e, (p-1)(q-1)) = 1$ (chosen by the PKG)
i: Unique public identity of Samantha
s_i: Private signing key of Samantha who owns the identity i
r: A random number satisfying $0 < r < N-1$ (chosen by Samantha)
$f(\cdot)$: A one-way function (chosen by the PKG)
D: Digital document of Samantha
$D^{sig} = (S_1, S_2)$: Digital signature of the digital document D signed by Samantha

Bellare, Namprempre, and Neven (2004) proposed that any digital signature algorithm can also be modified such that it can be converted to an ID-based digital signature algorithm. Two examples of the ID-based digital signature algorithms are Guillou–Quisquater digital signature algorithm and the Bellare–Namprempre–Neven digital signature algorithm, whose details can be found in Libert and Quisquater (2011).

6.3.3 Cryptanalysis of the ID-based public key cryptosystems and ID-based digital signature algorithms

Hoffstein et al. (2008) discussed some security issues regarding the security of the ID-based public key cryptosystems and digital signature algorithms. As provided in the second column of Tables 6.4 and 6.5, the "KeyGen" step is run by the PKG, which includes the creation of the user's private key by considering the PKG's master secret key msk and the user's unique public identity i. If the adversary Eve pretends the public unique identity i of Alice to be her own identity and requests the PKG to create the private decryption key d_i or the private signing key s_i, then she can recover the plaintexts by using the private key d_i of Alice or sign the documents by using the private signing key s_i of Alice, thus the PKG needs to keep track of the owners of the identities. Another much more dangerous possible attack mentioned in Hoffstein et al. (2008) is that Eve can send a lot of identities to the PKG and request the PKG to create the associated private keys. By using the knowledge of the private keys created by the PKG, Eve can recover the master secret key msk of the PKG.

Bellare et al. (2004) provided the security proofs for a large class of ID-based public key cryptosystems and digital signature algorithms. Please see Bellare et al. (2004) for details.

6.4 GOLDWASSER-MICALI PROBABILISTIC PUBLIC KEY CRYPTOSYSTEM AND ITS CRYPTANALYSIS

6.4.1 Goldwasser–Micali probabilistic public key cryptosystem

The Goldwasser–Micali public key cryptosystem is the first probabilistic public key cryptosystem. It is a "bit-by-bit encryption", which is based on the idea that both the plaintext bit m and the ephemeral key r are encrypted. Since the ephemeral key r is random, then the pair (m,r) will also be random. However, as explained in Section 2.4 of Chapter 2, it is sufficient to decrypt only m during the decryption process. Table 6.7 provides the steps of this public key cryptosystem for the encryption of one bit.

Basic parameters of Goldwasser-Micali probabilistic public key cryptosystem (adapted from Goldwasser & Micali, 1984; Gómez Pardo, 2013; Hoffstein et al., 2008; Sako, 2011a):

p,q: (Random) prime numbers (of length k) (chosen by Alice)
N: Integer number satisfying $N = p \cdot q$ (computed by Alice and sent to Bob by Alice)
a: Integer number satisfying $\left(\frac{a}{p}\right) = \left(\frac{a}{q}\right) = -1$ (chosen by Alice)
b: Plaintext bit (chosen by Bob)
r: Ephemeral key satisfying $1 < r < N$ (chosen by Bob)

Table 6.7 Goldwasser-Micali probabilistic public key cryptosystem

	Alice	*Bob*
Private: p, q Public: N, a	- Chooses a, p, q. - Computes $N = p \cdot q$. - Sends a and N to Bob.	
Encryption Private: b, r Public: c		- Chooses $b \in \{0,1\}$. - Chooses $1 < r < N$. - Computes $c = \begin{cases} r^2 \pmod{N} \text{ if } b = 0 \\ a \cdot r^2 \pmod{N} \text{ if } b = 1 \end{cases}$. - Sends c to Alice.
Decryption	- Determines b by considering $b = \begin{cases} 0 \text{ if } \left(\frac{c}{p}\right) = \left(\frac{c}{q}\right) = 1 \\ 1 \text{ if } \left(\frac{c}{p}\right) = \left(\frac{c}{q}\right) = -1 \end{cases}$	

Source: Adapted from Goldwasser and Micali (1984), Gómez Pardo (2013), and Hoffstein et al. (2008).

Although the Goldwasser–Micali public key cryptosystem is based on the hardness of the "quadratic residuosity problem" provided in Section 1.2.5 of Chapter 1, it may not be practical due to the bit-by-bit encryption (Bellare & Rogaway, 1995; Hoffstein et al., 2008). Since the basic ElGamal, elliptic curve ElGamal, GGH, and NTRU public key cryptosystems use the ephemeral key during the encryption process, they may also be called the probabilistic public key cryptosystems.

Example 6.5

We assume that Alice chooses $p = 29, q = 37$, and $a = 14$ such that $\left(\frac{14}{29}\right) = \left(\frac{14}{37}\right) = -1$ holds, which means there are no $c \in \mathbb{Z}$ and $d \in \mathbb{Z}$ values that satisfy $c^2 \equiv 14 \pmod{29}$ and $d^2 \equiv 14 \pmod{37}$. We also assume that Bob chooses $b = 1$ and $r = 18$. Then, the steps of the Goldwasser–Micali probabilistic public key cryptosystem will be as given in Table 6.8.

6.4.2 Cryptanalysis of Goldwasser–Micali probabilistic public key cryptosystem

Please recall the definition of the "quadratic residuosity problem" from Section 1.2.5 of Chapter 1 and the definition of "semantic security" from Section 2.11 of Chapter 2. The Goldwasser–Micali probabilistic public key cryptosystem is the first cryptosystem that achieved the "semantic security" against a passive eavesdropper under the assumption that solving the "quadratic residuosity problem" is hard (Sako, 2011b; Yan, 2008).

Table 6.8 An example for the Goldwasser–Micali probabilistic public key cryptosystem

	Alice	*Bob*
Encryption	- Chooses $a = 14, p = 29, q = 37$. - Computes $N = 29 \cdot 37 = 1073$. - Sends $a = 14$ and $N = 1073$ to Bob.	
		- Chooses $b = 1$. - Chooses $r = 18$. - Computes $c = 14 \cdot 18^2 \equiv 244 \pmod{1073}$ - Sends $c = 244$ to Alice.
Decryption	- Computes $\left(\frac{244}{29}\right) = \left(\frac{244}{37}\right) = -1$ - Determines $b = 1$.	

Some other probabilistic public key cryptosystems have also been proposed. As an example, the "Paillier public key cryptosystem" is a probabilistic public key cryptosystem based on the "composite residuosity class problem" (Paillier, 1999).

6.5 CONCLUSIONS

This chapter was related to other selected public key cryptosystems and digital signature algorithms including knapsack cryptosystems, ID-based public key cryptosystems, ID-based digital signature algorithms, and Goldwasser–Micali probabilistic public key cryptosystem. The single-iterated Merkle–Hellman knapsack cryptosystem is the first knapsack cryptosystem, whereas the Goldwasser–Micali probabilistic public key cryptosystem is the first probabilistic public key cryptosystem. The single-iterated Merkle–Hellman knapsack cryptosystem was totally broken, while the Goldwasser–Micali cryptosystem is semantically secure; however, it is not practical due to the bit-by-bit encryption. In addition to the basic structure of the ID-based public key cryptosystem and ID-based digital signature algorithm, the digital signature algorithm of Shamir and the basic cryptanalysis approaches were also provided in this chapter. The examples related to the single-iterated Merkle–Hellman knapsack cryptosystem, multiplicative knapsack cryptosystem, and the Goldwasser–Micali probabilistic public key cryptosystem show the practicality of the algorithms.

REFERENCES

Bellare, M., Namprempre, C., & Neven, G. (2004). Security proofs for identity-based identification and signature schemes. In C. Cachin & J. L. Camenisch (Eds.), *Advances in cryptology - EUROCRYPT 2004*. Lecture Notes in Computer Science, 3027. Berlin, Heidelberg: Springer. https://doi.org/10.1007/978-3-540-24676-3_1

Bellare, M., & Rogaway, P. (1995). Optimal asymmetric encryption. In A. De Santis (Ed.), *Advances in cryptology - EUROCRYPT'94*. Lecture Notes in Computer Science, 950. Berlin, Heidelberg: Springer. https://doi.org/10.1007/BFb0053428

Boneh, D., & Boyen, X. (2004). Efficient selective-ID secure identity-based encryption without random oracles. In C. Cachin & J. L. Camenisch (Eds.), *Advances in cryptology - EUROCRYPT 2004*. Lecture Notes in Computer Science, 3027. Berlin, Heidelberg: Springer. https://doi.org/10.1007/978-3-540-24676-3_14

Boneh, D., & Franklin, M. (2001). Identity-based encryption from the weil pairing. In J. Kilian (Ed.), *Advances in cryptology - CRYPTO 2001*. Lecture Notes in Computer Science, 2139. Berlin, Heidelberg: Springer. https://doi.org/10.1007/3-540-44647-8_13

Boneh, D., & Franklin, M. (2003). Identity-based encryption from the weil pairing. *SIAM Journal of Computing, 32*(3), 586–615.

Brickell, E. F., Lagarias, J. C., & Odlyzko, A. M. (1984). Evaluation of the Adleman attack on multiply iterated knapsack cryptosystems. In D. Chaum (Ed.), *Advances in cryptology*. Boston, MA: Springer. https://doi.org/10.1007/978-1-4684-4730-9_3

Chor, B., & Rivest, R. L. (1985). A knapsack type public key cryptosystem based on arithmetic in finite fields (preliminary draft). In G. R. Blakley & D. Chaum (Eds.), *Advances in cryptology. CRYPTO 1984*. Lecture Notes in Computer Science, 196. Berlin, Heidelberg: Springer. https://doi.org/10.1007/3-540-39568-7_6

Cocks, C. (2001) An identity based encryption scheme based on quadratic residues. In B. Honary (Ed.), *Cryptography and coding 2001*. Lecture Notes in Computer Science, 2260. Berlin, Heidelberg: Springer. https://doi.org/10.1007/3-540-45325-3_32

Desmedt, Y. (2011). Knapsack cryptographic schemes. In H. C. A. van Tilborg & S. Jajodia (Eds.), *Encyclopedia of cryptography and security*. Boston, MA: Springer.https://doi.org/10.1007/978-1-4419-5906-5_323.

Desmedt, Y. G. (1988). What happened with knapsack cryptographic schemes?. In J.K. Skwirzynski (Ed.), *Performance limits in communication theory and practice*. NATO ASI Series, 142. Dordrecht: Springer. https://doi.org/10.1007/978-94-009-2794-0_7

Goldwasser, S., & Micali, S. (1984). Probabilistic encryption. *Journal of Computer and System Sciences, 28*, 270–299.

Gómez Pardo, J. L. (2013). Public-key encryption. *Introduction to cryptography with maple*. Berlin, Heidelberg: Springer. https://doi.org/10.1007/978-3-642-32166-5_8.

Hoffstein, J., Pipher, J., & Silverman, J. H. (2008). *An introduction to mathematical cryptography*. Springer Science + Business Media, LLC.

Lagarias, J. C. (1984). Performance analysis of Shamir's attack on the basic Merkle-Hellman knapsack cryptosystem. In J. Paredaens (Ed.), *Automata, languages and programming. ICALP 1984*. Lecture Notes in Computer Science, 172. Berlin, Heidelberg: Springer. https://doi.org/10.1007/3-540-13345-3_28.

Lenstra, H. W. (1991). On the Chor-Rrivest knapsack cryptosystem. *Journal of Cryptology, 3*, 149–155. https://doi.org/10.1007/BF00196908

Libert, B., & Quisquater, J. J. (2011). Identity-based cryptosystems. In H. C. A. van Tilborg, S. Jajodia (Eds.), *Encyclopedia of cryptography and security*. Boston, MA: Springer. https://doi.org/10.1007/978-1-4419-5906-5_127.

Merkle, R. C., & Hellman, M. E. (1978). Hiding information and signatures in trapdoor knapsacks. *IEEE Transactions on Information Theory, 24*(5), 525–530.

Naccache, D. (2011). Multiplicative knapsack cryptosystem. In H. C. A. van Tilborg & S. Jajodia (Eds.), *Encyclopedia of cryptography and security*. Boston, MA: Springer. https://doi.org/10.1007/978-1-4419-5906-5_513

Naccache, D., & Stern, J. (1997). A new public-key cryptosystem. In W. Fumy (Ed.), *Advances in cryptology - EUROCRYPT '97*. Lecture Notes in Computer Science, 1233. Berlin, Heidelberg: Springer. https://doi.org/10.1007/3-540-69053-0_3

Odlyzko, A. M. (1990). *The rise and fall of knapsack cryptosystems, Cryptology and computational number theory, Proceedings of symposia in applied mathematics 42*, Providence, RI: AMS.
Paillier, P. (1999). Public-key cryptosystems based on composite degree residuosity classes. In J. Stern (Ed.), *Advances in cryptology - EUROCRYPT '99*. Lecture Notes in Computer Science, 1592. Berlin, Heidelberg: Springer. https://doi.org/10.1007/3-540-48910-X_16
Sako, K. (2011a). Goldwasser-Micali encryption scheme. In H. C. A. van Tilborg & S. Jajodia (Eds.), *Encyclopedia of cryptography and security*. Boston, MA: Springer. https://doi.org/10.1007/978-1-4419-5906-5_19
Sako, K. (2011b). Semantic security. In H. C. A. van Tilborg & S. Jajodia (Eds.), *Encyclopedia of cryptography and security*. Boston, MA: Springer. https://doi.org/10.1007/978-1-4419-5906-5_23
Shamir, A. (1984). A polynomial-time algorithm for breaking the basic merkle-hellman cryptosystem, *IEEE Transactions on Information Theory, 30*(5), 699–704. https://doi.org/10.1109/TIT.1984.1056964
Shamir, A. (1985). Identity-based cryptosystems and signature schemes. In G. R. Blakley & D. Chaum (Eds.), *Advances in cryptology. CRYPTO 1984*. Lecture Notes in Computer Science, 196. Berlin, Heidelberg: Springer. https://doi.org/10.1007/3-540-39568-7_5
Shamir, A., & Zippel, R. (1980). On the security of the Merkle-Hellman cryptographic scheme. *IEEE Transactions on Information Theory, 26*(3), 339–340. https://doi.org/10.1109/TIT.1980.1056197
van Tilborg, H. C. A. (1988). *The knapsack system. An introduction to cryptology*. Kluwer Academic Publishers.
Yan, S. Y. (Ed.). (2008). RSA public-key cryptography. In *Cryptanalytic attacks on RSA*. Boston, MA: Springer. https://doi.org/10.1007/978-0-387-48742-7_2

Printed in the United States
by Baker & Taylor Publisher Services